The Scarecrow Author Bibliographies

WILLIAM DEAN HOWELLS
A Bibliography

Compiled by

Vito J. Brenni

The Scarecrow Author Bibliographies, No. 9

The Scarecrow Press, Inc.
Metuchen, N.J.   1973

A
012
H859b
1973

Library of Congress Cataloging in Publication Data

Brenni, Vito Joseph, 1923-
  William Dean Howells: a bibliography.

  (The Scarecrow author bibliographies, no. 9)
  1. Howells, William Dean, 1837-1920--Bibliography.
Z8420.25.B74   016.818'4'09   73-4855
ISBN 0-8108-0620-7

Dedicated to

MY NEPHEWS AND NIECES

Who Gave Me

Many Happy Days

TABLE OF CONTENTS

PREFACE

In 1946 William Gibson and George Arms began to publish a bibliography of William Dean Howells in the New York Public Library Bulletin. It was included in several issues and later reprinted in book form with some revisions and corrections. It represents a distinguished achievement because the authors give full description for all first editions and provide many useful notes for many of the entries. They searched many old periodicals for his early writings, and in so doing made the task of this bibliographer much lighter. The checklists and the annual register in their bibliography are invaluable to the scholar who wants to know what Howells wrote in a particular year.

The fourth volume of Jacob N. Blanck's Bibliography of American Literature (New Haven, Yale University, 1963) contains a full description of the first editions and lists a great many of Howells' short writings, including introductions to books, anecdotes, speeches, letters, and poems. It does not include periodical articles except when they later appeared in books. It also contains a short list of biographical and critical articles.

In 1969 James Woodress and Stanley P. Andersen published a bibliography of writings about William Dean Howells in a special number of American Literary Realism 1870-1910. An item-by-item check has not been made against the list in this bibliography because it appeared long after this section had been completed. Conceivably it has some articles not included in this book, although every effort was made by the present compiler to find everything written about him.

Whereas the arrangement in the bibliographies by Gibson and Arms and by Blanck is chronological, the arrangement in this work is by form. The student of Howells can now secure a complete list of his short stories, poems, novels, plays, travel writings, criticism, etc. For a number of the publications listed more than one location is given in order to help students and others to find them in both small and large collections. Also for the first time the student can find in one book all the writings by and about Howells with a subject and author index. A subject index is also given for the columns which Howells wrote for Harper's Monthly, Harper's Weekly, and the Atlantic Monthly.

In so far as the compiler was able to do so, the entries were checked by personal examination and by a number of correspondents who were so kind to answer my letters. I am especially grateful to the British Museum, the Library of Congress, the New York Public Library, Vassar College, Rutgers University, Columbia University, Ohio State University, and the State University of New York colleges at Plattsburgh and New Paltz for permitting me to use their collections over a period of several years.

Much of Howells' writing still remains unread. The hope is that many more readers in the future will study this important critic and writer now that the bibliographic apparatus has been improved. If this book facilitates such study, the bibliographer will have accomplished his main purpose.

INTRODUCTION

William Dean Howells was born March 1, 1837 at Martin's Ferry, Belmont County, Ohio. Much of his boyhood was spent in his father's newspaper office as typesetter, compositor, and fledgling contributor of poems, sketches, and newsletters to the family paper, the Ashtabula Sentinel, and to local papers. In 1857, Howells became a correspondent for the Cincinnati Gazette and a year later a reporter, news editor, and editorial writer for the Ohio State Journal in Columbus. With a young friend, John James Piatt, Howells published Poems of Two Friends in 1859 and other verses in the Atlantic Monthly, the Cincinnati Dial and the Saturday Press.

His campaign book, Lives and Speeches of Abraham Lincoln and Hannibal Hamlin (1860), won for Howells the pleasurable commission of traveling to Canada, New England, and New York to report on leading industries. He turned his assignment into a literary pilgrimage to Boston to meet James T. Field, Atlantic Monthly editor, and James Russell Lowell. Through them he was introduced to other literary giants of the day. This visit he fondly described years later in his Literary Friends and Acquaintance (1900) and claimed the visit to be the turning point of his literary career.

He sought and obtained a post as United States consul in Venice in 1861. During his four years abroad he married Elinor Gertrude Mead and continued contributing articles to The Boston Advertiser, published later as Venetian Life (1866) and Italian Journeys (1867).

In 1866, Howells was offered the assistant editorship of the Atlantic Monthly by Fields. In 1871, upon Fields' resignation, Howells became editor-in-chief, a position he held until 1881. Because of his work on the Atlantic, Howells was able to meet, encourage, and sometimes befriend leading writers of his day. He had made many friends among the older generation (Lowell, Holmes, Longfellow--to name a few) early in his career, and his kindly, sensitive appreciation of the new writers, especially Henry James, Mark Twain, and Bret Harte, developed into personal friendships which lasted for years. Among these many friends was Thomas Wentworth Higginson, minister-turned-reformer, colonel in the Civil War, and distinguished man of letters.

Higginson had been contributing to the Atlantic Monthly from its inception in 1858 and, when Howells assumed editorship, he carried on an intermittent correspondence with Howells for over thirty years. The letters from Howells (1869-1901) were preserved by Higginson and published in 1927 by George S. Hellman in "The Letters of Howells to Higginson," Twenty-Seventh Annual Report of The Bibliophile Society, 1901-1929 (Boston, 1929).

Although the correspondence adds nothing significant to a Howells' biography, the friendship between Howells and Higginson marked by these letters has been largely overlooked. A summary overview of the correspondence might be of interest to students of Howells. Most of the letters are on the business at hand: reviews assigned to Higginson, correction of manuscripts, comments about Higginson's essays, and expressions of appreciation to Higginson for his favorable articles and speeches about Howells' fiction.

In 1869, Higginson must have asked Howells for the Atlantic's principles for reviewing books. Howells answered that he himself did most of the reviewing and "I try not to let any really important American book go unmentioned." His only principle of selection was, "I see such books as [have] something interesting to be written about.... If you'll look over the magazine for a year, you'll find the facts of American book-making pretty well reflected in it" (Dec. 24, 1869, p. 24). A perusal of the table of contents for the 1869 Atlantic reveals such names as Bret Harte, S. Lanier, Gail Hamilton, Longfellow, Lowell, Motley, and Stedman.

Higginson's task, it seems, was often as reviewer of books that Howells felt too onerous to handle himself: "H. H. [Helen Hunt] whom I was puzzled how to dispose of" (Jan. 7, 1871, p. 28). Other requests for reviews of H. H.'s work were "because I knew you were her friend, and I wanted a more cordial review of her work than I knew how to get otherwise" (Feb. 16, 1872 and April 6, 1873, p. 31). Howells accepted Higginson's review of John James Piatt's Western Windows and Other Poems ("refined sentiment and subtle expression," Atlantic Monthly, April, 1869), commenting wryly, "The doubt of his future is all I could have asked you to leave out of his notice" (April 1, 1869, p. 22).

When a book on Thoreau by William Ellery Channing appeared, Howells asked Higginson to review it. Howells, since his first visit to Thoreau in 1860 (Literary Friends), had not taken kindly to him. When the Channing book came to his notice, Howells wrote that he "was not in sympathy with either of them, but I'm quite willing to believe that there are good and fine things which I don't like, even in literature" (Oct. 12, 1873, p. 32). Howells, it seems, preferred Higginson to review books which would be given kindlier treatment than Howells himself could manage.

Besides reviewing books, Higginson continued contributing familiar essays and literary criticism to the Atlantic, most of which met with Howells' approval. Higginson, in turn, was pleased with Howells' use of the familiar and commonplace and must have seen in Howells' novels a strong contrast to the sentimental and moralistic novels of the day. Howells commented, "I think there may very well be novels of purpose--and sermons. But neither ought to be read on weekdays" (March 17, 1870, p. 26).

Between 1870 and 1879 Higginson followed Howells' literary career with interest and admiration, but frequently disagreed with Howells' theory of realism. He saw Howells preferring the unheroic, the neurotic character, as in A Foregone Conclusion, to the whole, mature character Higginson would have preferred. However, when an approving review by Higginson appeared in the World in 1879, Howells was grateful, "because I know that you have not always liked my things." As for the sentimental and moralistic in fiction, Howells wrote in the same letter, "It may or may not surprise you if I say that while I despise the Tendenz romanskt as much as anybody, I should be ashamed and sorry if my words did not unmistakably teach a lenient, generous, and liberal life: that is, I should feel degraded merely to amuse people" (Sept. 17, 1879, p. 38).

In the 1880's Howells saw the influence of the French and Russian realists on the newer generation of writers. He was troubled that Higginson disliked it:

> I ought to be willing you should dislike my literary creed, or my preaching it. But I can't. I don't

> mind people's trying to raise apples and peaches,
> but I insist upon pears now because it is not
> "apple year," and because all the peaches I taste
> have "got the gathers." They've run out.
>
> To drop the metaphor I mean that no reader of
> mine shall suppose that the true and natural way
> of writing fiction which is now universal, wherever
> the fiction is worth reading, is any longer to be
> taken on sufferance. It has come to stay. [Aug.
> 31, 1886, p. 44.]

The correspondence of the later years treats of matters no deeper than points of grammar and style which Higginson must have questioned. His use of the preposition at the end of a sentence Howells defended as a matter of taste and reason. "It makes a lighter and pleasanter movement in the prose, and it is more conformable to good colloquial usage, to do so" (Nov. 5, 1891, p. 49). As for his views on the use of colloquial English, Howells did not find the participial construction natural English and believed that "it is better to write as sensibly as we speak, unless indeed we speak as formally as we write" (May 20, 1894, p. 53). After Howells resigned from the Atlantic Monthly in 1881, he assumed the "Editor's Study" for Harper's in 1886, a column he continued until 1892 when he became co-editor for four months of Cosmopolitan. Higginson also contributed articles to Harper's; among them, "Women and Men" drew applause from Howells (Oct. 20, 1895, pp. 54-55).

Altogether, the letters leave one with an impression of Howells as a generous-minded person who could have business-like candor about Higginson's work: "I think some of those Oldport papers among the most charming essays we have; but the stories I did not like so well" (Oct. 18, 1873, p. 33). He could be sensitive to Higginson's criticism but could look upon even the adverse ones as those of a friend: "I wish you had sent me your praises. I would much rather have my sins left with God; though this is asking a good deal of one's friends, perhaps, and I am sure you are one of mine" (Nov. 5, 1891, p. 50). For some reason the correspondence ends abruptly in 1901 even though Higginson continued publishing until his death in 1911 and Howells produced several books within that decade.

During the 1880's and 1890's Howells' growing concern over the many social injustices in American life finds reflection in his bold defense of the Chicago Anarchists in

the New York Tribune (1887) and in such novels as Annie
Kilburn (1888), A Hazard of New Fortunes (1890), and A
Traveler from Altruria (1894). In 1900 he began the
"Editor's Easy Chair" for Harper's in which he discussed
social problems, literature, and matters that struck his
fancy. The column resulted in graceful, urbane essays
which Howells continued until his death in New York City
in May 1920.

Howells' last years were filled with honors and
recognitions. For his many novels, critical essays, travel
books, plays, and poetry, he was awarded honorary degrees
by Yale (1901), Oxford (1904), Columbia (1905), and Prince-
ton (1912). He was elected first president of the American
Academy of Arts and Letters (1908) and given a gold medal
for fiction by that organization in 1915. By the 1920's,
however, his theory of criticism, summarized in Criticism
and Fiction (1891), had been superseded by the stark
naturalism of Norris, Dreiser, Garland, and Crane. He
had, nevertheless, made his mark on American letters by
introducing to his readers the French and Russian realists
whom he admired, by asserting and practicing his own
views on realism, and by encouraging the best of two gen-
erations of American novelists.

Mary Anne Brennan, O. P.
Siena Heights College
Adrian, Michigan

THE BIBLIOGRAPHY

NOVELS

1 Annie Kilburn. N. Y. , Harper, 1889. 331p.
   First published in Harper's monthly, June-Nov.
   1888.
2 April hopes. Edinburgh, Douglas, 1887. 484p.
   First published in Harper's monthly, Feb. -Nov.
   1887.
3 A chance acquaintance. Boston, Osgood, 1873. 279p.
   Appeared also in Atlantic monthly, Jan. -June 1873.
4 The coast of bohemia. N. Y. , Harper, 1893. 340p.
   First printed in Ladies' home journal, Dec. 1892-
   Oct. 1893.
5 The day of their wedding. N. Y. , Harper, 1896. 158p.
   First published in Harper's bazaar, Oct. --Nov.
   1895. The novel was published in 1896 by David
   Douglas in Edinburgh under the title Idyls in drab.
   It also included A parting and a meeting.
6 Dr. Breen's practice. Boston, Osgood, 1881. 272p.
   First published in Atlantic monthly, Aug. 1881--
   Dec. 1881.
7 "A fearful responsibility. " In A fearful responsibility
   and other stories. 1900. p. 1-164.
   First published in Scribner's 22:276-93, 390-414,
   June, July 1881.
8 Fennel and rue. N. Y. and London, Harper, 1908.
   130p.
9 The flight of Pony Baker; a boy's town story. N. Y.
   and London, Harper, 1902. 223p.
   Portions of this novel appeared in Youth's companion, Dec. 1, 1898; Nov. 16, 23, 1899; and
   May 10, 1900; and in Harper's weekly, July 5,
   1902.
10 A foregone conclusion. Boston, Osgood, 1875. 265p.
    Appeared first in the Atlantic monthly, July--
    Dec. 1874.
11 A hazard of new fortunes. Edinburgh, Douglas, 1889.
    2v.
         The first American edition was published by
         Harper in 1890 in its Franklin Square Library,
         new series, no. 661. The novel appeared for

the first time in Harper's weekly, Mar. 1889--
Nov. 1889.

12 An imperative duty. N. Y. , Harper, 1892 (i. e. 1891).
150p.
First published in Harper's monthly, July--Oct.
1891.

13 Indian summer. Boston, Ticknor, 1886. 395p.
First published in Harper's monthly, July 1885--
Feb. 1886.

14 The Kentons. N. Y. and London, Harper, 1902. 317p.

15 The lady of the Aroostook. Boston, Houghton, Osgood,
1879. 326p.

16 The landlord at lion's head. N. Y. , Harper, 1897.
461p.
First published in Harper's weekly, July 4, 1896-
Dec. 1896.

17 The leatherwood god. N. Y. , Century, 1916. 236p.
Appeared also in Century magazine, April--Nov.
1916.

18 No entry.

19 Mercy see The quality of mercy

20 The minister's charge or the apprenticeship of Lemuel
Barker. Boston, Ticknor, 1887. 463p.
Published first in Century magazine, Feb. --Dec.
1886. Published also in 1886 in book form by
David Douglas in Edinburgh.

21 Miss Bellard's inspiration. N. Y. and London, Harper,
1905. 224p.

22 Mrs. Farrell. N. Y. and London, Harper, 1921. 266p.
Contains an introduction by Mildred Howells. The
novel appeared first in the Atlantic monthly in
1875 and 1876 under the title Private theatricals.
See Ricus, "A suppressed novel of Mr. Howells, "
Bookman 32:201-03, Oct. 1910. See also Blanck's
Bibliography of American literature, entry no.
9864.

23 A modern instance. Boston, Osgood, 1882. 514p.
Serialized in Century magazine, Dec. 1881--Oct.
1882. The British edition was issued a few days
before the American.

24 An open-eyed conspiracy; an idyll of Saratoga. N. Y. ,
Harper, 1897. 181p.
First published in Century magazine, July--Oct.
1896.

25 A parting and a meeting. N. Y. , Harper, 1896. 99p.
First published in Cosmopolitan, Dec. 1894--Feb.
1895.

18

26 The quality of mercy, a story of contemporary life.
        New York Sun, Oct. 4, 1891--Jan. 3, 1892.
            Published by Harper in 1892; also published by
            David Douglas in 1892 in Edinburgh under the title
            of Mercy.
27 Ragged lady. N. Y. and London, Harper, 1899. 357p.
28 The rise of Silas Lapham. Boston, Ticknor, 1885.
        515p.
            Serialized in Century magazine, Nov. 1884--Aug.
            1885. Lillian K. Sabine wrote a four-act play
            based on the novel in 1927. The play was pub-
            lished by Samuel French.
29 The shadow of a dream. N. Y., Harper, 1890. 218p.
            Appeared also in Harper's monthly, Mar. -- May
            1890.
30 The son of Royal Langbrith. N. Y. and London, Harper,
        1904. 369p.
            Appeared also in the North American review,
            Jan. --Aug. 1904.
31 The story of a play. N. Y. and London, Harper, 1898.
        312p.
            Published first in Scribner's magazine, Mar. --
            Aug. 1897.
32 Their silver wedding journey. N. Y. and London,
        Harper, 1899. 2v.
            Appeared in Harper's monthly, Jan--Dec. 1899.
            A condensation of the novel was published in
            Germany in 1920 under the title of Hither and
            thither in Germany.
33 Their wedding journey. Boston, Osgood, 1872. 287p.
            First published in the Atlantic monthly, July--
            Dec. 1871. The Atlantic published a supplement
            to this novel in the May issue of 1883 under the
            title "Niagara revisited, twelve years after their
            wedding journey." In the following year Dalziel
            in Chicago published the item as a separate. It
            was suppressed. See essay by Rudolf and Clara
            Kirk in Essays in literary history, presented to
            J. Milton French. N. Y., Russell and Russell,
            1965 (c1960). p. 177-95.
34 Through the eye of the needle. N. Y. and London,
        Harper, 1907. 233p.
            A portion of the novel appeared in the Cosmopoli-
            tan, Apr. --Sept. 1894.
35 A traveler from Altruria. N. Y., Harper, 1894. 318p.
            First appeared in the Cosmopolitan, Nov. 1892--
            Oct. 1893.

36 The undiscovered country. Boston, Houghton, Mifflin,
    1880. 419p.
        First appeared in the Atlantic monthly, Jan. --
        July 1880.
37 The vacation of the Kelwyns; an idyll of the middle
    eighteen seventies. N. Y. and London, Harper,
    1920. 257p.
38 "The whole family, a novel in twelve parts; chapter one:
    the father." Harper's bazaar 41:1161-70, Dec.
    1907.
        Howells wrote only this first chapter.
39 A woman's reason. Boston, Osgood, 1883. 466p.
        Appeared also in Century magazine, Feb. --Oct.
        1883.
40 The world of chance. N. Y., Harper, 1893. 375p.
        First published in Harper's monthly, Mar. --Nov.
        1892.

SHORT STORIES

COLLECTIONS

41 Between the dark and the daylight; romances. N.Y.
   and London, Harper, 1907. 185p.
42 Christmas every day and other stories told for children.
   N.Y., Harper, 1893. 150p.
43 The daughter of the storage and other things in prose
   and verse. N.Y. and London, Harper, 1916. 352p.
44 A day's pleasure and other sketches. Boston, Houghton
   Mifflin, 1881. 240p.
45 Doorstep acquaintance and other sketches. N.Y.,
   Houghton Mifflin, 1900. 92p.
46 A fearful responsibility and other stories. Boston, Osgood, 1881. 255p.
47 The Howells story book. Edited by Mary E. Burt and
   Mildred Howells. N.Y., Scribner's, 1900. 161p.
48 A pair of patient lovers. N.Y. and London, Harper,
   1901. 368p.
49 Questionable shapes. N.Y. and London, Harper, 1903.
   219p.
50 Suburban sketches. N.Y., Hurd and Houghton, 1871.
   234p.
51 Suburban sketches. New and enlarged edition. Boston,
   Osgood, 1872. 255p.

INDIVIDUAL STORIES

52 "After the wedding." Harper's monthly 114:64-69, Dec.
   1906.
      Appears as "The father and the mother" in The
      mother and the father, dramatic passages.
53 "The amigo." Harper's monthly 112:51-53, Dec. 1905.
      Also in Daughter of the storage..., 1916. p.161-
      72.
54 "The angel of the Lord." In Questionable shapes. 1903.
   p.109-58.
      First published as "At third hand, a psychological
      inquiry" in Century magazine 61:496-506, Feb. 1901.

55 "At the sign of the savage." Atlantic monthly 40:36-48,
      July 1877.
            Also in A fearful responsibility... 1900. p.165-
            208.
56 "The bag of gold." Ashtabula sentinel 32:1, Apr. 22,
      1863.
            Unsigned.
57 "The boarders." Harper's monthly 132:540-43, Mar.
      1916.
            Also in The daughter of the storage... 1916.
            p.127-40.
58 "Bobby, study of a boy." Ohio state journal 22:1, Dec.
      14, 1858.
58a "Busily engaged; a plot for a farce." Ashtabula sentinel
      35:1, Oct. 3, 1866.
59 "Braybridge's offer." Harper's monthly 112:229-36,
      Jan. 1906.
            Also in Between the dark and the daylight. 1907.
            p.147-66.
60 "Butterflyflutterby and flutterbybutterfly." In Christmas
      every day... 1893. p.111-50.
61 "Buying a horse." Atlantic monthly 43:741-50, June
      1879.
            Also in Golden book 8:169-77, Aug. 1928. In-
            cluded in A day's pleasure... 1881. p.93-138.
            Published as a separate by Houghton Mifflin in
            1916.
62 "By horse-car to Boston." In Suburban sketches. 1901.
      p.91-114.
63 "A case of metaphantasmia." Harper's weekly 49:20-22,
      40-41, Dec. 16, 1905.
            Also in Between the dark and the daylight. 1907.
            p.125-43. Included in Harper, Wilhelmina, comp.
            Off duty. N.Y., Century, 1919. p.225-41.
64 "The chick of the Easter egg." Harper's weekly 50:
      509-12, Apr. 14, 1906.
            Also in Between the dark and the daylight. 1907.
            p.169-85.
65 "Christmas every day." Saint Nicholas magazine 13:
      163-67, Jan. 1886.
            Also in Christmas every day... 1893. p.3-24.
            Included in The Howells story book. 1900. p.3-
            17. Contained in Watts, F., ed. The complete
            Xmas book. rev. ed. Watts, 1961. Also in A
            St. Nicholas anthology, the early years. Ed. by
            Burton C. Frye. N.Y., Meredith Press, 1969.
            p.195-99.

66   "A circle in the water."   Scribner's magazine 17:293-
        303, 428-40, Mar.-Apr. 1895.
            Also in A pair of patient lovers. 1901. p.1-78.
66a "City and country in the fall; a long distance eclogue."
        Harper's weekly 46:1792, Nov. 29, 1902.
67   "The critical bookstore."   Harper's monthly 127:431-42,
        Aug. 1913.
            Also in The daughter of the storage... 1916.
        p.185-226.
68   "The daughter of the storage."   Harper's monthly 123:
        572-83, Sept. 1911.
            Also in The daughter of the storage... 1916. p.3-
        44.
69   "A day's pleasure."   Atlantic monthly, July-Sept. 1870.
            Also in A day's pleasure... 1881. p.7-91. In-
        cluded in Suburban sketches. 1901. p.115-70.
70   "Dick Dowdy, study of a first-rate fellow."   Ohio state
        journal 22:2, Dec. 6, 1858.
71   "Difficult case."   Atlantic monthly 86:24-36, 205-17,
        July-Aug. 1900.
            Also in A pair of patient lovers. 1901. p.145-220.
72   "Doorstep acquaintance."   Atlantic monthly 23:484-93,
        Apr. 1869.
            Also in Doorstep acquaintance... 1900.   Included
        in Suburban sketches. 1901. p.35-59.
73   "A dream."   Knickerbocker 58:146-50, Aug. 1861.
74   "Editha."   Harper's monthly 110:214-24, Jan. 1905.
            Also in Between the dark and the daylight. 1907.
        p.125-43.   Included in Burrell, J.A. and Cerf,
        B.A., eds.   Bedside book of famous American
        stories. N.Y., Random House, 1936. p.316-27.
        Contained in Burrell, J.A. and Cerf, B.A., eds.
        Anthology of famous American stories.   N.Y.,
        Modern Library, 1953. p.316-27.   Also in Ungar,
        Frederick, ed. To mother with love.   N.Y.,
        Stephen Daye, 1951. p.272-89.
75   "The eidolons of Brooks Alford."   Harper's monthly
        113:387-97, Aug. 1906.
            Also in Between the dark and the daylight. 1907.
        p.65-90.
76   "The emigrant of 1802."   Ashtabula sentinel, Feb. 9,
        Mar. 9, 30, Apr. 20, 1854.
77   "Escapade of grandfather."   In Daughter of the storage
        ... 1916. p.269-84.
78   "An experience."   In Daughter of the storage... 1916.
        p. 117-26.
78a "Fast and firm--a romance at Marseilles."   Ashtabula
        sentinel 35:1, Jan. 24, 31, 1866.

79 "The father." In The mother and the father, dramatic
     passages. N.Y., Harper, 1909.
         First published as "Father and mother, a mystery."
     Harper's monthly 100:869-74, May 1900.
80 "The father and the mother" see "After the wedding."
81 "A feast of reason." In Daughter of the storage...
     1916. p. 227-40.
82 "Flitting." Atlantic monthly 26:734-39, Dec. 1870.
         Also in Suburban sketches. 1901. p. 241-55.
         Included in A day's pleasure... 1881. p. 139-66.
83 "The fulfillment of the pact." Harper's weekly 56:9-10,
     Dec. 14, 1912.
84 "His apparition." Harper's monthly 104:621-48, Mar.
     1902.
         Also in Questionable shapes. 1903. p. 5-108.
85 "Hot." Ohio state journal 23:2, June 29, 1859.
         Also in The indicator; a Hesperian leaflet. North
     Bend, Ohio, John Scott, 1901. p. 26-28.
86 "How I lost a wife, an episode in the life of a bachelor."
     Ashtabula sentinel, May 18, 1854, p. 1.
86a "Incident." Pellet, no. 2, Apr. 17, 1872, p. 4.
         Harvard University has the Pellet, an occasional
     newspaper published in Boston by the Massachusetts
     Homeopathic Hospital Fair.
87 "The independent candidate." Ashtabula sentinel, Nov.
     23, 30, Dec. 7, 21, 28, 1854; Jan. 4, 11, 18, 1855,
     p. 1.
88 "The journeyman's secret." Ashtabula sentinel, Nov. 3,
     1853, p. 1.
89 "Jubilee days." Atlantic monthly 24:245-54, Aug. 1869.
         Also in Suburban sketches. 1901. p. 195-219.
90 "The lost child--a street scene." Ohio state journal
     22:1, Mar. 4, 1859.
91 "The magic of a voice." Lippincott's magazine 64:901-
     28, Dec. 1899.
         Also in A pair of patient lovers. 1901. p. 221-84.
92 "Making love between heaven and earth." Ohio state
     weekly journal 48:4, Mar. 1, 1859.
93 "A memory that worked overtime." Harper's monthly
     115:415-18, Aug. 1907.
         Also in Between the dark and the daylight. 1907.
     p. 93-103.
94 "Mrs. Johnson." Atlantic monthly 21:97-106, Jan. 1868.
         Also in Suburban sketches. 1901. p. 11-34.
95 "Mother." Harper's monthly 106:21-26, Dec. 1902.
         Also in The mother and the father, dramatic pas-
     sages.

96 "The mother-bird." Harper's monthly 120:126-28, Dec.
    1909.
        Also in Daughter of the storage... 1916. p. 151-
        60.
97 "The mouse." In A day's pleasure... 1881. p. 167-80.
98 "Not a love story." Odd-fellows casket 1:222-24, Feb.
    1859.
99 "An old-time love affair." Ashtabula sentinel, Sept. 14,
    1854, p. 1.
100 "A pair of patient lovers." Harper's monthly 95:832-51,
    Nov. 1897.
        Also in A pair of patient lovers. 1901. p. 1-78.
101 "The pearl." Harper's monthly 133:409-13, Aug. 1916.
102 "Pedestrian tour." Atlantic monthly 24:591-603, Nov.
    1869.
        Also in Suburban sketches. 1901. p. 60-90.
103 "A perfect goose." Odd-fellows casket, Apr. 1859,
    p. 379-80.
        Signed Chispa.
104 "The pony engine and the pacific express." In Christ-
    mas every day... 1893. p. 51-70.
        Also in The Howells story book. 1900. p. 18-30.
105 "A presentiment" see "Talking of presentiments."
106 "The pumpkin-glory." In Christmas every day... 1893.
    p. 71-110.
        Also in The Howells story book. 1900. p. 31-54.
107 "The pursuit of the piano." Harper's monthly 100:725-
    46, Apr. 1900.
        Also in A pair of patient lovers. 1901. p. 79-144.
108 "The return to favor." Harper's monthly 131:278-80,
    July 1915.
        Also in Current opinion 61:57-58, July 1916. In-
        cluded in Daughter of the storage... 1916. p. 81-
        92.
109 "A romance of real life." Atlantic monthly 25:305-12,
    Mar. 1870.
        Also in Doorstep acquaintance... 1900. p. 58-74.
        Included in Suburban sketches. 1901. p. 171-89.
110 "Romance of the crossing." Odd-fellows casket 1:443-
    44, May 1859.
        Signed Chispa.
111 "Rotational tenants; a Hallowe'en mystery." Harper's
    monthly 133:770-77, Oct. 1916.
112 "Scene." Every Saturday 10:11, Jan. 7, 1871.
        Also in Suburban sketches. 1901. p. 190-94.
113 "A sleep and a forgetting." Harper's weekly 50:1781-
    84, 1862-65, 1899-1901; 51:24-27, Dec. 15--Jan. 5,
    1907.

Also in <u>Between the dark and the daylight.</u> 1917.
p. 3-61.

114 "Somebody's mother." <u>Harper's monthly</u> 131:523-26,
Sept. 1915.

Also in <u>The daughter of the storage...</u> 1916.
p. 93-106.

115 "A summer Sunday in a country village." <u>Odd-fellows</u>
<u>casket,</u> Apr. 1859, p. 354-57.

116 "Table talk." In <u>Daughter of the storage...</u> 1916.
p. 253-68.

117 "A tale of love and politics." <u>Ashtabula sentinel,</u>
Sept. 1, 1853.

118 "Tale untold." <u>Atlantic monthly</u> 120:236-42, Aug. 1917.

119 "Talking of presentiments." <u>Harper's monthly</u> 116:76-
81, Dec. 1907.

Appears as "A presentiment" in <u>The daughter of</u>
<u>the storage...</u> 1916. p. 45-63.

120 "Their first quarrel." In Clemens, Samuel L. <u>Women</u>
<u>and things.</u> N.Y., Harper, 1906. p. 170-75.

121 "Though one rose from the dead." <u>Harper's monthly</u>
106:724-38, Apr. 1903.

Also in <u>Questionable shapes.</u> 1903. p. 159-219.

122 "Tonelli's marriage." <u>Atlantic monthly</u> 22:96-110,
July 1868.

Also in <u>Doorstep acquaintance...</u> 1900. p. 24-57.
Included in <u>A fearful responsibility...</u> 1900.
p. 209-55.

123 "Turkeys turning the tables." In <u>Christmas every day</u>
... 1893. p. 25-50.

124 "Why he married." <u>Ashtabula sentinel</u> 35:1, Oct. 31,
1866.

Unsigned; believed to be by Howells.

PLAYS

COLLECTIONS

125 Complete plays. Edited with an introduction by Walter
J. Meserve. N.Y., New York University Press,
1960. 649p.
126 Minor dramas. Edinburgh, Douglas, 1907. 2v.
127 The mouse-trap and other farces. N.Y., Harper,
1889. 184p.
128 The sleeping car and other farces. Boston, Houghton
Mifflin, 1889.

INDIVIDUAL PLAYS

129 The Albany depot. N.Y., Harper, 1892. 68p.
Also in Complete plays. Edited by Walter J.
Meserve. 1960. p. 386-95. First published in
Harper's weekly 33:989 and supp. 1005-08, Dec.
14, 1889.
130 Bride roses; a scene. Boston, Houghton Mifflin, 1900.
48p.
Also in Complete plays. p. 431-37. First published
in Harper's monthly 87:424-31, Aug. 1893.
131 "Colonel Sellers as a scientist." In Complete plays.
p. 209-41.
Written in collaboration with Samuel L. Clemens.
132 A counterfeit presentiment. Boston, Osgood, 1877.
155p.
Also in Complete plays. p. 72-109. Appeared
originally in the Atlantic monthly, Aug.-Oct. 1877.
133 The elevator. Boston, Osgood, 1885. In Complete
plays. p. 302-13.
Included in The sleeping car and other farces.
1889. First published in Harper's monthly 70:111-
25, Dec. 1884.
134 Evening dress. N.Y., Harper, 1893. 59p.
Also in Complete plays. p. 409-18. First published in Cosmopolitan 13:116-27, May 1892.
135 "Five o'clock tea." In Complete plays. p. 366-73.
Included in The mouse trap and other farces. 1889.

First published in Harper's monthly 76:86-96, Dec.
1887.

136 "A foregone conclusion." In Complete plays. p.316-
37.
Written in collaboration with William Poel.

137 The garroters. N.Y., Harper, 1886. 90p.
Also in Complete plays. p.340-52. Included in
The mouse-trap and other farces. 1889. First
appeared in Harper's monthly 72:146-62, Dec.
1885.

138 "A hazard of new fortunes." In Complete plays. p.
532-50.

139 "Her opinion of his story." In Complete plays.
p.577-83.
Included in Minor dramas. 1907. v.2, p.398-
426. Appeared in Harper's bazaar 41:429-37, May
1907.

140 "The impossible, a mystery play." In Complete plays.
p.619-27.
First published in Harper's monthly 122:116-25,
Dec. 1910.

141 An Indian giver. Boston, Houghton Mifflin, 1900. 99p.
Also in Complete plays. p.467-80. First published in Harper's monthly 94:235-52, Jan. 1897.

142 A letter of introduction. N.Y., Harper, 1892. 62p.
Also in Complete plays. p.397-407. Appeared in
Harper's monthly 84:243-56, Jan. 1892.

143 "A likely story." In Complete plays. p.375-84.
Included in The mouse-trap and other farces.
1889.

144 "A masterpiece of diplomacy." In Complete plays.
p.439-50.
Included in Minor dramas. 1907. v.1, p.220-
69. First published in Harper's monthly 88:371-
85, Feb. 1894.

145 The mother and the father; dramatic passages. N.Y.
and London, Harper, 1909. 55p.
Also in Complete plays. p.563-75. The play is a
combination of the following: "Father and mother,
a mystery," Harper's monthly 100:869-74, May
1900; "The mother," Harper's monthly 106:21-26,
Dec. 1902; and "After the wedding," Harper's
monthly 114:64-69, Dec. 1906.

146 "The mouse trap." In Complete plays. p.355-64.
Included in The mousetrap and other farces. 1889.
First published in Harper's monthly 74:64-75, Dec.
1886.

147 "The night before Christmas." In Complete plays.
    p. 603-11.
        Included in Howells, William Dean. The daughter
        of the storage and other things in prose and verse.
        1916. p. 319-52. First published in Harper's
        monthly 120:207-16, Jan. 1910.
148 Out of the question. Boston, Osgood, 1877. 183p.
        Also in Complete plays. p. 35-68. Appeared in
        Atlantic monthly 39:195-208, Feb. 1877.
149 The parlor car. Boston, Osgood, 1876.
        Also in Complete plays. p. 25-33. Included in
        The sleeping car and other farces. 1889.
150 Parting friends. N.Y. and London, Harper, 1911.
    57p.
        Also in Complete plays. p. 613-17. First pub-
        lished in Harper's monthly 121:670-77, Oct. 1910.
151 A previous engagement. N.Y., London, 1897. 65p.
        Also in Complete plays. p. 452-65. First pub-
        lished in Harper's monthly 92:28-44, Dec. 1895.
152 "Priscilla: a comedy." In Complete plays. p. 141-
    204.
153 The register. Boston, Osgood, 1884. 91p.
        Also in Complete plays. p. 255-68. Included in
        The sleeping car and other farces. 1889. First
        published in Harper's monthly 68:70-86, Dec. 1883.
154 "The rise of Silas Lapham." In Complete plays.
    p. 484-517.
        Written in collaboration with Paul Kester.
155 Room Forty-five. Boston, Houghton Mifflin, 1900. 61p.
        Also in Complete plays. p. 552-60. First pub-
        lished in Frank Leslie's popular monthly 49:132-
        48, Dec. 1899.
156 "Saved: an emotional drama." In Complete plays.
    p. 585-92.
        First published in Harper's weekly 52:22-24, Dec.
        26, 1908.
157 A sea change or Love's stowaway; a lyricated farce.
    Boston, Osgood, 1884.
        Also in Complete plays. p. 272-99. Appeared in
        Harper's weekly 32:505 and supp. 521-24, July 14,
        1888. Published also by Ticknor in 1888 with ad-
        ditions and changes from the text in Harper's
        weekly.
158 "Self-sacrifice: a farce tragedy." In Complete plays.
    p. 629-40.
        First published in Harper's monthly 122:748-57,
        Apr. 1911.

159 The sleeping car. Boston, Osgood, 1883.   74p.
     Also in Complete plays.   p. 243-53.
160 The smoking car.   Boston, Houghton Mifflin, 1900.
     70p.
     Also in Complete plays.   p. 519-28.   First pub-
     lished in Frank Leslie's popular monthly 47:183-99,
     Dec. 1898.
161 "A true hero."   In Complete plays.   p. 594-601.
     First published in Harper's monthly 119:866-75,
     Nov. 1909.
162 The unexpected guests.   N. Y., Harper, 1893.   54p.
     Also in Complete plays.   p. 420-29.   Appeared in
     Harper's monthly 86:211-25, Jan. 1893.
163 "Yorick's love."   In Complete plays.   p. 115-39.
     Adapted and translated from the Spanish of Esta-
     benez.   The play remained unpublished.

POEMS

COLLECTIONS BY HOWELLS

164 Poems. Boston, Osgood, 1873. 172p.
165 Poems. Boston, Ticknor, 1886. 223p.
Reprint except for "Pordenone" and "The long
days."
166 Poems of two friends. By John J. Piatt and William
Dean Howells. Columbus, Ohio, Follett, Foster,
1860. 132p.
Howells's poems are on p. 83-132.
167 Stops of various quills. N.Y., Harper, 1895. 58
leaves.

ANTHOLOGIES

168 The poets and poetry of the West. By William T.
Coggeshall. Columbus, Ohio, Follett, Foster, 1860.
688p.
169 An American anthology 1787-1900. Edited by Edmund
C. Stedman. Boston, Houghton Mifflin, 1900. 878p.

INDIVIDUAL POEMS

170 "All four." (In Poems of two friends. 1860. p. 97).
171 "All the long August afternoon."
An unpublished holograph poem laid in the Newberry
Library copy of William Dean Howells's The flight
of Pony Baker published in 1902.
172 "Andenken." Atlantic monthly 5:100-02, Jan. 1860.
173 "Another day." Harper's monthly 82:608, Mar. 1891.
Also in Stops of various quills. 1895. Included
in Warner, Charles D., ed. Library of the world's
best literature. N.Y., Peale and Hill, 1897.
p. 7657.
174 "At the circus." Saturday press 2:3, Dec. 31, 1859.
175 "The autumn land." Signed Godfrey Constant (pseud.)
Ohio farmer 6:188, Nov. 21, 1857.
Also in Poems of two friends. 1860. p. 95.

176 "Avery." (In Poems. 1873. p.143-47).
First published in William Dean Howells's Their
wedding journey. Boston, Houghton Mifflin, 1871.
p.139-41. In the 1968 edition by John K. Reeves,
published by Indiana University Press, the poem
is on p. 86-88.

177 The battle in the clouds; song and chorus inscribed to
the Army of the Cumberland. Written by William
Dean Howells and composed by M. Keller. 1864.
Also in Poems. 1873. Included in Stevenson,
Burton E., ed. Poems of American history. rev.
ed. Boston, Houghton Mifflin, 1922. p.506-07.
The poem is about the Battle of Lookout Mountain,
Nov. 24, 1863.

178 "Before the gate." Atlantic monthly 24:176, Aug. 1869.
Also in Poems. 1873. p.84-85.

179 "Bereaved." Ohio state journal 23:4, Mar. 2, 1860.
Also in Poems. 1873. p.136-37.

180 "Bewildered guest." Harper's monthly 86:548, Mar.
1893.
Also in Warner, Charles D., ed. Library of the
world's best literature. N.Y., Peale and Hill,
1897. p.7656. Included in Markham, Edwin,
comp. The book of American poetry. N.Y., Wise,
1934. p.191.

181 "The bird song." Signed Wilhelm Constant (pseud.)
National era, Dec. 2, 1858, p.189.
Appears as "The bird" in Poems of two friends.
1860. p.127.

182 "Black Cross Farm (to F.S.)" In Howells, William
Dean. The daughter of the storage and other things
in prose and verse. N.Y., Harper, 1916. p.173-
81.

183 "The bobolinks are singing." Saturday press 3:1, Feb.
11, 1860.
Also in Poems. 1873. p.110-12. Also in The
poets and poetry of the West. 1860. p.681.

184 "Bopeep: a pastoral." In The Atlantic Almanac 1870.
Boston, Fields, Osgood, 1869. p.12-16.
Included in Poems. 1873. p.148-59.

185 "Breakfast is my best meal." Frank Leslie's magazine
48:388-91, Aug. 1899.
Also in Howells, William Dean. The daughter of
the storage and other things in prose and verse.
N.Y., Harper, 1916. p.141-50.

186 "Bubbles." Atlantic monthly 7:415, Apr. 1861.
Also in Poems. 1873. p.29-30.

187 "The burden."   Harper's monthly 91:517, Sept. 1895.
     Also in Stops of various quills.   1895.
188 "By the sea."   Commonwealth 1:1, May 1863.
     Also in Poems.   1873.   p. 97.   Set to music by
     F. Boott and published by Ditson in 1872 under the
     title of The song of the sea.
189 "The caged robin."   In Poems of two friends.   1860.
     p. 119-20.
190 "Calvary."   Harper's monthly 90:39, Dec. 1894.
     Also in Stops of various quills.   1895.   Included
     in Clark, Thomas C. and Clark, Hazel D., eds.
     Christ in poetry.   N. Y., Association Press, 1952.
     p. 132.
191 "Caprice," Saturday press 3:1, Apr. 14, 1860.
     Also in Kronenberger, Louis, ed.   An anthology of
     light verse.   N. Y., Modern Library, 1935.   p. 148-
     49.   Included in Poems.   1873.   p. 49-50.
192 "Captain Dunlevy's last trip."   In Howells, William
     Dean.   The daughter of the storage and other things
     in prose and verse.   N. Y., Harper, 1916, p. 67-77.
193 "Change."   Harper's monthly 90:38, Dec. 1894.
     Also in Stops of various quills.   1895.   Included
     in An American anthology, 1787-1900.   1900.
     p. 386.   The poem appears under the title "Some-
     times when after spirited debate" (first line of
     poem) in Richard Le Gallienne's The Le Gallienne
     book of English and American poetry.   N. Y.,
     Garden City Publishing Co., 1935.
194 "Christmas."   Harper's weekly 47:1982, Dec. 12, 1903.
195 "The Christmas spirit."   Harper's weekly 46:1822-24,
     Dec. 6, 1902.
     (Not verified.)
196 "A Christmas story."   Casket 2:235-37, Dec. 1853.
197 "Clement."   Galaxy 1:210-12, June 1, 1866.
     Also in Poems.   1873.   p. 86-96.
198 "The coming."   Ohio state journal 23:4, Jan. 23, 1860;
     Bookman 35:510-14, July 1912.
     Reprinted in part in William Dean Howells's Years
     of my youth.   N. Y., Harper, 1916.
199 "Company."   Harper's monthly 86:547, Mar. 1893.
     Also in Stops of various quills.   1895.
200 "Compliment."   In Poems of two friends.   1860.
     p. 113.
201 "Conscience."   Harper's monthly 90:39, Dec. 1894.
     Also in Stops of various quills.   1895.   Included
     in Warren, Ina R. ed., Notable single poems of
     American authors.   Buffalo, Charles W. Moulton
     [1895].

202 "Consolation." Saturday press, Oct. 17, 1865, p.157.
203 "Convention." Dial 1:371, June 1860.
      Also in Poems. 1873. p.171.
204 "Dead." Saturday press 2:1, Nov. 12, 1859.
      Also in Poems of two friends. 1860. p.116-117.
      Included in The poets and poetry of the West.
      1860. p.680.
205 "The death of May." National era, June 21, 1855,
     p. 97.
      Also in Poems of two friends. 1860. p.111-12.
206 Don't wake the children. Words by William Dean
    Howells and music by Clarence W. Bowers. Jeffer-
    son, Ohio, J.A. Howells, 1895.
207 "Dorothy Dudley." In Theatrum majorum. The Cam-
    bridge of 1776. Boston, Hurd and Houghton, 1876.
    p. 1.
208 "A double-barreled sonnet to Mark Twain." Harper's
    weekly 46:1943, Dec. 13, 1902.
209 "The doubt." National era, Sept. 16, 1858 p.145; also
    in Ashtabula sentinel 27:297, Sept. 23, 1858.
      Included in Poems of two friends. 1860. p.121.
      Contained also in Poems. 1873. p.127-28. Ap-
      peared in the National era under the pseudonym of
      Wilhelm Constant.
210 "The dream." Signed Will Narlie. Ohio farmer 7:304,
    Sept. 18, 1858.
      Also in Cady, Edwin H. The road to realism; the
      early years 1837-1885 of William Dean Howells.
      Syracuse, N.Y., Syracuse University Press, 1956.
      p. 58.
211 "Drifting away." Saturday press 2:1, Sept. 10, 1859.
      Also in Poems of two friends. 1860. p.114. In-
      cluded in The poets and poetry of the West. 1860.
      p. 678-79.
212 "Drowned." In Poems of two friends. 1860. p.123.
213 "Elegy on John Butler Howells." Ashtabula sentinel
    33:1, June 29, 1864.
      Also in Poems. 1873. p.100-04.
214 "The emigrant's last meal in the old house." Ohio
    state journal 15:1, June 3, 1852.
      This is Howells's second published poem.
215 "The empty house" see "The old homestead."
216 "Equality." In Stops of various quills. 1895.
217 "Evening voices." Ashtabula sentinel, May 20, 1858,
     p. 153.
      Also in Poems of two friends. 1860. p.104.

218 "Except as little children." In Hill, Martha S. , ed.
     Fame's tribute to children, being a collection of auto-
     graph sentiments contributed by famous men and
     women for this volume. Done in facsimile and pub-
     lished for the benefit of the Children's Home of the
     World's Columbian Exposition. Chicago, Hayes and
     Co. , 1893. pt. 2, p. 24.
          A four-line poem, appearing first in this publica-
     tion, written in Howells's own hand and signed.
219 "Experience." Harper's monthly 108:929, May 1904.
220 "The face at the window." Harper's weekly 51:1825,
     Dec. 14, 1907.
          Also in Howells, William Dean. The daughter of
     the storage and other things in prose and verse.
     N. Y. , Harper, 1916. p. 107-13.
221 "Faith" see "What shall it profit?"
222 "The faithful of the Gonzaga." In Poems. 1873.
     p. 59-76.
          First printed in the New York Ledger 1865(?)
     See Frederic C. Marsten, Jr. "The early life of
     William Dean Howells: a chronicle 1837-1871."
     Ph. D. dissertation, Brown University, 1944.
     p. 280.
223 "Feuerbilder." Saturday press 3:1, Jan. 14, 1860.
          Also in Poems. 1873. p. 141-42.
224 "The first blue violet."
          Located in the Ohio farmer (date not given). It is
     the third poem published by Howells according to
     Edwin H. Cady, The road to realism; the early
     years 1837-1885 of William Dean Howells. Syra-
     cuse, N. Y. , Syracuse University Press, 1956.
     p. 41.
225 "The first cricket." Atlantic monthly 24:351, Sept.
     1869.
          Also in Poems. 1873. p. 77-78. Set to music
     by F. Boott and published by Ditson in 1876.
226 "For one of the killed." In Poems. 1873. p. 133.
          Set to music by Mabel W. Daniels and published
     by Arthur P. Schmidt in 1923. The title of the
     sheet music is Glory and endless years.
227 "Forlorn." Nation 3:134-35, Aug. 16, 1866.
          Also in Poems. 1873. p. 13-18. For brief his-
     tory of poem, see William Dean Howells's Literary
     friends and acquaintance. N. Y. , Harper, 1900.
     p. 85.
228 "Friends and foes." Harper's monthly 86:547, Mar.
     1893.
          Also in Stops of various quills. 1895. A Spanish

translation is contained in Pan American magazine
27:38-39, May 1918.
229 "From generation to generation." Harper's monthly
86:548, Mar. 1893.
Also in Stops of various quills. 1895. Included
in An American anthology 1787-1900. p.386. Contained in Benet, William R., ed. Poems for youth.
N.Y., Dutton, 1925. p.149.
230 "Gerrit Smith." Ohio state journal 23:2, Nov. 15, 1859.
Gerrit Smith was an upstate New York philanthropist.
The poem is anti-slavery.
231 Glory and endless years see "For one of the killed."
232 "Gone." In Poems. 1873. p.122.
Also in Poems of two friends. 1860. p.93. Set
to music by E.A. McDowell and included in Eight
songs with pianoforte accompaniment. N.Y.,
Breitkopf and Hartel, 1893. (i.e. 1894).
233 "Good society" see "Society."
234 "The heaven-wreath" see "The wreath in heaven--a
fancy."
235 "Heinesque." Ohio state journal 23:2, Nov. 23, 1859.
236 "Heredity." Harper's monthly 90:37, Dec. 1894.
Also in Stops of various quills. 1895. Included
in Markham, Edwin, comp. The book of American
poetry. N.Y., Wise, 1934. p.192.
237 "Hope." Harper's monthly 86:549, Mar. 1893.
A poem of twelve lines, the first one beginning "Yes,
death is at the bottom of the cup." Appears under
the title of "If" in Stops of various quills. 1895.
Also in An American anthology 1787-1900. Boston,
Houghton Mifflin, 1915. p.171.
238 "Hope." Harper's monthly 91:517, Sept. 1895.
Also in An American anthology 1787-1900. 1900.
p.387.
239 "If" see "Hope."
240 "In August" see "Pleasure-pain."
241 "In earliest spring." Atlantic monthly 29:619, May
1872.
Also in Poems. 1873. p.108-09. Included in
George, David L., ed. Family book of best-loved
poems. Garden City, N.Y., Hanover House, 1952.
p.284.
242 "In the dark." Harper's monthly 90:37, Dec. 1894.
Also in Stops of various quills. 1895.
243 "Judgment day." In Stops of various quills. 1895.
Also in An American anthology 1787-1900. 1900.
p.387. Included in Benét, William R., comp.

Poems for youth. N.Y., Dutton, 1925. p.148-49.
Contained in The first book of the Authors Club.
N.Y., 1893. p.288.
244 "The king dines." In Stops of various quills. 1895.
245 "Labor and capital." In Stops of various quills. 1895.
246 "Leonora." Saturday press 9:60, Apr. 12, 1855.
Renamed "Sonnet" in Poems of two friends. 1860.
p.110.
247 "Liebeswonne." Saturday press 2:1, Oct. 22, 1859.
Also in Poems of two friends. 1860. p.108.
248 "Life." Harper's monthly 82:608, Mar. 1891.
Also in Stops of various quills. 1895.
249 "The little children." In Wharton, Edith, ed. Le
livre des sansfoyer. N.Y., Scribner's, 1916. p.17.
250 "Living." Harper's monthly 86:547, Mar. 1893.
Also in Stops of various quills. 1895.
251 "The long days." Atlantic monthly 33:663, June 1874.
Also in Poems. 1886. p.223.
252 "Lost beliefs." Atlantic monthly 5:486, Apr. 1860.
Also in Poems. 1873. p.31.
253 "Louis Lebeau's conversion." Atlantic monthly 10:534-
38, Nov. 1862.
Also in Poems. 1873. p.32-48.
254 "Materials of a story." Harper's monthly 84:942, May
1892.
Also in Stops of various quills. 1895.
255 "Midnight rain." In Poems of two friends. 1860.
p.125-26.
According to William M. Gibson and George W.
Arms's Bibliography of William Dean Howells, the
poem first appeared in the Ohio farmer (no date
given) and later reprinted under the title of "Nightly rain" in Ashtabula sentinel 23:1, Oct. 5, 1854.
The poem was signed Will Narlie.
256 "Midway." Harper's monthly 90:39, Dec. 1894.
Also in Stops of various quills. 1895.
257 "Misanthropy." Dial 1:555, Sept. 1860.
258 "Moods." Harper's monthly 82:608, Mar. 1891.
259 "The moonlight is full of the fragrance." Dial 1:708,
Nov. 1860; Saturday press 3:1, Nov. 10, 1860; Ohio
state journal 24:4, Nov. 14, 1860.
260 "Mortality." Harper's monthly 82:848-49, May 1891.
Also in Stops of various quills. 1895.
261 "Mortuaviva." Saturday press 2:1, Dec. 10, 1859.
A part of this poem appears as "While she sang"
in Poems. 1873. p.160-62.
262 "The movers." In Poems of two friends. 1860.

p. 85-89.
> Also in Poems. 1873. p. 115-19. Contained in
> The poets and poetry of the West. 1860. p. 679-
> 80.

263 "The mulberries." Atlantic monthly 27:377-79, March
1871.
> Also in Poems. 1873. p. 79-83.

264 "The mysteries." In Poems of two friends. 1860.
p. 101.
> Also in Poems. 1873. p. 130.

265 "Naming the bird." In Poems. 1873. p. 163-69.

266 "Nightly rain" see "Midnight rain."

267 "No love lost, a romance of travel. N. Y., Putnam, 1869.
58p.
> A poem in blank verse. Appeared originally in
> Putnam's magazine 2:641-51, Dec. 1868.

268 "November--impression." Harper's monthly 83:906,
Nov. 1891.
> Also in Stops of various quills. 1895.

269 "The old bouquet." In Poems of two friends. 1860.

270 "Old Brown." Ashtabula sentinel, Jan. 25, 1860; Commonwealth, June 24, 1865.
> Included in Redpath, James. Echoes of Harper's
> Ferry. Boston, Thayer and Eldridge, 1860.
> p. 316. A single leaf of the poem, presumably pub-
> lished in Columbus, Ohio, in 1859, is listed and
> reproduced in Blanck's Bibliography of American
> literature, vol. 4, p. 384 and facing page. An ex-
> tract of the poem under the title of "Success and
> unsuccess" is in The Hesperian tree; an annual of
> the Ohio Valley 1900. Edited by John J. Piatt.
> Cincinnati, Ohio, George C. Shaw, 1900. p. 38.

271 "The old farmer's elegy." Unsigned. Ashtabula sentinel, May 25, 1854. p. 1.

272 "The old homestead." Atlantic monthly 7:213, Feb.
1861.
> Appears as "The empty house" in Poems. 1873.
> p. 27-28.

273 "Old winter, loose thy hold on us." Ohio state journal
15:2, Mar. 23, 1852.
> The poem is signed V. M. H. and represents Howells's
> first publication. It appeared also in the Cincinnati
> commercial 15:4, Apr. 24, 1852, under the title of
> "Old winter, let go thy hold on us."

274 "On a bright winter day." Harper's monthly 127:835,
Nov. 1913.

275 "Our thanksgiving accept" see "Thanksgiving."

276 "Parable."   Harper's monthly 91:519, Sept. 1895.
     Also in Stops of various quills. 1895.
277 "The passengers of a retarded submersible." North
     American review 204:741-42, Nov. 1916.
          Also in Clarke, George H. A treasury of war
          poetry. Boston, Houghton Mifflin, 1917. p.136-
          38.
278 "Peonage."   Harper's monthly 82:609, Mar. 1891.
     Also in Stops of various quills. 1895.
279 "Phantoms."   Saturday press 3:4, Mar. 17, 1860.
280 "The pilot's story."   Atlantic monthly 6:323-25, Sept.
     1860.
          Also in Poems. 1873. p.3-12.
281 "Pistol, Nym, and Bardolph discuss the terrors of
     heat."   Ashtabula sentinel, Aug. 24, 1854, p.4.
          The poem contains thirty-five lines of blank verse.
282 "Pleasure-pain."   Atlantic monthly 5:468-70, Apr. 1860.
          Reprinted in part in Poems. 1873. p.19-25.
          The last four stanzas appear under the title of
          "Summer dead" in The poets and poetry of the
          West. 1860. p.681. The same lines appear
          under the title of "In August" in Poems. 1873.
          p.26.
283 "A poet."   Dial 1:371, June 1860; also in Common-
     wealth 1:1, Feb. 14, 1863.
          Included in Poems. 1873. p.170.
284 "The poet's friends."   Atlantic monthly 5:185, Feb.
     1860.
          Also in Poems. 1873. p.172. Included in The
          poets and poetry of the West. 1860. p.680.
          Contained in Cady, Edwin H. The road to real-
          ism; the early years 1837-1885 of William Dean
          Howells. Syracuse, N.Y., Syracuse University
          Press, 1956. p.70.
285 [Poem translated into Italian by the Abbé Fratini. Uni-
     versity of Padua Printing Office, Padua, 1863].
          The English text appears under the title "A spring-
          time" in Poems. 1873. p.106-07. Additional
          information about the poem appears in Life in let-
          ters of William Dean Howells, vol. 1, p.76.
286 "Pordenone."   Harper's monthly 65:829-35, Nov. 1882.
          Also in Poems. 1886. p.201-22.
287 "A prayer: Lord for the erring thought" see "Thanks-
     giving."
288 "Prelude."   In Poems of two friends. 1860. p.83-84.
          Also in Poems 1873. p.113-14.

289 "Question." Harper's monthly 86:546, Mar. 1893.
 Also in Stops of various quills. 1895.
290 "Race." Critic 24 (ns 21): 220, Mar. 31, 1894;
 Harper's monthly 88:677, Apr. 1894.
 Also in Stops of various quills. 1895.
291 "Rapture." In Poems. 1873. p.124. Reprinted from
 "Liebeswonne" in Poems of two friends.
292 "Respite." Harper's monthly 86:549, Mar. 1893.
 Also in Stops of various quills. 1895.
293 "Reward and punishment." Harper's monthly 91:518,
 Sept. 1895.
 Also in Stops of various quills. 1895.
294 "Rhyme of the new year." Ashtabula sentinel 33:1,
 Dec. 28, 1864.
295 "The robin and the cows." In Untermeyer, Louis, ed.
 Golden treasury of poetry. N.Y., Golden Press,
 1959. p.60.
296 "The royal portraits." Harper's monthly 32:43, Dec.
 1865.
 Also in Poems. 1873. p.54-58.
297 "Saint Christopher." Harper's monthly 28:1-2, Dec.
 1863.
 Also in Poems. 1873. p.98-99.
298 "The sarcastic fair." In Poems of two friends. 1860.
 p.103.
 Also in Poems. 1873. p.123.
299 "A seasonable moral." Harper's weekly 48:42, Dec.
 10, 1904.
300 "Sir Philip Sydney." In Poems of two friends. 1860.
 p.132.
301 "The snow birds." Ohio farmer 9:32, Jan. 28, 1860.
 Also in Poems. 1873. p.138.
302 "Society." Harper's monthly 90:36, Dec. 1894.
 This is a four-line poem beginning "Yes, I suppose
 it is well to make some sort of exclusion." It appears under the title of "Good society" in Stops of
 various quills. 1895.
303 "Society." Harper's monthly 90:360, Mar. 1895.
 Also in Warner, Charles D., ed. Library of the
 world's best literature. N.Y., Peale and Hill,
 1897. The poem has twenty-eight lines and begins
 "I looked and saw a splendid pageantry / Of beautiful women and lordly men."
304 "Solitude." Harper's monthly 90:38, Dec. 1894.
 Also in Stops of various quills. 1895.
305 "Some one else." Harper's monthly 82:609, Mar. 1891.
 Also in Stops of various quills. 1895.

306 "Sometimes when after spirited debate"   see   "Change."
307 "The song the oriole sings"   see   "While the oriole
       sings."
308 "Sonnet"   see   "Leonora."
309 "Sonnet to Mark Twain."   Harper's weekly 49:1884,
       Dec. 23, 1905.
            Also in Mark Twain's seventieth birthday: record
            of a dinner given in his honor.   N.Y., Harper
            [1905; i.e. 1906].
310 "Sorrow, my sorrow."   Harper's monthly 108:147, Dec.
       1903.
            Also in Book news monthly, June 1908, p.732.
311 "Sphinx."   Harper's monthly 90:35, Dec. 1894.
            Also in Stops of various quills. 1895.
312 "Spring."   National era, May 3, 1855, p.70.
            Also in Poems of two friends. 1860. p.118.
313 "The spring fever (in suitable hexameters)" Ohio state
       journal 22:2, Apr. 14, 1859.
314 "A springtime."   Commonwealth 2:1, Apr. 1, 1864.
            Also in Poems. 1873. p.106-07. Appeared orig-
            inally in Italian. See entry 285.
315 "Statistics."   Harper's monthly 91:520, Sept. 1895.
            Also in Stops of various quills. 1895.
316 "The straw hat."   In Poems of two friends. 1860.
       p.131.
317 "Success--a parable."   Ohio farmer 9:144, May 5, 1860.
            Also in The Hesperian tree; an annual of the Ohio
            Valley 1903. Edited by John J. Piatt. Columbus,
            Ohio, S.F. Harriman, 1903. p.50.
318 "Success and unsuccess"   see   "Old Brown."
319 "Summer dead"   see   "Pleasure-pain"
320 "Sweet clover."   Harper's monthly 32:322, Feb. 1866.
            Also in Poems. 1873. p.51-53.
321 "Sympathy."   Harper's monthly 91:518, Sept. 1895.
            Also in Stops of various quills. 1895.
322 "Temperament."   Harper's monthly 82:608, Mar. 1891.
            Also in Stops of various quills. 1895.
323 "Thanksgiving."   Nation 1:708, Dec. 7, 1865.
            Also in Stevenson, Burton E., ed. The home book
            of verse. 9th ed. N.Y., Holt, 1953. vol. 2,
            p.2933. Appears under the title "Our thanksgiving
            accept" in Le Row, Caroline B., comp. Places
            for every occasion. Hinds, Noble, and Eldridge,
            1901. p.362. Included under the title "A prayer:
            Lord for the erring thought" in Hill, Caroline, ed.
            World's great religious poetry. N.Y., Macmillan,
            1939. p.447. Published under the title "The

undiscovered country" in Morrison, James D., ed.
Masterpieces of religious verse. N.Y., Harper,
1948. p.122.

324 "Thistles." In Poems of two friends. 1860. p.99.

325 "The thorn." Saturday press 2:1, Dec. 3, 1859.
Also in Poems of two friends. 1860. p.122. Included in Poems. 1873. p.129.

326 "The throstle." Ashtabula sentinel 27:41, Aug. 5, 1858.

327 "Through the meadow." In Poems. 1873. p.120-21.
Also in Poems of two friends. 1860. p.92.

328 "Time." Harper's monthly 9:36, Dec. 1894.
Also in Stops of various quills. 1895.

329 "Tomorrow." Harper's monthly 86:547, Mar. 1893.
Also in Stops of various quills. 1895.

330 "Twelve p.m." Harper's monthly 90:35, Dec. 1894.
Also in Stops of various quills. 1895.

331 "The two wives." Boston daily advertiser 104:2, Nov.
12, 1864.
Also in Poems. 1873. p.134-35.

332 "Under the locusts." Saturday press 2:1, June 18,
1859.
Also in Poems of two friends. 1860. p.124.

333 "The undiscovered country" see "Thanksgiving."

334 "Vagary." Saturday press 3:4, Mar. 24, 1860.
Also in Poems. 1873. p.139-40.

335 "The violets." In Poems of two friends. 1860.

336 "Vision." Harper's monthly 91:518, Sept. 1895.
Also in Stops of various quills. 1895. Included
in An American anthology 1787-1900. 1900.
p.387. Contained in Kreymborg, Alfred, ed.
Lyric America. N.Y., Coward-McCann, 1930.
p.155-56.

337 "Weather-breeder." Harper's monthly 82:609, Mar.
1891.
Also in Stops of various quills. 1895.

337a "We wept when we saw in the meadow" [first line].
Saturday press 3:1, May 26, 1860.

338 "What shall it profit?" Harper's monthly 82:384, Feb.
1891.
Also in Stops of various quills. 1895. Included
in An American anthology 1787-1900. 1900. p.387.
Appears under the title of "Faith" in Morrison,
James D., ed. Masterpieces of religious verse.
N.Y., Harper, 1948. p.387.

339 "While she sang" see "Mortuaviva."

340 "A winter's evening tale." Ashtabula sentinel, Dec.
14, 1854.

341 "While the oriole sings." Atlantic monthly 34:83-84,
     July, 1874.
          Appears as "The song the oriole sings" in Poems.
          1886. p.199-200.
342 "The Wit supreme and sovereign Sage." New York
     times, May 1, 1892. p.2.
          Also in Critic 20:270, May 7, 1892. A four-line
          poem.
343 "Words of warning." In Poems of two friends. 1860.
     p.129.
344 "The wreath in heaven--a fancy." Ohio farmer 4:84,
     May 26, 1855.
          Signed Will Narlie, a pseudonym. Appears in
          Poems of two friends. 1860. p.106 under the
          title of "The heaven-wreath."
345 "Ye child and ye angell." Signed Will Narlie. Ashta-
     bula sentinel, Aug. 31, 1854, p.1.

TRAVEL WRITINGS

BOOKS

346 Certain delightful English towns with glimpses of the pleasant country between. N.Y. and London, Harper, 1906. 290p.

347 Familiar Spanish travels. N.Y. and London, Harper, 1913. 327p.

348 Italian journeys. N.Y., Hurd and Houghton, 1867. 320p.

349 A little Swiss sojourn. N.Y., Harper, 1892. 120p.

350 London films. N.Y. and London, Harper, 1905. 241p.
   Appeared also in Harper's monthly, Dec. 1904, Mar., and June through Aug. 1905.

351 Niagara revisited. Chicago, Dalziell, 1884.
   First published in Atlantic monthly 51:598-610, May 1883.

352 Roman holidays and others. N.Y. and London, Harper, 1908. 303p.
   Most of the volume is reprinted from the New York Sun, 1908.

353 Seven English cities. N.Y. and London, Harper, 1909. 201p.

354 Three villages. Boston, Osgood, 1884. 198p.

355 Tuscan cities. Boston, Ticknor, 1886. 251p.

356 Venetian life. N.Y., Hurd and Houghton, 1866. 359p.

357 Venetian life. 2d ed. N.Y., Hurd and Houghton, 1867.
   Contains a new chapter on the history of Venetian commerce.

358 Venetian life. new and enl. ed. Boston, Osgood, 1872.
   Reprint except for "Our last year in Venice" p.399-434.

ARTICLES (in Books and Periodicals)

359 "Aberystwyth, a Welsh watering place." In Seven English cities. 1909. p.121-38.

360 "Afternoons in Wells and Bristol." In Certain delight-
     ful English towns. 1906. p. 103-21.
361 "Algeciras and Tarifa." In Familiar Spanish travels.
     1913. p. 311-27.
362 "Ashore at Genoa." In Roman holidays and others.
     1908. p. 25-36.
363 "At Padua." Atlantic monthly 20:25-32, July 1867.
     Also in Italian journeys. 1878. p. 196-215.
364 "The austere attraction of Burgos." Harper's monthly
     124:813-27, May 1912.
        Also in Familiar Spanish travels, p. 31-52, under
     the title of "Burgos and the bitter cold."
365 "Back at Genoa." In Roman holidays and others.   1908.
     p. 272-83.
366 "A Bermudan sojourn." Harper's monthly 124:16-27,
     Dec. 1911.
367 "By way of Southampton to London." Harper's monthly
     113:892-903, Nov. 1906.
        Also in Certain delightful English towns.   1906.
     p. 122-42.
368 "Capri and Capriotes." Nation 3:14-15, 33-34, July 5,
     12, 1866.
        Also in Italian journeys. 1878. p. 116-35.
369 "Certain things in Naples." Nation 2:108-110, Jan. 25,
     1866.
        Also in Italian journeys. 1878. p. 75-88.
370 "The city of the royal pavilion." North American re-
     view 194:602-11, Oct. 1911.
371 "A confession of St. Augustine." Harper's monthly
     134:680-88, 877-85, Apr. --May 1917.
372 "Cordova and the way there." Harper's monthly 126:
     112-25, Dec. 1912.
        Also in Familiar Spanish travels. 1913. p. 165-
     95.
373 "An English country town and country house." Harper's
     monthly 113: 165-75, July 1906.
        Also in Certain delightful English towns.   1906.
     p. 83-102.
374 "A day at Doncaster and an hour at Durham." Harper's
     monthly 115:58-66, June 1907.
        Also in Seven English cities. 1909. p. 80-96.
375 "A day at Henley." Harper's weekly 49:826-28, 841,
     June 10, 1905.
376 "A day at White Sulphur." Ohio state journal 23:2,
     July 6, 1859.
        Signed Chispa.

377 "A day in Pompeii." Nation 1:430-32, Oct. 5, 1865.
    Also in Italian journeys. 1878. p. 89-105.
378 "Ducal Mantua." In Italian journeys. 1878. p. 321-
    98.
      Another version appears as no. 39 of The Mono-
    graph series, published by Q. P. Index, Bangor,
    Maine and J. W. Christopher, New York.
379 "Eden after the fall." In Roman holidays and others.
    1908. p. 284-303.
379a "En passant." Ohio state journal, July 24, 28, 31,
    Aug. 4, 6, 7, 1860.
380 "English feeling toward Americans." North American
    review 179:815-23, Dec. 1904.
381 "English idiosyncrasies." North American review
    181:649-64, 897-911, Nov.--Dec. 1905.
382 "Experiences of a true Baconian in Shakespeare's town."
    North American review 195:120-27, Jan. 1912.
383 "First days in Seville." Harper's monthly 126:568-81,
    Mar. 1913.
      Also in Familiar Spanish travels. 1913. p. 196-
    225.
384 "Floating down the river on the O-Hi-o." In Literature
    and life... 1902. p. 309-22.
      Taken from "Editor's easy chair" Harper's monthly
    105:146-51, June 1902.
385 "A Florentine mosaic." Century magazine, Feb.--June
    1885.
      Also in Tuscan cities. 1894. p. 1-141.
386 "Fortnight in Bath." Harper's monthly 111:811-24, Nov.
    1905.
387 "Forza Maggiore." Atlantic monthly 19:220-27, Feb.
    1867.
388 "From New York into New England." In Literature and
    life... 1902. p. 222-27.
389 "From Venice to Florence and back again." Boston
    advertiser 101:2, May 25, 1863.
390 "A glimpse of Genoa." Atlantic monthly 19:359-63,
    Mar. 1867.
      Also in Italian journeys. 1878.
391 "A glimpse of the English Washington country." Har-
    per's monthly 112:651-61, Apr. 1906.
392 "Glimpses of English character." In Seven English
    cities. 1909. p. 159-200.
392a "Glimpses of summer travel." Cincinnati gazette,
    July 24, 27, 31, Aug. 1, 6, 9, 1860.

393 "Gnadenhutten." Atlantic monthly 23:95-115, Jan. 1869.
        Also in Three villages. 1884. p.117-98.
394 "The great gridiron of St. Lawrence." In Familiar
        Spanish travels. 1913. p.150-64.
395 "A half-hour at Herculaneum." Nation 2:429-30, Apr.
        5, 1866.
        Also in Italian journeys. 1878. p.106-15.
396 "The human interest of Buxton." North American re-
        view 194:227-38, Aug. 1911.
        Also in Cornhill magazine, n.s.31:203-14, Aug.
        1911.
397 "I visit Camp Harrison." Ohio state journal 23:2, Aug.
        31, 1859.
        Signed Chispa.
398 "In Charleston." Harper's monthly 131:747-57, Oct.
        1915.
399 "In Folkestone out of season." Harper's monthly 109:
        821-30, Nov. 1904.
        Also in Certain delightful English towns. 1906.
        p.143-72.
400 "In smokiest Sheffield." In Seven English cities. 1909.
        p.27-40.
401 "Industrious Lucca." In Tuscan cities. 1894. p.241-
        56
402 "Kentish neighborhoods, including Canterbury." Harper's
        monthly 113:550-63, Sept. 1906.
        Also in Certain delightful English towns. 1906.
        p.173-92.
403 "The landing of a pilgrim." Harper's monthly 110:707-
        18, Apr. 1905.
        Also in Certain delightful English towns. 1906.
        p.1-21.
404 "Last days in a Dutch hotel." In Literature and life...
        1902. p.95-109.
        Taken from "Life and letters" Harper's weekly
        41:1134, 1147, Nov. 13-20, 1897.
404a "Letter from Europe." Ohio state journal, Jan. 9,
        30, 31, 1862.
404b "Letters from Venice." Boston advertiser, Mar. 27,
        June 29, July 28, Sept. 11, Sept. 29, Nov. 21, Nov.
        26, Dec. 8, 1863; Jan. 18, Feb. 4, 6, 27, Mar. 5,
        12, 19, 26, Apr. 7, 22, May 7, June 16, 25, July
        2, 9, 16, 23, 1864.
405 "Lexington." Longman's 1:41-61, Nov. 1882.
        Also in Three villages. 1884. p.11-68.
406 "A little German capital." Nation 2:11-13, Jan. 4,
        1866.

407 "Llandudno, another Welsh watering place." In Seven
English cities. 1909. p. 139-58.
408 "Malvern among her hills." In Certain delightful English towns. 1906. p. 237-56.
409 "A memory of San Remo." Harper's monthly 140:321-
27, Feb. 1920.
410 "Men and manners on the way from Ferrara to Genoa."
Nation 2:205-07, Feb. 15, 1866.
411 "Minor Italian travels." Atlantic monthly 20:337-48,
Sept. 1867.
412 "A modest liking for Liverpool." In Seven English
cities. 1909. p. 3-14.
413 "The mother of the American Athens." Harper's
monthly 117:514-25, Sept. 1908.
414 "My first visit to New England." Harper's monthly
88:816-24; 89:40-52, 228-35, 441-51, May--Aug. 1894.
415 "Naples and her joyful noise." In Roman holidays and
others. 1908. p. 37-54.
416 "Niagara, first and last." In The Niagara book; a
complete souvenir of Niagara Falls, containing
sketches, stories and essays. By W. D. Howells,
Mark Twain, pseud., Prof. Nathaniel S. Shaler and
others. Buffalo, Underhill and Nichols, 1893. 225p.
417 "A night and a day in Toledo." Harper's monthly
125:429-42, Aug. 1912.
Also in Familiar Spanish travels. 1913. p. 124-
49.
418 "Nine days' wonder in York." Harper's monthly 116:
349-61, Feb. 1908.
Also in Seven English cities. 1909. p. 41-68.
419 "Our last year in Venice." In Venetian life. 1872.
p. 399-434.
420 "Our nearest point in antiquity." Harper's monthly
113:99-109, June 1906.
421 "Over at Pisa." In Roman holidays and others. 1908.
p. 259-71.
422 "Oxford." North American review 183:620-38, Oct. 5,
1906.
Also in Certain delightful English towns. 1906.
p. 193-218.
423 "A pair of pageants." North American review 195:
607-17, May 1912.
424 "Panforte di Siena." In Tuscan cities. 1894. p. 142-
210.
425 "Phases of Madrid." North American review 196:608-
34, Nov. 1912.

426 "A pilgrimage to Petrarch's house at Arquà." In
      Italian journeys. 1878. p. 216-34.
427 "Pistoja, Prato, and Fiesole." In Tuscan cities. 1894.
      p. 257-72.
428 "Pitiless Pisa." In Tuscan cities. 1894. p. 211-40.
429 "Pompeii revisited." In Roman holidays and others.
      1908. p. 55-67.
430 "The road to Rome and home again." Boston adver-
      tiser 105:2,1,2, Mar. 4, Apr. 13, May 3, 1865.
431 "The road to Rome from Venice." In Italian journeys.
      1878. p. 9-177.
432 "Roman holidays." In Roman holidays and others.
      1908. p. 68-238.
433 "Roman pearls." Nation 3:253-54, 433-35, 523-25,
      Sept. 27, Nov. 29, Dec. 27, 1866.
          Also in Italian journeys. 1878. p. 151-77.
434 "Roundabout to Boston." Harper's monthly 91:427-38,
      Aug. 1895.
          Also in Literary friends and acquaintance. 1900.
      p. 91-112.
435 "San Sebastian and beautiful Biscay." In Familiar
      Spanish travels. 1913. p. 8-30.
436 "A sennight of the centennial." Atlantic monthly 38:
      92-107, July 1876.
437 "A Shaker village." Atlantic monthly 37:699-710, June 1876.
          Appears under the title of "Shirley" in Three villages.
      1884. p. 69-116.
438 "Shrewsbury by way of Worcester and Hereford." In
      Certain delightful English towns. 1906. p. 257-74.
439 "Some last drops in Tunbridge Wells." North Amer-
      ican review 193:879-92, June 1911.
440 "Some literary memories of Cambridge." Harper's
      monthly 101:823-39, Nov. 1900.
441 "Some Sevillan incidents." Harper's monthly 127:71-86,
      June 1913.
          Appears under the title of "Sevillan aspects and inci-
      dents" in Familiar Spanish travels. 1913. p. 226-66.
442 "Stopping at Vicenza, Verona, and Parma." In Italian
      journeys. 1878. p. 293-320.
443 "Summer isles of Eden." In Literature and life...
      1902. p. 78-88.
          Taken from "Editor's easy chair" in Harper's
      monthly 103:146-51, June 1901.
444 "The surprise of Ronda." In Familiar Spanish travels.
      1913. p. 296-310.
445 "Three English capitals of industry." Harper's monthly
      118:891-902, May 1909.

The three cities are Manchester, Liverpool, and Sheffield.

446 "To and in Granada." North American review 197: 501-21, Apr. 1913.

Also in Familiar Spanish travels. 1913. p. 267-95.

447 "Twenty-four hours at Exeter." Harper's monthly 111:497-506, Sept. 1905.

448 "Two little English episodes." Harper's monthly 119: 241-44, July 1909.

449 "Two up-town blocks into Spain." In Roman holidays and others. 1908. p. 14-24.

450 "Up and down Madeira." In Roman holidays and others. 1908. p. 1-13.

451 "The variety of Valladolid." Harper's monthly 125: 165-78, July 1912.

452 "A visit to the Cimbri." Nation 1:495-97, Oct. 19, 1865.

Also in Italian journeys. 1878. p. 235-50.

453 "The waters of Blackpool." North American review 194:872-81, Dec. 1911.

454 "A week at Leghorn." In Roman holidays and others. 1908. p. 239-58.

455 "A year in a Venetian palace." Atlantic monthly 27: 1-14, Jan. 1871.

BOOKS

456 Criticism and fiction. N.Y., Harper, 1891. 188p.
   The essays are taken from the "Editor's study" in
   Harper's monthly.
457 Heroines of fiction. N.Y., Harper, 1901. 2v.
   Most of the essays appeared in Harper's bazaar,
   May 5, 1900 through Jan. 1902. An index to both
   volumes was done by H. Robinson Shipherd and is
   located in the N.Y. Public Library.
458 Literature and life; studies. New York and London,
   Harper, 1902. 322p.
459 Modern Italian poets; essays and versions. N.Y.,
   Harper, 1887. 370p.
460 My literary passions. N.Y., Harper, 1895. 261p.
   First published in Ladies home journal, Dec. 1893
   --March 1895.
461 My Mark Twain; reminiscences and criticisms. N.Y.,
   Harper, 1910. 187p.
   Contains essays from the Atlantic monthly 1869,
   1872, 1875, 1876, 1880; from Century 1882; from
   the North American review 1901; Harper's monthly
   1890, 1910 and Harper's weekly 1896 and 1905.
462 The seen and unseen at Stratford-on-Avon; a fantasy.
   New York and London, Harper, 1914. 112p.

ARTICLES (in Books and Periodicals)

463 "Aleardo Aleardi." In Modern Italian poets. 1887.
   p. 333-59.
   First printed as "Modern Italian poets" in the
   North American review 104:352-53, Apr. 1867.
464 "Allessandro Manzoni." In Modern Italian poets. 1887.
   p. 126-74.
   Part of this essay appeared in the North American
   review 104:317-23, Apr. 1867.
465 "American literature in exile." In Literature and life.
   1902. p. 202-05.
   Also in Literature ns 1:169-70, Mar. 3, 1899.

466 "Anthony Trollope's Lily Dale." In Heroines of fiction.
     1901. v. 2, p. 94-108.
467 "Anthony Trollope's Lucy Robarts and Griselda Grant-
     ly." In Heroines of fiction. 1901. v. 2, p. 109-21.
468 "Anthony Trollope's Mrs. Proudie." In Heroines of
     fiction. 1901. v. 2, p. 122-37.
469 "The art of Longfellow." North American review
     184:472-85, Mar. 1, 1907.
470 [The art of authorship] In Bainton, George, comp. The
     art of authorship. N. Y., Appleton, 1890. p. 334-35.
471 "Bardic symbols." Ohio state journal, Mar. 28, 1860,
     p. 2.
472 "A belated guest." In Howells, William D. Literary
     friends and acquaintance. N. Y., Harper, 1911.
     p. 289-305.
473 "The Canadian habitant in recent fiction." Literature
     ns 1:337-38, Apr. 21, 1899.
474 "Certain of the Chicago school of fiction." North Amer-
     ican review 176:734-46, May 1903.
         Edith Wyatt, George Ade, F. P. Dunne; references
     to Fuller, Will Payne, Robert Herrick, Brand
     Whitlock, and Frank Norris.
475 "Cervantes." In My literary passions. 1895. p. 20-
     27.
476 "Charles Kingsley's Hypatia." In Heroines of fiction.
     1901. v. 2, p. 1-13.
477 "Charles Reade." In My literary passions. 1895.
     p. 191-97.
478 "A conjecture of intensive fiction." North American
     review 204:869-80, Dec. 1916.
479 "Cooper's novels." Ohio state weekly journal 49:3,
     Apr. 5, 1859.
480 "A critical comment on Mark Twain's work." Harper's
     weekly 54:10, Apr. 30, 1910.
         Contains excerpts from article in North American
     review, Feb. 1901.
481 "Criticism and fiction." In Criticism and fiction and
     other essays. Edited by Clara and Rudolf Kirk.
     N. Y., New York University Press, 1959. p. 9-87.
     Published as a separate in 1891 by Harper.
482 "Curtis, Longfellow, Schlegel." In My literary pas-
     sions. 1895. p. 145-49.
483 "DeForest, James, Erckmann-Chatrian, Björnson."
     In My literary passions. 1895. p. 222-28.
484 De Quincey, Goethe, Longfellow." In My literary pas-
     sions. 1895. p. 175-82.

485 "Dickens." In My literary passions. 1895. p. 88-103.
486 "Dickens's later heroines." In Heroines of fiction.
     1901. v. 1, p. 148-60.
487 "Diversions of the higher journalist, the apotheosis of
     M. Rostand." Harper's weekly 47:1112, July 4, 1903.
488 "Diversions of the higher journalist, a grain of wheat
     in the heap of chaff." Harper's weekly 47:1093, June
     27, 1903.
489 "The earlier heroines of Charles Dickens." In Heroines
     of fiction. 1901. v. 1, p. 125-35.
490 "Edgar Allan Poe." Harper's weekly 53:12-13, Jan.
     16, 1909.
491 "Edward Bellamy." Atlantic monthly 82:253-56, Aug.
     1898.
492 "Emile Zola." North American review 175:587-96,
     Nov. 1902.
     Also in the introduction to Havelock Ellis's trans-
     lation of Germinal by Zola.
493 "The fiction of Eden Phillpotts." North American re-
     view 190:15-22, July 1909.
494 "The fiction of John Oliver Hobbes." North American
     review 183:1251-61, Dec. 21, 1906.
     Hobbes is a pseudonym. The author's real name
     is Mrs. Pearl Richards, a Massachusetts novelist
     and playwright (1867-1906).
495 "The fiction of Leonard Merrick." North American
     review 185:378-86, June 21, 1907.
496 "First American notice." In Thornton, Richard, ed.
     Recognition of Robert Frost. N. Y., Holt, 1937.
     p. 44-45.
     Reprint of article in Harper's monthly, Sept. 1915.
497 "First fiction and drama." In My literary passions.
     1895. p. 34-37.
498 "First impressions of literary New York." Harper's
     monthly 91:62-74, June 1895.
     Also in Literary friends and acquaintance. 1911.
     p. 67-90.
499 "The Florentine satirist, Giusti." North American
     review 115:31-47, July 1872.
500 "Frances Burney's Evelina." In Heroines of fiction.
     1901. v. 1, p. 13-23.
501 "Francesco Dall'Ongaro." In Modern Italian poets.
     1887. p. 300-22.
     First published in North American review 106:26-
     42, Jan. 1868.
502 "Frank Norris." North American review 175:769-78,
     Dec. 1902.

503 "A French poet of the old regime." Atlantic monthly
　　　41:332-43, Mar. 1878.
504 "A French view of Byron." Ohio state weekly journal
　　　48:1, Mar. 15, 1859.
　　　Editorial unsigned.
505 "The future of the American novel." Harper's monthly
　　　124:634-37, Mar. 1912.
　　　Also in Criticism and fiction and other essays.
　　　Edited by Clara and Rudolf Kirk. N.Y., New
　　　York University Press, 1959. p. 345-49.
506 "George Eliot, Hawthorne, Goethe, Heine." In My
　　　literary passions. 1895. p. 183-90.
507 "George Eliot's Gwendolyn Harleth and Janet Dempster."
　　　In Heroines of fiction. 1901. v. 2, p. 79-93.
508 "George Eliot's Maggie Tulliver and Hetty Sorel." In
　　　Heroines of fiction. 1901. p. 44-64.
509 "George Eliot's Rosamond Vincy and Dorothea Brooke."
　　　In Heroines of fiction. 1901. v. 2, p. 65-78.
510 "Giacomo Leopardi." In Modern Italian poets. 1887.
　　　p. 244-74.
　　　Appeared as "The laureate of death" in the Atlantic
　　　monthly 56:311-22, Sept. 1885.
511 "Giambattista Niccolini." In Modern Italian poets.
　　　1887. p. 196-243.
　　　Appeared as "Niccolini's anti-papal tragedy."
　　　North American review 115:333-66, Oct. 1872.
512 "Giovanni Prati." In Modern Italian poets. 1887.
　　　p. 323-32.
513 "Giulio Carcano, Arnaldo Fusinato, and Luigi Mercanti-
　　　ni." In Modern Italian poets. 1887. p. 360-68.
　　　First published as "Modern Italian poets" in the
　　　North American review 104:352-53, Apr. 1867.
514 "Giuseppe Parini." In Modern Italian poets. 1887.
　　　p. 25-50.
　　　First published as "An obsolete fine gentleman."
　　　Atlantic monthly 36:98-106, July 1875.
515 "Goldoni, Manzoni, D'Azeglio." In My literary pas-
　　　sions. 1895. p. 206-15.
516 "Goldsmith." In My literary passions. 1895. p. 10-
　　　19.
517 "Gordon A. Stewart." In Coggeshall, William T.
　　　Poets and poetry of the West. Columbus, Follett,
　　　Foster, 1860. p. 612.
518 "Have we household poetry in the West? Literary mat-
　　　ters." Ohio state journal 22:2, Nov. 20, 1858.
　　　Unsigned. Attributed to Howells by A Bibliography

of William Dean Howells by William Gibson and George Arms, p. 80.

519 "Hawthorne's Hester Prynne." In Heroines of fiction. 1901. v. 1, p. 161-74.

520 "Hawthorne's Zenobia and Priscilla, and Miriam and Hilda." In Heroines of fiction. 1901. p. 175-89.

521 "Heine." In My literary passions. 1895. p. 165-74.

522 "Helen Louisa Bostwick." In Coggeshall, William T. Poets and poetry of the West. Columbus, Follett, Foster, 1860. p. 550.

523 "Henry James, Jr." Century magazine 25:25-29, Nov. 1882.
Also in Mordell, Albert, ed. Discovery of a genius: William Dean Howells and Henry James. N. Y., Twayne, 1961. p. 112-22.

524 "Henry Wadsworth Longfellow." Harvard register 3:1-2, Jan. 1881.

525 "A heroine of Bulwer's." In Heroines of fiction. 1901. v. 1, p. 113-24.

526 "The heroine of Kate Beaumont." In Heroines of fiction. 1901. p. 152-63.

527 "The heroine of The initials." Harper's bazaar 35: 302-09, Aug. 1901.
Also in Heroines of fiction. 1901. v. 2, p. 138-51. The initials was written by the Baroness Taut-phoeus.

528 "Heroines of Charles Dickens's middle period." In Heroines of fiction. 1901. p. 136-47.

529 "Heroines of Miss Ferrier, Mrs. Opie, and Mrs. Radcliffe." In Heroines of fiction. 1901. v. 1, p. 79-89.

530 "Hjalmar Hjorth Boyesen." Harper's bazaar 29:70-71, Jan. 25, 1896.

531 "Ik Marvel." In My literary passions. 1895. p. 82-87.
Ik Marvel is the author of Reveries of a bachelor and Dream life.

532 "Irving." In My literary passions. 1895. p. 28-33.

533 "Impressions of Emerson." Harper's weekly 47:784, May 16, 1903.

534 "In memory of Mark Twain." American Academy proceedings 1:5-6, 11-12, 15, 18, 21, 24, 29, Nov. 1, 1911.
Published also in Public meetings under the auspices of the American Academy and the National Institute of Arts and Letters held at Carnegie Hall, N. Y., Nov. 30, 1910, in memory of Samuel Lang-

horne Clemens. N. Y. , American Academy of
Arts and Letters, 1922.

535 "Is New York City a 'city without a face'?" New York
herald, Feb. 3, 1901, p. 6.

536 "Jane Austen's Anne Eliot and Catherine Morland." In
Heroines of fiction. 1901. v. 1, p. 49-64.

537 "Jane Austen's Elizabeth Bennet." In Heroines of fiction. 1901. p. 37-48.

538 "John Hay in literature." North American review 181:
343-51, Sept. 1905.

539 "John Herbert A. Bone." In Coggeshall, William T.
Poets and poetry of the West. Columbus, Follett,
Foster, 1860. p. 589.

540 "Lamartine and American literature." Ohio state
journal 24:2, Nov. 3, 1860.

541 "Lazarillo de Tormes." In My literary passions.
1895. p. 139-44.

542 "Literary Boston thirty years ago." Harper's monthly
91:865-79, Nov. 1895.

543 "Literary criticism." Round table 3:49, Jan. 27, 1866.

544 "Literary gossip." Ohio state journal, Jan. 17, 1860,
p. 1; Apr. 26, 1860, p. 1; Jan. 18, 28, Feb. 4, 9,
11, 13, 20, 23, 1861.

545 "Literary gossip." Atheneum, Nov. 25, 1882, p. 700.
Letter on Dickens and Thackeray in reference to
article on Henry James, Jr. in Century magazine,
Nov. 1882.

546 "The literary outlook." Harper's weekly 46:1407, Oct.
4, 1902.
About Henry James and N. S. Shaler.

547 "The literary outlook and inlook." Harper's weekly
47:607-08, Apr. 11, 1903.

548 "Literary recollections." North American review 195:
551-58, Apr. 1912.

549 "A little mistake." Harper's weekly 46:1029, Aug. 2,
1902.

550 "Longfellow's Spanish student." In My literary passions. 1895. p. 38-40.

551 "Lyof N. Tolstoy." North American review 188:842-
59, Dec. 1908.
Also in the North American review, Dec. 1910,
p. 729-45.

552 "Macaulay." In My literary passions. 1895. p. 114-
18.

553 "The man of letters as a man of business." Scribner's
magazine 14:429-45, Oct. 1893.

Also in Literature and life... 1902. p.1-35. In-
cluded in Criticism and fiction and other essays.
Ed. by Clara and Rudolf Kirk. N.Y., New York
University Press, 1959. p.298-309.

554 "Mark Twain." New York times, Nov. 17, 1900,
p.789.
Contains the introduction to Twain's Lotos Club
speech.

555 "Mark Twain." Century magazine 24:780-83, Sept.
1882.

556 "Mark Twain; an inquiry." North American review
172:306-21, Feb. 1901; 191:836-50, June 1910.
Also in Howells, William D. European and American masters. Edited by Clara and Rudolf Kirk.
N.Y., Collier Books, 1963. p.149-54.

557 "Mary R. Whittlesey." In Coggeshall, William T.
Poets and poetry of the West. Columbus, Follett,
Foster, 1860. p.640.

558 "Massimo d'Azeglio." Nation 2:202-04, Feb. 15, 1866.
The Italian author was born Massimo Taparelli.

559 "Meetings with Clarence King." In Clarence King
Memoirs. The helmet of Mambrino. N.Y., Putnam,
1904. p.135-56.
Clarence King, American geologist (1842-1901),
was the author of the seven-volume Report of the
geological exploration of the 40th parallel (1870-
1880). He was the first director of the U.S. Geological Survey.

560 "Mr. Aldrich's fiction." Atlantic monthly 46:695-98,
Nov. 1880.

561 "Mr. Bret Harte's Miggles and Mr. T.B. Aldrich's
Marjorie Daw." In Heroines of fiction. 1901. v.2,
p.225-33.

562 "Mr. Charles W. Chesnutt's stories." Atlantic month-
ly 85:699-701, May 1900.
Charles W. Chesnutt (1858-1932) was born in
Cleveland, Ohio.

563 "Mr. G.W. Cable's Aurora and Clotilde Nancanou."
In Heroines of fiction. 1901. v.2, p.234-44.

564 "Mr. Garland's books." North American review 196:
523-38, Oct. 1912.
Also in Howells, William D. European and American masters. N.Y., Collier Books, 1963. p.193-
99.

565 "Mr. H.B. Fuller's Jane Marshall and Miss M.E.
Wilkins's Jane Field." In Heroines of fiction. 1901.
v.2, p.245-59.

566 "Mr. Harben's Georgia fiction." North American re-
     view 191:356-63, Mar. 1910.
     Will N. Harben (1858-1919) was a Georgia novelist
     who wrote about Georgia.
567 "Mr. Henry James's later work." North American re-
     view 176:125-37, Jan. 1903.
     Also in Mordell, Albert, ed. Discovery of a
     genius: William Dean Howells and Henry James.
     N.Y., Twayne, 1961. p.192-207. Contained in
     Dupee, F.W. The question of Henry James; a
     collection of critical essays. N.Y., Holt, 1945.
     p. 6-19.
568 "Mr. Howells on Tourgueneff." Critic 26:204, Mar.
     16, 1896.
569 "Mr. Henry Ward's heroines." In Heroines of fiction.
     1901. v.2, p.260-74.
570 "Mr. James's Daisy Miller." In Heroines of fiction.
     1901. v.2, p.164-76.
571 "Mr. Pett Ridge's clever books." North American
     review 191:64-74, Jan. 1910.
572 "Mr. Thomas Hardy's Bathsheba Everdene and Paula
     Power." In Heroines of fiction. 1901. v.2, p.193-
     210.
573 "Mr. Thomas Hardy's heroines." In Heroines of fic-
     tion. 1901. v.2, p.177-92.
574 "My favorite novelist and his best book." In Howells,
     William D. European and American masters. Edited
     by Clara and Rudolf Kirk. N.Y., Collier Books,
     1963. p.28-30.
     Appeared first in Munsey's magazine, Apr. 1897.
575 "My memories of Mark Twain." Harper's monthly
     121:165-78, 340-48, 512-29, July-Sept. 1910.
576 "The nature of American literary criticism." Litera-
     ture 3:378-79, 424-25, Nov. 5, 1898.
577 "The nature of Charles Reade's heroines." In Heroines
     of fiction. 1901. v.2, p.14-27.
578 "The new historical romances." North American re-
     view 171:935-48, Dec. 1900.
579 "The new poetry." North American review 168:581-92,
     May 1899.
580 "The new sort of stories." Literature ns 1:457-58,
     May 26, 1899.
581 "New York low life in fiction." In Howells, William D.
     European and American masters. N.Y., Collier
     Books, 1963. p.205-11.
     The article is about Stephen Crane's Maggie and
     Cahan's Yekl. It was originally published in the
     New York world, July 26, 1896.

582 "Novel-writing and novel-reading. An impersonal expla-
      nation." Bulletin of the New York Public Library
      62:15-34, Jan. 1958.
           Also in Howells and James: a double billing.
           Novel-writing and novel-reading. An impersonal
           explanation. Edited by William M. Gibson. Henry
           James and the Bazaar letters. Edited by Leon
           Edel and Lyall H. Powers. N.Y., New York Pub-
           lic Library, 1958.
583 "The novels of Robert Herrick." North American re-
      view 189:812-20, June 1909.
           Robert Herrick (1868-1938) wrote novels relating
           to Chicago.
584 "Oliver Wendell Holmes." Harper's monthly 94:120-34,
      Dec. 1896.
           Also in Howells, William D. Literary friends and
           acquaintance. N.Y., Harper, 1900. p.146-77.
585 "Ossian." In My literary passions. 1895. p.66-68.
586 "The passing of a poet." Literature ns 1:217-19, Mar.
      17, 1899.
587 "Pastor Fido, Aminta, Romola, Yeast, Paul Ferroll."
      In My literary passions." 1895. p.216-21.
588 "Paul Lawrence Dunbar." Bookman 23:185-86, Apr.
      1906.
           Reprint of introduction by William D. Howells to
           Dunbar's Lyrics of lowly life.
589 "A personal retrospect of James Russell Lowell."
      Scribner's magazine 28:363-78, Sept. 1900.
           Also in Current literature 30:48-51, Jan. 1901.
           Contained in Howells, William D. Literary friends
           and acquaintance. N.Y., Harper, 1900.
590 "The philosophy of Tolstoy." In Howells, William D.
      Criticism and fiction and other essays. N.Y., New
      York University Press, 1959. p.167-78.
591 "The poetry of love." Round table 3:81-82, Feb. 17,
      1866.
592 "The poetry of Mr. Madison Cawein." North American
      review 187:124-28, Jan. 1908.
           Howells had high regard for Madison Cawein, a
           Kentucky poet (1865-1914).
593 "A political novelist and more." North American re-
      view 192:93-100, July 1910.
           The novelist is Brand Whitlock (1869-1934).
594 "Pope." In My literary passions. 1895. p.48-59.
595 "Problems of existence in fiction." In Howells, Wil-
      liam D. Criticism and fiction and other essays.
      Edited by Clara and Rudolf Kirk. N.Y., New York
      University Press, 1959. p.336-38.

Originally appeared in Literature ns 1:193-94,
Mar. 10, 1899.
596 "A psychological countercurrent in recent fiction."
North American review 173:872-88, Dec. 1901.
597 "Puritanic influences on American literature." Harper's
weekly 46:1110, Aug. 16, 1902.
598 "Puritanism in fiction." Literature ns 2:563-64, May
14, 1898.
Also in Literature and life... 1902. p. 278-83.
599 "Recent Russian fiction, a conversation." North American review 196:85-103, July 1912.
600 "The romantic imagination." Atlantic monthly 82:253-
56, Aug. 1898.
Also in Howells, William D. European and American masters. Ed. with introduction by Clara and
Rudolf Kirk. N.Y., Collier, 1963. p. 184-93.
Included in Howells, William D. Criticism and
fiction and other essays. Ed. by Clara M. Kirk
and Rudolf Kirk. N.Y., New York University
Press, 1959. p. 250-55.
601 "Scott." In My literary passions. 1895. p. 40-43.
602 "Scott's Jeanie Deans and Cooper's lack of heroines."
In Heroines of fiction. 1901. v. 1, p. 102-12.
603 "Scott's Rebecca and Rowena Lucy Ashton." In Heroines of fiction. 1901. p. 90.
604 "Shakespeare." In My literary passions. 1895. p. 68-
81.
605 "Silvio Pellico, Tommaso Grossi, Luigi Carver, and
Giovanni Berchet." In Modern Italian poets. 1887.
p. 175-95.
606 "Some anomalies of the short story." North American
review 173:422-32, Sept. 1901.
Also in Literature and life... 1902. p. 110-24.
607 "Some Arcadian shepherds." Atlantic monthly 29:84-89,
Jan. 1872.
A portion is reprinted in Modern Italian poets.
608 "Some literary memories of Cambridge." Harper's
monthly 101:823-39, Nov. 1900.
609. "Some nineteenth century heroines in the eighteenth
century." In Heroines of fiction. 1901. v. 1,
p. 1-12.
610 "Some western poets of today, Helen L. Bostwick."
Ohio state journal 24:2, Oct. 1, 1860.
611 "Some western poets of today, William Wallace Harney."
Ohio state journal 24:1, Sept. 25, 1860.
612 "The southern states in recent American literature."
Literature 3:231-32, 257-58, 280-81, Sept. 10, 17,
24, 1898.

613 "Stockton and all his works." Book buyer 20:19-21,
     Feb. 1900.
614 "Tennyson." In My literary passions. 1895. p.150-
     64.
615 "A terrible suspicion." Ohio state weekly journal,
     March 29, 1859, p.4.
            Contains a criticism of Saxe's poem "Love."
616 "Thackeray." In My literary passions. 1895. p.129-
     38.
617 "Thackeray's bad heroines." In Heroines of fiction.
     1901. v.1, p.190-202.
618 "Thackeray's Ethel Newcome and Charlotte Bronte's
     Jane Eyre." In Heroines of fiction. 1901. v.1,
     p.215-27.
619 "Thackeray's good heroines." In Heroines of fiction.
     1901. v.1, p.203-14.
620 "Tourgenieff, Auerbach." In My literary passions.
     1895. p.229-33.
621 "Tribute to Warner." In Fields, James T. Charles
     Dudley Warner. N.Y., McClure, Phillips, 1904.
     p.199-208.
622 "The turning of the tide." Harper's weekly 46:907,
     July 12, 1902.
            The article is about N.S. Shaler's Phi Beta Kappa
     poem.
623 "The two Catherines of Emily Bronte." In Heroines of
     fiction. 1901. v.1, p.228-39.
624 "Two heroines of Maria Edgeworth." In Heroines of
     fiction. 1901. v.1, p.24-36.
625 "Uncle Tom's cabin." In My literary passions. 1895.
     p.63-65.
626 "Unworthy Mr. Thackeray." Ohio state weekly journal
     49:1, May 17, 1859.
            Unsigned. About The Virginians by Thackeray.
627 "Valera, Valdes, Galdos, Verga, Zola, Trollope,
     Hardy." In My literary passions. 1895. p.243-49.
628 "Variations of Reade's type of heroines." In Heroines
     of fiction. 1901. p.14-27.
629 "Vincenzo Monti and Ugo Foscolo." In Modern Italian
     poets. 1887. p.102-25.
630 "When Mark Twain missed fire." Golden book 20:97-
     98, July 1934.
631 "The white Mr. Longfellow." Harper's monthly 93:
     327-43, Aug. 1896.
            Also in Howells, William D. Literary friends and
     acquaintance. N.Y., Harper, 1900. p.178-211.

632 "Will the novel disappear?" North American review
     175:291-94, Sept. 1902.
633 "William Black's Gertrude White." In Heroines of fic-
     tion. 1901. v. 2, p. 211-24.
     Gertrude White is a character in Macleod of Dare.
634 "Wordsworth, Lowell, Chaucer." In My literary pas-
     sions. 1895. p. 104-13.
635 "An appreciation." In Crane, Stephen. Maggie, a
     child of the streets. London, Heinemann, 1896.
     p. v-vii.
636 "An appreciation." In Howe, E. W. The story of a
     country town. N. Y., Harper, 1917. p. v-vi.
     Appeared first as "Two notable novels" in Century
     28:632-33, Aug. 1884.
637 "Carlo Goldoni." In Autobiography. Memoirs of Carlo
     Goldoni. Tr. from the original French by John
     Black. Boston, Osgood, 1877. p. 5-29.
638 "Edward Gibbon." In Autobiography. Memoirs of Ed-
     ward Gibbon, Esq. Boston, Osgood, 1877. p. 5-41.
     Also in Atlantic monthly 41:99-111, Jan. 1878.
639 "Edward Lord Herbert." In Autobiography. Lives of
     Lord Herbert of Cherbury and Thomas Ellwood.
     Boston, Osgood, 1877. p. 1-14.
640 "Emile Zola." In Zola, Emile. Germinal. Tr. from
     the French by Havelock Ellis. N. Y., Boni and Live-
     right, 1923. p. v-xviii.
     First published in North American review 175:587-
     96, Nov. 1902.
641 "George Du Maurier." In Du Maurier, George. Eng-
     lish society. N. Y., Harper, 1897. p. 1-9.
642 "Jean François Marmontel." In Autobiography. Mem-
     oirs of Jean François Marmontel. Boston, Houghton,
     Osgood, 1878. vol. 1, p. 5-27.
643 "Leo Tolstoi." In Tolstoi, Leo. Sebastopol. Tr. from
     the French by Frank D. Millet. N. Y., Harper,
     1887. p. 5-12.
     Appeared as "Lyof Tolstoi" in Harper's weekly
     31:299-300, Apr. 23, 1887.
644 "A letter to the publisher." In Howells, William D.
     Minor dramas. Edinburgh, Douglas, 1907. vol. 1,
     p. v-xii.
645 "One of the public to the author." In The Henry James
     year book. Selected and arranged by Evelyn G.
     Smalley. Boston, Gorham Press, 1911. p. 10-11.
646 "The poetry of Madison Cawein." In Cawein, Madison.
     Poems. N. Y., Macmillan, 1911. p. xiii-xix.

647 "Preface." In Garland, Hamlin. They of the high
     trails. N.Y., Harper, 1916. p.xi-xvi.
648 "Introduction." In Gould, F.J. The children's
     Plutarch; tales of the Romans. N.Y., Harper, 1910.
     p.vii-xi.
649 "Introduction." In Howells, William C. Recollections
     of life in Ohio, from 1813 to 1840. Cincinnati, Rob-
     ert Clarke, 1895. p.iii-viii.
          William Dean Howells also wrote the conclusion of
          the book, p.196-207.
650 [entry omitted]
651 "Introductory sketch." In Howells, William D. The
     coast of Bohemia. Biographical edition. N.Y.,
     Harper, 1899. p.iii-vii.
652 "Introduction." In Howells, William D. A little girl
     among the old masters. Boston, Osgood, 1884.
653 "Introduction." In Howells, William D. Modern Ital-
     ian poets. N.Y., Harper, 1887. p.1-10.
654 "Introduction." In Hughes, Thomas. Tom Brown's
     school-days. N.Y., Harper, 1911. p.ix-xii.
655 "Introduction." In Ibanez, Vicente Blasco. The shad-
     ow of the cathedral. Tr. by Mrs. W.A. Gillespie.
     N.Y., Dutton, 1919. p.v-xiv.
656 "Introduction." In James, Henry. Daisy Miller. N.Y.,
     Harper, 1906; i.e. after Feb. 28, 1916.
657 "Introduction." In Living truths from the writings of
     Charles Kingsley. Selected by E.E. Brown. Boston,
     Lothrop, 1882. p.3-4.
658 "Introduction." In Mark Twain's library of humor.
     N.Y., Webster, 1888.
          The introduction was written by the associate edi-
          tors.
659 "Introduction." In Mark Twain's speeches. N.Y.,
     Harper, 1910. p.vii-viii.
660 "Introduction." In Merrick, Leonard. The actor-man-
     ager. London, Hodder and Stoughton, 1918. p.v-xiv.
661 "Introduction." In The poems of George Pellew.
     Edited by William Dean Howells. Boston, W.B.
     Clarke, 1892. p.v-xi.
          First published in Cosmopolitan 13:527-30, Sept.
          1892.
662 "Prefatory sketch." In Bellamy, Edward. The blind-
     man's world and other stories. Boston, Houghton
     Mifflin, 1898. p.v-xiii.
          First published in the Atlantic monthly 82:253-56,
          Aug. 1898.
663 "The prose poem." In ... Pastels in prose. Tr. by
     Stuart Merrill. N.Y., Harper, 1890. p.v-viii.

664 "A reminiscent introduction." In Howells, William D.,
      ed. The great modern American stories; an anthol-
      ogy. N.Y., Boni and Liveright, 1920. p.vii-xiv.
665 "Sketch of George Fuller's life." In George Fuller, his
      life and works. Ed. by J.B. Millet. Boston,
      Houghton Mifflin, 1886. p.1-52.
666 "Thomas Ellwood." In Autobiography. Lives of Lord
      Herbert of Cherbury and Thomas Ellwood. Boston,
      Osgood, 1877. p.169-79.
667 "Valera and Dona Luz." In Valera, Juan. Dona Luz.
      Tr. by Mary J. Serrano. N.Y., Appleton, 1891.
      p.3-4.
668 "Wilhelmine." In Memoirs of Frederica Sophia Wilhel-
      mina, Princess Royal of Prussia, margravine of Bai-
      reuth, sister of Frederick the Great. Boston, Os-
      good, 1877. vol. 1, p.1-28.
669 "Introduction." In Andersen, Hans. Fairy tales and
      wonder stories. N.Y., Harper, 1914. p.xi-xiii.
670 "Introduction." In Austen, Jane. Pride and prejudice.
      N.Y., Scribner's, 1918. p.v-xviii.
671 "Introduction." In De Maupassant, Guy. The second
      odd number; thirteen tales. Tr. by Charles H.
      White. N.Y., Harper, 1917. p.vii-xii.
672 "Introduction." In Dunbar, Paul L. Lyrics of a lowly
      life. N.Y., Dodd, Mead, 1896. p.xiii-xx.
      Also in Bookman 23:185-86, Apr. 1906.
673 "Introduction." In Galdos, B. Perez. Dona Perfecta.
      Tr. by Mary J. Serrano. N.Y., Harper, 1896.
      p.v-xiii.
674 "Introduction." In Garland, Hamlin. Main-travelled
      roads. Cambridge, Mass., Stone and Kimball, 1893.
      p.1-6.
      Appeared first in "Editor's study" in Harper's
      monthly 83:638-40, Sept. 1891.
675 "Introduction." In Stoddard, Charles W. South-sea
      idyls. N.Y., Scribner, 1892.
676 "Introduction." In Swift, Jonathan. Gulliver's travels.
      N.Y., Harper, 1913. p.xv-xvi.
677 "Introduction." In Tolstoy, Leo. Master and man.
      Tr. by A.H. Beaman. N.Y., Appleton, 1895. p.v-
      xv.
678 "Introduction." In Valdes, A.P. The joy of Captain
      Ribot. Tr. by Minna C. Smith. N.Y., Brentano,
      1900.
      The introduction comes from a review which
      Howells wrote for Literature, May 1899.

679 "Introduction." In Verga, Giovanni. The house by the
        medlar-tree. Tr. by Mary A. Craig. N.Y., Harper,
        1890. p.iii-vii.
680 "Introduction." In Artemus Ward's best stories. Ed.
        by Clifton Johnson. N.Y., Harper, 1912. p.vii-xvi.
681 "Introduction." In Wyss, David. The Swiss Family
        Robinson. N.Y., Harper, 1909. p.xi-xiii.

The following titles belong to a series called "Harper's novelettes." They were edited by William Dean Howells and
Henry Mills Alden. Howells wrote the introductions.

682 Different girls. N.Y., Harper, 1906. p.v-vii.
683 The heart of childhood. N.Y., Harper, 1906. p.iii-iv.
684 Quaint courtships. N.Y., Harper, 1906. p.v-vi.
685 Shapes that haunt the dusk. N.Y., Harper, 1907.
        p.v-vii.
686 Southern lights and shadows. N.Y., Harper, 1907.
        p.v-vi.
687 Their husbands' wives. N.Y., Harper, 1906. p.v-vi.
688 Under the sunset. N.Y., Harper, 1906. p.v-vii.

BOOK REVIEWS

The following abbreviations are used in the citations below:

AM   Atlantic Monthly
CM   Century Magazine
HM   Harper's Monthly
HW   Harper's Weekly
Lit   Literature
NAR   North American Review
RT   Round Table
ec   "Editor's Easy Chair," Harper's Monthly
es   "Editor's Study," Harper's Monthly

689 Abbott, A.O. Prison life in the South. AM, Oct.
    1866.
690 Adams, Brooks. Emancipation of Massachusetts. HM,
    May 1887, es.
691 Adams, Charles F. Autobiography. HM, Aug. 1916,
    ec.
692 Adams, Henry. History of the United States. HM,
    May 1890, es.
             . The education of Henry Adams. HM, Feb.
    1919, ec.
693 Adams, W.D. Dictionary of English literature. AM,
    Mar. 1890.
694 Afterglow, no name series. AM, July 1877.
695 Agassiz, Louis. A journey in Brazil. AM, Mar 1868.
696 Aiken, Conrad. Earth triumphant. HM, Sept. 1915,
    ec.
697 Alec-Tweedie, Ethel B. America as I saw it. HM,
    Feb. 1914, ec.
698 Alden, H.M. A study of death. HW 39:965, Oct. 12,
    1895.
699 Aldrich, A.R. The rose of flame. HM, Sept. 1889,
    es.
700 Aldrich, Thomas B. Ballad of Babie Bell. SP 2:1,
    Sept. 17, 1859.
             . Flower and thorn. AM, Jan 1877.
             . Marjorie Daw and other people. AM, Nov.
    1873.
             . Poems. AM, Aug. 1866.

65

_____ . Prudence Palfrey. AM, Aug. 1874.
_____ . The queen of Sheba. AM, Jan. 1878.
_____ . The sister's tragedy. HM, May 1891, es.
_____ . The story of a bad boy. AM, Jan. 1870.
_____ . Wyndham Towers. HM, Apr. 1890, es.
701 Allan-Olney, Mary. The private life of Galileo. AM,
      Sept. 1870.
702 Allen, Grant. Babylon. HM, Feb. 1886, es.
703 Allibone, S. A. A critical dictionary of English litera-
      ture. AM, Aug. 1890.
704 An American anthology. Edited by E. C. Stedman.
      NAR 172:148-60, Jan. 1901.
705 The American architect and building news, vol. 1. AM,
      Mar. 1877.
706 American poems. Ed. by H. E. Scudder. AM, Mar.
      1880.
707 American prose. Ed. by H. E. Scudder. AM, July
      1880.
708 American sonnets. Ed. by William Sharp. HM, Sept.
      1889, es.
709 Ames, Mary C. A memorial of Alice and Phoebe Cary.
      AM, Mar. 1873.
710 Andersen, H. C. In Spain and a visit to Portugal. AM,
      Sept. 1870.
_____ . O. T., A Danish romance. AM, Sept. 1870.
_____ . Only a fiddler. AM, Nov. 1870.
_____ . The story of my life. AM, Sept. 1871.
711 Arnaud, Giuseppe. I contemporanei italiani. NAR,
      Oct. 1866.
_____ . I poeti patriottici dell'Italia. NAR, Oct.
      1866.
712 L'art, quatrième année, tome III. AM, Jan. 1879.
713 Audoux, Marguerite. Marie-Claire. HM, June 1911.
714 Auerbach, Berthold. Edelweiss. Trans. by Ellen
      Frothingham. AM, June 1869.
715 Austin, Henry. Vagabond verses. HM, May 1891, es.
716 Avery, B. P. Californian pictures. AM, Dec. 1877.

717 Bacon, A. M. Japanese girls and women. HM, Oct.
      1891, es.
718 Bacon, F. W. and Burgess, N. Vim. HM, July 1889,
      es.
719 Bacon, L. W. A life worth living; memorials of Emily
      Bliss Gould. AM, July 1879.
720 Bacourt, M. De. Souvenirs of a diplomate. HM, Feb.
      1886, es.
721 Badeau, Adam. Aristocracy of England. HM, Sept.
      1886, es.

722 Baker, G. A., Jr. Point-lace and diamonds. AM,
     July 1875.
723 Baker, W. M. Moses Evans. AM, Aug. 1874.
     _____. The new Timothy. AM, Oct. 1870.
724 Balestier, Walcott. A victorious defeat. HM, July
     1886, es.
725 Ballard, J. P. Insect lives. AM, Jan. 1880.
726 Balzac, Honoré de. The duchesse de Langeais. HM,
     May 1886, es.
     _____. Sons of the soil. HM, Sept. 1890, es.
727 Bangs, J. K. A houseboat on the Styx. HW 40:223,
     Mar. 1896.
728 Barnard, Charles and Burgess, Neil. The country fair.
     HM, July 1889.
729 Barras, Paul F. J. N. de. Memoirs. Ed. by George
     Duruy. HW 39:556-57, June 15, 1895.
730 Bartlett, John. Familiar quotations. AM, Nov. 1868.
731 Bates, Arlo. A wheel of fire. HM, Jan. 1886, es.
732 Baylor, F. C. Behind the Blue Ridge. HM, Nov. 1887,
     es.
733 Bazan, Emilia. Morrina. HM, Apr. 1891, es.
734 Beecher, H. W. Norwood. AM, June 1868.
735 Bell, Lilian. The instinct of step-fatherhood. Lit,
     Dec. 31, 1898.
736 Bellamy, Edward W. Looking backward. HM, June
     1888, es.
     _____. Miss Ludington's sister. CM, May 1886;
     HM, May 1886.
737 Bellezza, Paolo. Humour. NAR, Oct. 1901.
738 Bellows, H. W. The old world in its new face. AM,
     July 1868.
739 Benjamin, W. Contemporary art in Europe. AM,
     Jan. 1878.
740 Bennett, Arnold. Hilda Lessways. HM, June 1912, ec.
     _____. Your U. S. HM, Apr. 1913, ec.
741 Benson, E. F. The relentless city. HW, Nov. 28,
     1903.
742 Besant, Walter. Fifty years ago. HM, Dec. 1888, es.
743 Bigelow, John. William Cullen Bryant. HM, May
     1890, es.
744 Birukoff, Paul. Leo Tolstoy, his life and works. HM,
     Feb. 1907.
745 Bishop, N. H. The pampas and the Andes. AM, Mar.
     1869.
746 Bishop, W. H. Detmold, a romance. AM, Aug. 1879.
     _____. The golden justice. HM, Apr. 1887, es.

747   Bisland, Elizabeth. <u>A flying trip around the world.</u>
      HM, Oct. 1891, es.
748   Björnson, Björnstjerne. <u>Arne.</u> AM, Apr. 1870.
      _____. <u>The fisher-maiden.</u> AM, Apr. 1870.
      _____. <u>The happy boy.</u> AM, Apr. 1870.
      _____. <u>In God's ways.</u> HM, Feb. 1891, es.
      _____. <u>The railroad and the churchyard.</u> Tr. by
      Carl Larsen. AM, Nov. 1870.
749   Black, William. <u>White heather.</u> HM, Feb. 1886, es.
750   Boileau, Nicolas. <u>Les heros de roman.</u> Ed. by T. F.
      Crane. HM, May 1903, ec.
751   Boswell, James. <u>Life of Johnson.</u> Ed. by G. B. Hill.
      HM, Feb. 1890, es.
752   Botta, Vincenzo. <u>Dante.</u> RT, n. s. , no. 4, p. 51-52,
      Sept. 30, 1865.
753   Bourget, Paul. <u>Outre-mer.</u> HW 39:485, May 25,
      1895.
754   Boyesen, H. H. <u>Essays on Scandinavian literature.</u>
      HW 39:460, May 18, 1895.
      _____. <u>Gunnar.</u> AM, Nov. 1874.
      _____. <u>The mammon of unrighteousness.</u> HM,
      July 1891, es.
      _____. <u>Story of Norway.</u> HM, Aug. 1886, es.
755   Boyland, G. H. <u>Six months under the Red Cross.</u> AM,
      Dec. 1873.
756   Brighouse, H. <u>Hobson's choice.</u> HM, Mar. 1916, ec.
757   Brinton, D. G. <u>The myths of the new world.</u> AM, Oct.
      1868.
758   Brooke, Rupert. <u>Letters from America.</u> HM, Aug.
      1916, ec.
759   Brown, Alice. <u>Meadow-grass.</u> HW, Nov. 30, 1895.
760   Brown, Kenneth and Boone, H. B. <u>Eastover courthouse.</u>
      HM, Oct. 1901, ec.
761   Brown, M. E. <u>Musical instruments and their homes.</u>
      HM, Apr. 1889, es.
762   Browning, Robert. <u>Asolando.</u> HM, Apr. 1890, es.
      _____. <u>The inn album.</u> AM, Mar. 1876.
      _____. <u>Red cotton night-cap country.</u> AM, July
      1873.
763   Bryant, William C. <u>Letters of a traveller.</u> <u>Ohio</u>
      <u>state journal</u> 22:2, Apr. 16, 1859.
      _____. <u>Orations and addresses.</u> AM, Oct. 1873.
      _____. <u>Thanatopsis.</u> AM, Jan. 1879.
764   Bryce, James. <u>The American commonwealth.</u> HM,
      Mar. 1889, es.
765   Bugbee, J. M. and Holmes, O. W. <u>Memorial, Bunker</u>
      <u>Hill.</u> AM, Aug. 1875.

766   Bunner, H. C. Midge. HM, Aug. 1887, es.
767   Bunsen, Frances. A memoir of Baron Bunsen. AM,
      Jan. 1869.
768   Burne-Jones, Philip. Democracy and dollars. HM,
      Sept. 1904.
769   Burnet, Dana. Poems. HM, Sept. 1915, ec.
770   Burroughs, John. Locusts and wild honey. AM, July
      1879.
      _____. Wakerobin. AM, Aug. 1871.
771   Bury, J. D. A daughter of Thespis. HW, May 2,
      1903.
772   Butler, W. A. Nothing to wear and other poems. Lit,
      n. s. 2:225-26, Sept. 15, 1899.
773   Butterfield, C. W. An historic account of the expedi-
      tion against Sandusky. AM, Feb. 1874.
774   Byron, George Noel Gordon, Lord. Works, vol. 1:
      Letters 1804-13, Ed. by W. E. Henley. HW 41:270,
      Mar. 13, 1897.

775   Cable, G. W. Bonaventure. HM, Oct. 1888, es.
      _____. Grandissimes. HM, Oct. 1888, es.
776   Cabot, J. E. Memoir of Ralph Waldo Emerson. HM,
      Feb. 1888, es.
777   Cahan, Abraham. Yekl. New York world, July 26,
      1896, p. 18.
      _____. The imported bridegroom and other stories.
      Lit, Dec. 31, 1898.
778   Calhoun, L. G., ed. Modern women and what is said
      of them. AM, Nov. 1868.
779   Campbell, Helen. Prisoners of poverty abroad. HM,
      Aug. 1889, es.
780   Campbell, W. W. Lake lyrics. HM, Jan. 1892, es.
781   Cantu, Cesare. Della letteratura italiana. NAR, Oct.
      1866.
782   Carlyle, Jane Welsh. Letters and memorials. HM,
      July 1903, ec.
783   Carlyle, Thomas. Letters. Ed. by C. E. Norton.
      HM, Aug. 1889, es.
      _____. Early letters of Thomas Carlyle. Ed. by
      C. E. Norton. HM, May 1887, es.
784   Carpenter, E. B. South county neighbors. HM, Jan.
      1888, es.
785   Casgrain, H. R. Francis Parkman. AM, Oct. 1872.
786   Castiglione, Baldassare. The courtier. HM, May
      1902, ec.
787   Cawein, Madison. Accolon of Gaul. HM, Sept. 1889,
      es.

_____. Days and dreams. HM, Jan. 1892, es.
_____. Myth and romance. Lit, n.s. 2:153-54,
Aug. 25, 1899.
_____. Poems. NAR, Jan. 1908.
_____. The triumph of music and other lyrics.
HM, Feb. 1888, es.
789 Cervantes. Don Quixote. Tr. by John Ormsby. HM,
Feb. 1888, es.
790 Chaplin, H.W. Five hundred dollars. HM, Apr. 1888,
es.
791 Chapman, J.J. Causes and consequences. Lit 3:474-
75, Nov. 19, 1898.
792 Chapman, Maria W. Harriet Martineau's autobiography.
AM, May 1877.
793 Charnwood, G.R.B. Abraham Lincoln. HM, Dec.
1918, ec.
794 Chastellux, Francois J. Travels in North America.
HM, Apr. 1913, ec.
795 Chatfield-Taylor, H.C. Life of Goldoni. HM, Mar.
1914, ec.
796 Cherbuliez, Victor. Joseph Noirel's revenge. Tr. by
W. F. West. AM, Jan. 1873.
797 Chesnutt, C.W. Frederick Douglass. NAR, Aug. 1901.
798 Clark, George R. Sketch of his campaign in the Illinois
in 1778-79. AM, Nov. 1869.
799 Clay, C.M. The life of Cassius Marcellus Clay. HM,
Nov. 1886, es.
800 Clemens, Samuel L. The prince and the pauper. New
York tribune, Oct. 25, 1881.
_____. The adventures of Tom Sawyer. AM, May
1876.
_____. Sketches. AM, Dec. 1875.
_____. Mark Twain's letters. HM, Mar. 1918, ec.
_____. Mark Twain's library of American humor.
HM, Feb. 1889, es.
801 Cleveland, H.W. Voyage of a merchant navigator.
HM, Dec. 1886, es.
802 Codman, J.T. Brook Farm. HW 39:796, Aug. 24,
1895.
803 Collins, G.L. Putnam place. HW, May 2, 1903.
804 Collins, Wilkie. The queen of hearts. AM, May 1876.
805 Colquhoun, A.R. Greater America. HM, Sept. 1904.
806 Colvin, Sidney. Life of John Keats. HM, Sept. 1887,
es.
_____. John Keats. 2d ed. HM, July 1918, ec.
807 Conrad, Joseph. Almayer's folly. HW 39:508, June
1, 1895.

808 Conway, M. D. Life and papers of Edmund Randolph.
HM, Mar. 1889, es.
_____. Autobiography. HM, Jan. 1906, ec.
809 Cooke, R. T. Huckleberries. HM, Feb. 1892, es.
_____. Steadfast. HM, May 1889, es.
_____. Poems. HM, Sept. 1888, es.
810 Cooper, James F. The pioneers. Ohio state journal,
Apr. 5, 1859, p. 3
_____. The red rover. Ohio state journal, Apr.
5, 1859, p. 3.
811 Coppée, Francois. Tales. Ed. by Guy de Maupassant.
HM, Apr. 1891, es.
812 Corbin, C. F. Belle and the boys. AM, Jan. 1880.
813 Corbin, John. The Elizabethan Hamlet. HW 39:868-69,
Sept. 14, 1895.
814 Cornavo, Luigi. The temperate life. HM 108:640-44,
Mar. 1904.
815 Cornwall, Barry. Charles Lamb. AM, Dec. 1866.
816 Courthope, W. J. Liberal movement in English literature. HM, Mar. 1886, es.
817 Cozzens, Frederick S. Works. AM, Mar. 1871.
818 Craddock, C. E. Phantoms of the footbridge. HW
39:508, June 1, 1895.
_____. In the clouds. HM, Apr. 1887, es.
819 Cranch, C. P. Satan, a libretto. AM, Mar. 1874.
820 Crane, Stephen. The black riders. HW 40:79, Jan.
25, 1896.
_____. The red badge of courage. HW, Oct. 26,
1895.
_____. Maggie. HW, June 8, 1895; New York
world, July 26, 1896, p. 18.
821 Cross, Wilbur L. Life and times of Laurence Sterne.
NAR 191:273-76, Feb. 1910.
822 Croy, Henry. Boone stop. HM, Jan. 1919, ec.
823 Curtis, W. E. Capitals of South America. HM, Oct.
1888, es.
824 Custer, E. B. Following the guidon. HM, Oct. 1890,
es.

825 Dall, W. H. Alaska and its resources. AM, Aug. 1870.
826 Dandridge, Danske. Rose Brake. HM, May 1891, es.
827 Dante. Divine comedy. Tr. by H. W. Longfellow.
Nation 4:492-94, June 20, 1867.
_____. Divine comedy. Tr. by C. E. Norton. HM,
Feb. 1892, es.

_____. The first canticle of the Divine comedy of Dante. Tr. by T.W. Parsons. AM, Dec. 1867.

828 Darley, F.O.C. Compositions in outline from Hawthorne's Scarlet letter. AM, Jan. 1880.

829 Darlington, W.M. An account of the life and travels of Colonel James Smith. AM, Oct. 1870.

830 Darwin, C.R. What Darwin saw. AM, Jan. 1880.

831 Davis, A.J. The children's progressive lyceum, a manual. RT, n.s., no.8, p.116, Oct. 28, 1865.

832 Davis, Reuben. Recollections of Mississippi and Mississippians. HM, May 1890, es.

833 Davis, Rebecca H. Dr. Warrick's daughters. HW 40:342, Apr. 11, 1896.

_____. Gallegher. HM, Sept. 1891, es.

834 Day, Holman. The skipper and the skipped. HM, July 1911.

835 De Forest, John W. Kate Beaumont. AM, Mar. 1872.

_____. A lover's revolt. Lit, Dec. 17, 1898.

_____. The Wetherel affair. AM, Aug. 1874.

836 De Maupassant, Guy. Notre coeur. HM, Feb. 1891, es.

_____. The odd number. HM, Feb. 1890, es.

837 Denison, T.S. The man behind. HM, Oct. 1888, es.

838 De Normandie, James. Portsmouth book. Lit, n.s. 2:273-74, Sept. 29, 1899.

839 De Schweinitz, Edmund. The life and times of David Zeisberg. AM, Dec. 1870.

840 De Vere, Aubrey. Alexander the Great. AM, Oct. 1874.

841 Diaz, A.M. The Jimmyjohns. AM, Jan. 1878.

842 Dickens, Charles. Our mutual friend. RT, n.s., no. 13, p.200-01, Dec. 2, 1865.

_____. American notes. HM, Apr. 1913, ec.

843 Dickinson, A.E. What answer? AM, Jan. 1869.

844 Dickinson, Emily. Poems. Ed. by M.L. Todd. HM, Jan. 1891, es.

845 Dixon, W.H. Her majesty's tower. AM, May 1869.

_____. Her majesty's tower. second series. AM, Dec. 1869.

846 Dostoievsky, Feodor M. Le crime et le châtiment. HM, Sept. 1886, es.

_____. Les humilies et offenses. HM, Sept. 1886, es.

847 Dowie, M.M. A girl in the Carpathians. HW, May 4, 1895.

848 Drachmann, Holger. Paul and Virginia of a northern zone. HW 40:342, Apr. 11, 1896.

849   Drake, Daniel.   Pioneer life in Kentucky.   AM, Oct.
      1870.
850   Du Maurier, George.   The Martian.   HW 41:730, July
      24, 1897.
851   _____. Peter Ibbetson.   HM, Feb. 1892, es.
      Dunbar, P. L.   Majors and minors.   HW 40:630, Jan.
      27, 1896.
852   Dupuy, M. E.   Les grands maîtres de la litterature
      russe.   HM, June 1886, es.
853   Dunning, Charlotte.   A step aside.   HM, Apr. 1887,
      es.
854   Durand, John.   Italy, Rome, and Naples, from the
      French of Henri Taine.   AM, July 1868.
855   Dwight, Wilder.   Life and letters of Wilder Dwight.
      AM, Apr. 1868.
856   Dyer, Louis.   Machiavelli and the modern state.   HM,
      Apr. 1905.

857   Echegary, Jose.   Mariana.   HW 39:677, July 20,
      1895.
858   Eggleston, Edward.   The circuit rider.   AM, June
      1874.
      _____. The end of the world.   AM, Dec. 1872.
      _____. The Graysons.   HM, Feb. 1889, es.
      _____. The Hoosier schoolmaster.   AM, Mar. 1872.
859   Eggleston, G. C.   A rebel's recollection.   AM, Feb.
      1875.
      _____. The signal boys.   AM, Jan. 1878.
860   Eliot, George.   The legend of Jubal.   AM, July 1874.
      _____. The Spanish gypsy.   AM, Sept. 1868.
861   Ely, R. T.   Land, labor and taxation.   HM, Apr. 1888,
      es.
      _____. Social aspects of Christianity.   HM, Feb.
      1890, es.
862   Emerson, R. W.   May-day and other pieces.   AM,
      Sept. 1867.
      _____. Letters of Ralph Waldo Emerson to a friend.
      Lit, n. s. 2:201-02, Sept. 8, 1899.
863   Emerson, E. W.   Emerson in Concord.   HM, Aug.
      1889, es.
864   Emiliani-Giudiei.   Storia della letteratura italiana.
      NAR, Oct. 1866.
865   Espy, John and others.   Miscellanies.   AM, Aug.
      1871.

866   Faed, Thomas.   The Faed gallery.   AM, Jan. 1878.

867 Fambri, Paolo. The free press and dwelling in Italy.
       NAR, June 1869, p. 299-302.
868 Fawcett, Edgar. Fantasy and passion. AM, May 1878.
       _____. Social silhouettes. HM, Jan. 1886, es.
869 Felton, C. C. Greece, ancient and modern. AM, May
       1867.
870 Fetridge, W. P. Harper's hand-book for travelers in
       Europe and the East, fifth year. AM, Mar. 1867.
871 Field, Eugene. Little book of western verse. HM,
       May 1891, es.
872 Field, M. E., ed. The wings of courage. AM, Jan.
       1878.
873 Fielding, Henry. Voyage to Lisbon. HM, Jan. 1911,
       ec.
874 Fields, J. T. Yesterdays with authors. AM, Apr.
       1872.
875 Fields, J. T. and Whipple, E. P., eds. The family li-
       brary of British poetry. AM, Dec. 1878.
876 Fisher, G. P. Life of Benjamin Silliman. AM, July
       1866.
877 Fiske, John. Myth and mythmakers. AM, Feb. 1873.
       _____. The destiny of man. HM, Apr. 1886, es.
878 Foote, M. H. The cup of trembling. HW 40:223, Mar.
       7, 1896.
879 Ford, J. L. The brazen calf. HW, Dec. 19, 1903.
880 Forster, John. The life of Charles Dickens. AM, Feb.
       1872, Feb. 1873, May 1874.
881 Fox, John, Jr. A Cumberland vendetta. HW, Nov.
       30, 1895.
882 Franklin, Benjamin. Autobiography. Ed. by John
       Bigelow. AM, July 1868.
883 Frederic, Harold. In the valley. HM, Oct. 1890.
       _____. The Lawton girl. HM, Oct. 1890.
       _____. Seth's brother's wife. HM, Oct. 1890.
884 Frith, W. P. My autobiography. HM, Mar. 1888, es.
885 Froissart, Jean. The boys' Froissart. Ed. by Sidney
       Lanier. AM, Jan. 1880.
886 Frost, Robert. North of Boston. HM, Sept. 1915, ec.
       _____. A boy's will. HM, Sept. 1915, ec.
887 Froude, J. A. Oceana. HM, May 1886, es.
888 Fuller, Henry B. The cliff-dwellers. Harper's bazaar
       26:883, Oct. 28, 1893.
       _____. The last refuge. HM, Oct. 1901, ec.
       _____. With the procession. HW 39:508, June 1,
       1895.

889 Galdos, Perez. Dona Perfecta. Harper's bazaar 28:
     886, Nov. 2, 1895.
     _____. Leon Roch. HM, May 1888, es.
890 Gannett, W.C. Ezra Stiles Gannett, Unitarian minister.
     AM, May 1875.
891 A garden of Hellas. Tr. by L.C. Perry. HM, Jan.
     1892, es.
892 Garland, Hamlin. Main-travelled roads. HM, Sept.
     1891, es.
     _____. Rose of Dutcher's Coolly. HW 40:223,
     Mar. 7, 1896.
     _____. Son of the middle border. New York times,
     Aug. 30, 1917.
     _____. They of the high trails. HM, Sept. 1916,
     ec.
     _____. Ulysses S. Grant, his life and character.
     Lit, n.s. 1:73-74, Feb. 3, 1899.
     _____. The trail of the goldseekers. Lit, n.s 2:
     177-78, Sept. 1, 1899.
893 Gautier, Theophile. Romance of the mummy. Ohio
     state journal 23:2, Apr. 2, 1860.
894 Gayarre, Charles. Philip II of Spain. AM, May
     1867.
895 Gibbons, P.H. Pennsylvania Dutch and other essays.
     AM, Oct. 1872.
896 Gilder, J.L. Representative poems of living poets.
     HM, Oct. 1886.
897 Gilder, R.W. The new day. AM, Jan. 1876.
     _____. Two worlds and other poems. HM, Jan.
     1892, es.
898 Gilson, R.R. In the morning glow. HW, Nov. 15,
     1902.
899 Giovanitti, Arturo. Arrows in the gale. HM, Oct.
     1914.
900 Gobright, L.A. Recollections of men and things at
     Washington. AM, July 1869.
901 God in his world. HM, Apr. 1890, es.
902 Godkin, Edwin L. Life and letters. Ed. by Rollo
     Ogden. NAR, May 3, 1907.
903 Goethe, Johann Wolfgang von. Faust. Tr. by Bayard
     Taylor. AM, Feb. 1871, July 1871.
     _____. Correspondence between Goethe and Carlyle.
     Ed. by C.E. Norton. HM, Aug. 1887, es.
904 Goldschmidt, M. The flying mail. AM, Nov. 1870.
905 Gooch, F.C. Face to face with the Mexicans. HM,
     Jan. 1889, es.

906 Goodale, Elaine and Goodale, Dora. In Berkshire with
      wild flowers. AM, Jan. 1880.
907 Gosse, Edmund. From Shakespeare to Pope. HM,
      Mar. 1886, es.
      _____. Raleigh. HM, Dec. 1886, es.
908 Graham, Kenneth. The golden age. HW 40:223, Mar.
      7, 1896.
909 Graham, M. C. Story of the foothills. HW, Oct. 26,
      1895, ec.
910 Grant, Robert. The law and the family. HM, Mar.
      1920, ec.
911 Gray, David. Gallops. Lit, Dec. 31, 1898.
      _____. Letters, poems, and selected writings. HM,
      Apr. 1889, es.
912 Gray, G. Z. The children's crusade. AM, Feb. 1871.
913 Greeley, Horace. Recollections of a busy life. AM,
      Feb. 1869.
914 Greeley, A. W. Three years of Arctic service. HM,
      Aug. 1886, es.
915 Greene, B. C. A New England conscience. HM, Jan.
      1886, es.
916 Greene, G. W. The life of Nathaniel Greene. AM,
      Apr. 1868, Oct. 1871.
      _____. A short history of Rhode Island. AM, Sept.
      1877.
917 Greenough, Horatio. Letters of Horatio Greenough to
      his brother Henry Greenough. HM, Sept. 1887, es.
918 Griswold, W. M. Descriptive lists of novels. HM,
      Feb. 1892, es.
919 Gronlund, Laurence. Ca ira. HM, Apr. 1888, es.
      _____. Cooperative commonwealth. HM, Apr.
      1888, es.

920 Hale, Edward E. If, yes, and perhaps. AM, Nov.
      1868.
      _____. The Ingham papers. AM, July 1869.
921 Hall, F. H. Social usages at Washington. HM, Apr.
      1907.
      _____. Memories grave and gay. HM, Feb. 1919,
      ec.
922 Hall, Gertrude. The hundred and other stories. Lit,
      Dec. 31, 1898.
      _____. Verses. HM, Jan. 1892, es.
923 Hamerton, P. G. French and English. HM, Jan. 1890,
      es.

924 Hapgood, Isabel. Russian rambles. HW 39:485, May
      25, 1895.
925 Harben, Will. Westerfelt. HM, Oct. 1901, ec.
926 Harding, Chester. A sketch of Chester Harding drawn
      by his own hand. HM, Mar. 1891, es.
927 Hardy, Thomas. A group of noble dames. HM, Sept.
      1891, es.
 _____ . Jude the obscure. HW, Dec. 7, 1895.
 _____ . The mayor of Casterbridge. HM, Nov.
      1886, es.
 _____ . The woodlanders. HM, July 1887, es.
928 Harper, J.H. The house of Harper. HM, June 1912.
929 Harper's fifth reader. HM, Jan. 1890, es.
930 Harris, George. A century's change in religion. HM,
      Mar. 1915, ec.
931 Harrison, J.B. Dangerous tendencies in American life.
      AM, June 1880.
932 Harte, Bret. Echoes of the foothills. AM, Feb. 1875.
 _____ . Luck of roaring camp. AM, May 1870.
 _____ . Poems. AM, Mar. 1871.
 _____ . Sue. HW, Oct. 10, 1896.
933 Harvard memorials. Ed. by T.W. Higginson. AM,
      Jan. 1867.
934 Hassaurak, F. Four years among the Spanish Amer-
      icans. AM, Feb. 1868.
935 Hawthorne, Nathaniel. The scarlet letter. AM, Dec.
      1877.
 _____ . Marble Faun. Ohio state journal 23:2,
      Mar. 24, 1860.
 _____ . Passages from the French and Italian note-
      books of Nathaniel Hawthorne. AM, May 1872.
936 Hawthorne, Julian. Hawthorne and his circle. NAR
      177:873-82, Dec. 1903.
937 Hay, John. Castilian days. AM, Nov. 1871.
 _____ . Poems. HM, Sept. 1890, es.
938 Hayes, Henry. Margaret Kent. HM, Apr. 1886, es.
939 Hayes, I.I. The open polar sea. AM, Apr. 1867.
940 Hayne, P.H. Legends and lyrics. AM, Apr. 1872.
941 Hays, W.J. The princess Ioleways. AM, Jan. 1880.
942 Heard, A.F. The Russian church and Russian dissent.
      HM, Aug. 1887, es.
943 Hearn, Lafcadio. Youma. HM, Sept. 1890, es.
944 Heine, Heinrich. Scintillations from the prose works
      of Heinrich Heine. Tr. by S.A. Stern. AM, Aug.
      1873.
945 Henley, W.E. Book of verses. HM, Nov. 1888, es.

_____. Views and reviews. HM, Oct. 1890, es.
946 Hibbard, G. A. Iduna. HM, Feb. 1892, es.
947 Higginson, M. T. Memoir of Thomas Wentworth Hig-
     ginson. HM, July 1914, ec.
_____. Room for one more. AM, Jan. 1880.
948 Higginson, T. W. Army life in a black regiment. AM,
     Nov. 1869.
_____. Atlantic essays. AM, Nov. 1871.
_____. Larger history of the U. S. HM, Apr.
     1886, es.
_____. Old Cambridge. Lit, n. s. 1:505-06, June
     9, 1899.
949 Hilton, David. Brigandage in South Italy. NAR, July
     1865.
950 Hoffman, Charles F. Poems. AM, Feb. 1874.
951 Holland, F. M. Frederick Douglass. NAR, Aug. 1901.
952 Holland, J. G. Katherina. AM, Dec. 1867.
_____. Plain talks in familiar subjects. Nation 1:
     659, Nov. 23, 1865.
953 Holmes, John. Letters. HM, Mar. 1918. ec.
954 Holmes, Margaret. The chamber over the gate. HM,
     Apr. 1887, es.
955 Holmes, Oliver W. Before the curfew and other poems.
     HM, Sept. 1888, es.
_____. Mechanism in thought and morals. AM, May
     1871.
_____. A mortal antipathy. HM, Mar. 1886, es.
_____. Our hundred days in Europe. HM, Feb.
     1888, es.
_____. The poet at the breakfast table. AM, Dec.
     1872.
_____. Regimen sanitatis salernitanum. Tr. by
     John Ordronaus. AM, May 1871.
_____. The school-boy. AM, Jan. 1879.
_____. Songs of many seasons. AM, Jan. 1875.
956 Holt, Henry. On the cosmic relations. HM, Feb.
     1915, ec.
957 Hooker, Katherine. Wayfarers of Italy. HM, Jan.
     1903, ec.
958 Hope, Anthony. A change of air. HW, Oct. 26, 1895.
959 Hopkins, Tighe. Lady Bonnie's experiment. HW, Oct.
     26, 1895.
960 Horton, George. In unknown seas. HW 40:79, Jan.
     25, 1896.
_____. In Argolis. HW 47:1660, Oct. 17, 1903.
961 Hosmer, J. K. Life of young Sir Henry Vane. HM,
     Mar. 1889, es.

962 Houghton, R. M. Monographs, personal and social.
     AM, Aug. 1873.
963 House, Edward. Yone Santo. HM, May 1889, es.
964 Howard, Benjamin. Prisoners of Russia. HW, Feb.
     14, 1903.
965 Howe, E. W. The story of a country town. CM, Aug.
     1884.
966 Howell, James. Survey of the Signorie of Venice.
     HM, June 1904, ec.
967 Hudson, H. R. Poems. AM, July 1874.
968 Hudson, W. H. Far away and long ago. HM, Feb.
     1919, ec.
969 Hughes, Eilian. Some aspects of humanity. HM,
     Feb. 1890, es.
970 Hunt, Gaillard. Life in America one hundred years
     ago. HM, Aug. 1915, ec.
971 Hunt, Leigh. A day by the fire. AM, May 1870.
     _____. The wishing-cap papers. AM, May 1873.
972 Hunt, Leigh and Lee, S. A., eds. The book of the
     sonnet. AM, Apr. 1867.
973 Hunt, L. L. Memoir of Mrs. Edward Livingston. HM,
     Sept. 1886, es.
974 Hunt, Violet. A hard woman. HW 40:342, Apr. 11,
     1896.
975 Hutton, Lawrence. Curiosities of the American stage.
     HM, Mar. 1891, es.
976 Hutton, R. H. Brief literary criticism. NAR, Sept. 7,
     1906.

977 Ingelow, Jean. A story of doom. AM, Sept. 1867.
978 In Memoriam, General Steven Elliott. AM, July 1871.
979 Irvine, J. P. The green leaf and the gray. HM, Jan.
     1892, es.

980 Jaccaci, A. F. On the trail of Don Quixote. CM 56:
     177-85, June 1898.
981 James, Henry. French poets and novelists. AM,
     July 1878.
     _____. A passionate pilgrim. AM, Apr. 1875.
     _____. The reverberator. HM, Oct. 1888, es.
     _____. The secret of Swedenborg. AM, Dec. 1869.
     _____. Terminations. HW 39:701, July 27, 1895.
     _____. The tragic muse. HM, Sept. 1890, es.
982 James, William. The principles of psychology. HM,
     July 1891, es.
983 Jansen, C. W. The stranger in America. HM, Aug.
     1916, ec.

984 Janvier, T. A.   The Dutch founding of New York.   HW,
       Nov. 14, 1903.
       _____. The Mexican guide. HM, Jan. 1889, es.
       _____. The uncle of an angel. HM, Mar. 1886,
       es.
985 Jenner, W. A.   The publisher against the people.   HM,
       May 1908.
986 Jewett, Sarah O.   Deephaven.   AM, June 1877.
       _____. The king of Folly Island. HM, Oct. 1888,
       es.
       _____. The life of Nancy. HW, Nov. 30, 1895.
       _____. Strangers and wayfarers. HM, Apr. 1891,
       es.
       _____. A white heron and other stories. HM, Feb.
       1887, es.
987 Johnston, R. M.   Mr. Absalom Billingslea.   HM, Apr.
       1888, es.
       _____. The Corsican. HM, Dec. 1911.
988 Johnson, Samuel.   Rasselas.   HM, July 1915, ec.
989 Jones, H. A.   Michael and his lost angel.   HW 40:126,
       Feb. 8, 1896.
990 Judd, Sylvester.   Margaret, a tale of the real and ideal,
       of blight and bloom.   AM, Jan. 1871.
991 Jusserand, J. J.   With Americans of past and present
       days.   HM, Sept. 1916, ec.

992 Keeler, Ralph.   Vagabond adventures.   AM, Dec. 1870.
993 Keller, Helen.   The story of my life.   HM, June 1903,
       ec.
994 Kester, Paul.   His own country.   HM, Aug. 1917, ec.
995 Kester, Vaughan.   The manager of the B. and A.   HM,
       Oct. 1901, ec.
996 Kidder, D. P.   Brazil and the Brazilians.   Ohio state
       journal 22:2, Dec. 7, 1858.
997 King, Basil.   The war home.   HM, Jan. 1914, ec.
998 King, Charles.   Campaigning with Crook.   HM, Jan.
       1891, es.
999 King, Clarence.   Mountaineering in the Sierra Nevada.
       AM, Apr. 1872.
1000 Kingsley, Charles.   Charles Kingsley, his life and
       letters.   AM, June 1877.
1001 Kipling, Rudyard.   Mine own people.   HM, Sept.
       1891, es.
       _____. The seven seas. McClure's magazine
       8:453-55, Mar. 1897.
       _____. Departmental ditties. HM, Jan. 1891, es.

1002 Kirkland, Joseph. The McVeys. HM, May 1889, es.
           . Zury. HM, June 1888, es.
1003 Kirk, Ellen W. Queen money. HM, June 1888, es.
1004 Kravchinskii, Sergiei M. (Stepniak, Sergius, pseud.)
     The Russian peasantry. HM, Oct. 1888, es.

1005 Lamon, W.H. The life of Abraham Lincoln. AM,
     Sept. 1872.
1006 Lampman, Archibald. Among the millet and other
     poems. HM, Apr. 1889, es.
1007 Landor, Walter S. Cameos. Ed. by E.C. Stedman
     and T.B. Aldrich. AM, May 1874.
1008 Larcom, Lucy. An idyll of work. AM, Aug. 1875.
1009 Laszowska-Gerard, Mrs. E. The land beyond the
     forest. HM, Jan. 1889, es.
1010 Lathrop, G.P. Rose and roof-tree. AM, Jan. 1876.
           . Would you kill him. HM, Feb. 1890.
1011 Lathrop, R.H. Along the shore. HM, Nov. 1888, es.
1012 Laugel, August. The United States during the war.
     AM, Aug. 1866.
1013 Lea, H.C. History of the Inquisition of the middle
     ages. HM, Mar. 1888, May 1888, es.
           . Superstition and force. AM, Feb. 1867.
1014 Learned, Walter. Between the whiles. HM, Apr.
     1890, es.
1015 Lecky, W.E.H. History of European morals, from
     Augustus to Charlemagne. AM, Nov. 1869.
1016 Lee, Vernon. Baldwin. HM, Sept. 1886, es.
1017 Lefevre, Edwin. Wall Street stories. HM, Sept.
     1916, ec.
1018 Leland, C.G. Hans Breitmann's party. AM, Oct.
     1868.
1019 Letters from Muskoka. AM, Dec. 1878.
1020 Libraire de l'art, deuxieme annee. AM, Mar. 1877.
1021 Library of American literature. Ed. by E.C. Stedman
     and E.M. Hutchinson. HM, July 1888, es.
1022 Il libro dell'amore. Tr. by M.A. Canini. HM, Oct.
     1886, Nov. 1888.
1023 Life and correspondence of Louis Agassiz. HM, Feb.
     1886, es.
1024 Life and genius of Goethe. HM, June 1886, es.
1025 Lindsay, Vachel. Adventures while preaching the
     gospel of beauty. HM, Sept. 1915, ec.
1026 Memoir of Mrs. Edward Livingston. HM, Dec. 1886,
     es.
1027 Lloyd and Rosenfeld. The senator. HM, June 1890,
     es.

1028 Lodge, H.C.   Ballads and lyrics.   AM, July 1880.
————— .   George Washington.   HM, Oct. 1889, es.
1029 Lodge, Oliver.   Raymond Lodge.   HM, Nov. 1917.
1030 Longfellow, Henry W.   Aftermath.   AM, Nov. 1873.
————— .   The divine tragedy.   AM, Feb. 1872.
————— .   The hanging of the crane.   AM, Dec. 1874.
————— .   Keramos and other poems.   AM, July
1878.
————— .   The masque of Pandora.   AM, Jan. 1876.
————— .   The New England tragedies.   AM, Jan.
1869.
————— .   Poems of places.   AM, Mar. 1877.
————— .   Poems on slavery.   HM, June 1886, es.
————— .   The poets and poetry of Europe.   AM,
Jan. 1871.
————— .   Three books of song.   AM, July 1872.
————— .   Collected works.   NAR 104:531-40, Apr.
1867.
1031 Longfellow, Samuel.   Life of Longfellow.   HM, June
1886, es.
1032 Lounsbury, T.R.   Shakespeare as a literary artist.
HM, Mar. 1902, ec.
1033 Lowell, Amy.   Sword blades and poppy seeds.   HM,
Sept. 1915, ec.
1034 Lowell, James R.   Among my books, second series.
AM, Apr. 1876, June 1870.
————— .   The Bigelow papers.   2d series.   AM,
Jan. 1867.
————— .   Democracy and other addresses.   HM, May
1887, es.
————— .   Goethe's Hermann and Dorothea.   Tr. by
Ellen Frothington.   AM, June 1870.
————— .   Heartsease and rue.   HM, June 1888, es.
————— .   Letters.   HW 37:1102, Nov. 18, 1893.
————— .   My study windows.   AM, June 1871.
————— .   Poetical works.   AM, Jan. 1877.
————— .   Three memorial poems.   AM, Mar. 1877.
————— .   Under the willows.   AM, Feb. 1869.
————— .   Writings, vols. 7-10.   HM, June 1891, es.
1035 Lowell, Percival.   Chosen, the land of the morning
sun.   HM, Apr. 1886.
1036 Luffman, C.B.   A vagabond in Spain.   HW 39:677,
July 20, 1895.
1037 Lumholz, Carl.   Among cannibals.   HM, May 1890,
es.
1038 Luska, Sidney.   A Latin quarter courtship.   HM, May
1889, es.

_____. Grandison Mother. HM, May 1889, es.

1039 Lytton, E. B. The Parisians. AM, May 1874.

1040 Maartens, Maarten. My lady nobody. HW, Oct. 26, 1895.

1041 McAllister, Ward. Society as I have found it. HM, Mar. 1891, es.

1042 McBride, James. Pioneer biography. AM, Aug. 1871.

1043 McCarthy, Justin. Reminiscences. Lit, July 14, 1899.

1044 McClellan, G. B. The oligarchy of Venice. HM, June 1904, ec.

1045 McCracken, W. D. Little idyls of the big world. HW 40:223, Mar. 7, 1896.

1046 McFee, William. Casuals of the sea. HM, Aug. 1917, ec.

1047 McMaster, J. B. Life of Franklin. HM, Apr. 1888, es.

1048 Madison, Dolly. Memoirs and letters. HM, Dec. 1886, es.

1049 Mallock, W. H. The old order changes. HM, Apr. 1887, es.

1050 Markham, Edwin. The man with the hoe. Lit, n. s. 1:553-54, June 23, 1899.

1051 Marshall, H. R. Aesthetic principles. HW 39:726, Aug. 3, 1895.

1052 Martin, B. E. In the footprints of Charles Lamb. HM, Mar. 1891, es.

1053 Martineau, Harriet. Society in America. HM, Aug. 1916, ec.

1054 Mason, Walt. Prose poems. HM, June 1912.
_____. Business prose poems. HM, June 1912.

1055 Masters, Edgar Lee. Spoon River anthology. HM, Sept. 1915, ec.

1056 Matthews, Brander. An introduction to the study of American literature. HW 40:294, Mar. 28, 1896.
_____. His father's son. HW 39:725, Aug. 3, 1895, Oct. 26, 1895.
_____. These many years. New York times, Oct. 21, 1917.

1057 Maunder, E. W. Are the planets inhabited? HM, Dec. 1913, ec.

1058 Mayo, Katherine. The standard bearers. HM, Jan. 1919, ec.

1059 Megrue, R. C. and Glass, Montague. Abe and Maw-russ. HM, Mar. 1916, ec.

1060 Melville, Herman. Battle-pieces and aspects of the
      war. AM, Feb. 1867.
1061 Meredith, George. Beauchamp's career. HM, May
      1889, es.
1062 Meriwether, Lee. The tramp at home. HM, Aug.
      1889, es.
      _____. Tramp trip. HM, July 1887, es.
1063 Millais, J. E. The Millais gallery. AM, Jan. 1878.
1064 Miller, Joaquin. Songs of the Sierras. AM, Dec.
      1871.
      _____. Songs of the sunlands. AM, Jan. 1874.
1065 Minto, William. The literature of the Georgian era.
      HW, May 18, 1895.
1066 Mistral, Frederic. Mirèio. Tr. by H. W. Preston.
      AM, July 1872.
1067 Mitchell, D. G. English lands, letters and kings.
      HM, Feb. 1890, es.
1068 Mitchell, S. W. The cup of youth. HM, Sept. 1889,
      es.
      _____. In war time. HM, Jan. 1886, es.
      _____. A psalm of death. HM, July 1891, es.
1069 Moens, W. J. C. English travellers and Italian brigands.
      AM, Oct. 1866.
1070 Monnier, Marco. Notizie storiche documentate sul
      brigantaggio nelle provincie Napoletane. NAR, July
      1865.
      _____. L'Italie, est-elle la terre des morts?
      NAR, Oct. 1866.
1071 Montagu, Lady Mary. The letters of Lady Mary
      Wortley Montagu and The letters of Madame Sevigne
      to her daughter and friends. Ed. by Mrs. S. J.
      Hale. AM, Apr. 1869.
1072 Moore, C. L. Book of day-dreams. HM, Nov. 1888,
      es.
1073 Moore, George. Celibates. HW 39:701, July 27,
      1895.
      _____. Esther Waters. HW 39:701, July 27, 1895.
1074 Mordell, Albert. Dante and other waning classics.
      HM, May 1916, ec.
1075 Morley, John. Rousseau. AM, July 1873.
1076 Morris, William. The defence of Guinevere. AM,
      Aug. 1875.
      _____. Love is enough. AM, Mar. 1873.
1077 Morse, A. O. A vindication to the claim of Alexander
      M. W. Ball to the authorship of the poem Rock me
      to sleep Mother. AM, Aug. 1867.

1078   Morse, E. S.   Japanese homes and their surroundings.
       HM, Apr. 1886, es.
1079   Morse, J. T.   Life of Franklin.   HM, Jan. 1890, es.
       _____ .   Life and letters of Oliver Wendell Holmes.
       HW 40:510, May 23, 1896.
1080   Mother Goose's melodies.   Illustrations by Alfred
       Kappes.   AM, Jan. 1879.
1081   Motley, J. L.   Historic progress and American democ-
       racy.   AM, Apr. 1869.
       _____ .   History of the United Netherlands, vols.
       3 and 4.   AM, May 1868.
       _____ .   The rise of the Dutch republic.   AM, July
       1879.
1082   Moulton, L. C.   In the garden of dreams.   HM, Apr.
       1890, es.
       _____ .   Poems.   AM, May 1878.
1083   Murfree, Fanny.   Felicia.   HM, Sept. 1891, es.
1084   Murfree, M. N.   The despot of Broomsedge Cove.
       HM, May 1889, es.
       _____ .   Prophet of the great smoky mountain.
       HM, Jan. 1886, es.
       _____ .   Across the chasm.   HM, Jan. 1886, es.
1085   Murray, W. H.   Adventures in the wilderness.   AM,
       June 1869.

1086   Nelson, Meredith.   Short flights.   HM, Jan. 1892,
       es.
1087   Nevinson, Henry W.   Slum stories.   HW 39:508, June
       1, 1895.
1088   The new life of Dante Alighieri.   Tr. by C. E. Norton.
       AM, Nov. 1867.
1089   Nicolay, John and Hay, John.   Abraham Lincoln.   HM,
       Feb. 1891, es.
1090   Norman, Henry.   Peoples and politics of the Far
       East.   HW 39:485, May 25, 1895.
1091   Norris, Frank.   Moran of the Lady Letty.   Lit, Dec.
       17, 1898.
       _____ .   McTeague.   Lit, n. s. 1:241-42, Mar. 24,
       1899.
       _____ .   The octopus.   HM, Oct. 1901, ec.
       _____ .   The pit.   HW, Mar. 14, 1903.
1092   Norton, Charles E.   Letters.   Ed. by Sara Norton
       and M. A. de Wolf Howe.   NAR 198:836-48, Dec.
       1913.
1093   Norton, Eliot.   Lincoln, a lover of mankind.   HM,
       Apr. 1912.

1094 Noufflard, Georges. Berlioz et le mouvement de
      l'art contemporain. HM, May 1886, es.

1095 O'Connor, W. D. Good gray poet. RT 3:37, Jan. 20,
      1866.
1096 Old New England traits. Ed. by George Lunt. AM,
      Sept. 1873.
1097 Old songs. Ed. by E. A. Abbey and Alfred Parsons.
      HM, Apr. 1889, es.
1098 Oliphant, Margaret. The life of Lawrence Oliphant.
      HM, Oct. 1891, es.
1099 Onderdonk, J. C. A history of American verse. NAR,
      Jan. 1902.
1100 Ongaro, Francesco dall'. Poesie. NAR, Jan. 1868.
1101 Oppenheim, James. Songs for the new age. HM,
      Sept. 1915, ec.
1102 O'Reilly, J. B. Songs from the southern seas. AM,
      Jan. 1874.
1103 Orr, Mrs. Sutherland. The life and letters of Robert
      Browning. HM, Oct. 1891, es.
1104 Owen, R. D. Threading my way. AM, Feb. 1874.

1105 Palfrey, F. W. Memoir of William Francis Bartlett.
      AM, June 1878.
1106 Palfrey, J. G. A compendious history of New England.
      AM, Nov. 1872, June 1873.
1107 Parkman, Francis. The conspiracy of Pontiac. AM,
      Apr. 1871.
          . Count Frontenac and New France under
      Louis XIV. AM, Oct. 1877.
          . The discovery of the Great West. AM,
      Jan. 1870.
          . The Oregon trail. AM, Oct. 1872.
1108 Parkman, Francis, ed. Historical account of Bouquet's
      expedition. AM, Mar. 1869.
1109 Parton, James. Caricature and other comic art. AM,
      Jan. 1878.
          . Famous Americans of recent times. AM,
      May 1867.
          . Life of Thomas Jefferson. AM, July 1874.
1110 Pater, W. H. Studies in the history of the Renaissance.
      AM, Oct. 1873.
1111 Paul, C. K. , ed. Mary Wollstonecraft, letters to
      Imlay. AM, July 1879.
1112 Paulding, W. I. The literary life of James K. Pauld-
      ing. AM, July 1867.

1113 Payne, Will. The money captain. Lit, Dec. 17, 1898.

1114 Pellew, George. In castle and cabin. HM, Oct. 1888, es.

_____ . Life of John Jay. HM, Sept. 1890, es.

1115 Pennell, Joseph and Pennell (Mrs.) Our sentimental journey. HM, June 1888, es.

1116 Perry, T.S. English literature in the eighteenth century. HM, July 1886.

_____ . Evolution of the snob. HM, Dec. 1886, es.

_____ . From Opitz to Lessing. HM, July 1886, es.

_____ . History of Greek literature. HM, Apr. 1891, es.

1117 Phelps, E.S. Poetic studies. AM, July 1875.

1118 Piatt, J.J. Poems in sunshine and firelight. AM 17:653-55, May 1866.

_____ . Western windows and landmarks. AM, Jan. 1878.

1119 Piatt, S.M.B. Poems in company with children. AM, May 1878.

_____ . That new world. AM, Jan. 1877.

_____ . A voyage to the fortunate isles. AM, July 1874.

1120 Picard, G.H. A mission flower. HM, Jan. 1886, es.

1121 Pier, A.S. The sentimentalists. HM, Oct. 1901, ec.

1122 Pike, J.L. The prostrate state: South Carolina under Negro government. AM, Feb. 1874.

1123 Poole, Ernest. The harbor. HM, Apr. 1915, ec.

1124 Poore, B.P. Reminiscences. HM, Sept. 1887, es.

1125 Posnett, H.M. Comparative literature. HM, July 1886, es.

1126 Preston, H.W. Love in the nineteenth century. AM, Sept. 1873.

_____ . Year in Eden. HM, Apr. 1887, es.

1127 Purnell, Thomas. Literature and its professors. AM, Aug. 1867.

1128 Pyle, Howard. Rejected of men. HW, July 11, 1903.

1129 Racinet, Albert. Le costume historique. AM, July 1877, Dec. 1877, Jan. 1879.

1130 Ralph, Julian. People we pass. HW, Nov. 30, 1895.

1131 Reade, Charles. Griffith Gaunt. AM, Dec. 1866.

_____ . Memoirs. HM, July 1887, es.

           . A terrible temptation. AM, Sept. 1871.
1132 Reade, Charles and Boucicault, Dion. Foul play.
     AM, Aug. 1868.
1133 Real, Eduardo P. and Howells, Annie T. Popular
     sayings of old Iberia. AM, Sept. 1877.
1134 Reese, Lizette W. A branch of May. HM, Sept.
     1888.
1135 Reid, E. J. Judge Richard Reid. HM, Nov. 1886,
     es.
1136 Reid, Whitelaw. Ohio in the war. AM, Feb. 1868.
1137 Remington, Frederic. Sundown Leflare. Lit, n.s.
     1:121-22, Feb. 17, 1899.
1138 Richards, A. M. Letter and spirit. HM, July 1891,
     es.
1139 Richardson, A. D. A personal history of Ulysses S.
     Grant. AM, Nov. 1868.
1140 Richardson, A. S. The history of our country. AM,
     Aug. 1875.
1141 Ridge, W. P. A clever wife. HW 40:342, Apr. 1896.
1142 Riley, J. W. A child world. Daily tatler, Nov. 7,
     1896, p. 5-7.
           . Old-fashioned roses. HM, Jan. 1892, es.
           . Rhymes of childhood. HM, May 1891, es.
1143 Rizal, Jose. An eagle flight. HM, Apr. 1901.
1144 Robertson, Morgan. Spun-yarn. Lit, Dec. 31, 1898.
1145 Rollins, A. W. Uncle Tom's tenement. HM, Oct.
     1888, es.
1146 Roosevelt, Theodore. Winning of the West. HM,
     Oct. 1889, es.
           . Gouverneur Morris. HM, July 1888, es.
1147 Ropes, J. C. The first Napoleon. HM, Mar. 1886,
     es.
1148 Rosebery (Lord). Napoleon. HM, Feb. 1901, ec.
1149 Rosenfeld, Morris. Songs from the ghetto. Lit, n.s.
     1:97-98, Feb. 10, 1899.
1150 Rossetti, D. G. The Borzoi book of decorum. AM,
     July 1870.
           . Poems. AM, July 1870.
1151 Rossiter, W. S. An accidental romance. HW 40:223,
     Mar. 7, 1896.
1152 Royce, Josiah. History of California. HM, Aug.
     1886, es.
1153 Ruskin, John. Time and tide, by Weare and Tyne.
     AM, May 1868.
1154 Russell, A. P. Library notes. AM, Dec. 1875.
1155 Rydberg, Victor. The last Athenian. Tr. by Widgery
     Thomas. AM, June 1869.

1156 Saint Jorioz. Il brigantaggio alla frontiera pontificia
      dal 1860 al 1863. NAR, July 1865.
1157 Salter, W. M. Ethical religion. HM, Aug. 1889, es.
1158 Samuels, Samuel. From the forecastle to the cabin.
      HM, July 1887, es.
1159 Sarmiento, Domingo F. Life in the Argentine republic.
      AM, Sept. 1868.
1160 Schevill, Rudolph. Cervantes. HM, Sept. 1919, ec.
1161 Schock, George. Hearts contending. HM, Aug. 1910,
      ec.
1162 Schreiner, Olive. The story of an African farm. HM,
      Jan. 1889, es.
1163 Scidmore, E. R. Jinriksha days. HM, Oct. 1891, es.
1164 Scollard, Clinton. Old and new world lyrics. HM,
      Apr. 1889, es.
1165 Scott, Sir Walter. Journal. HM, Mar. 1891, es.
1166 Scudder, H. E. The Bodleys afloat. AM, Jan. 1880.
_____. The Bodley's on wheels. AM, Jan. 1879.
_____. Mr. Bodley abroad. AM, Jan. 1881.
_____. James Russell Lowell. HM, Feb. 1902.
_____. Men and manners in America one hundred
      years ago. AM, Aug. 1876.
_____. Stories from my attic. AM, Dec. 1869.
1167 William Winston Seaton, of the National intelligencer.
      AM, July 1871.
1168 Seeley, J. R. A short history of Napoleon the first.
      HM, Apr. 1886, es.
1169 Semmes, Raphael. Memoirs of service afloat during
      the war between the states. AM, Apr. 1869.
1170 Shaler, N. S. The individual. HM, May 1901, ec.
1171 Sharp, William. Romantic ballads and poems of
      phantasy. HM, Sept. 1889, es.
_____. Sosperi di Roma. HM, Jan. 1892, es.
1172 Sherman, F. D. Lyrics for a lute. HM, May 1891,
      es.
_____. Madrigals and catches. HM, Apr. 1889,
      es.
1173 Shigemi, Shinkichi. A Japanese boy. HM, Sept.
      1890, es.
1174 Shorter, C. E. George Borrow and his circle. HM,
      May 1914, ec.
1175 Sienkiewicz, Henryk. Children of the soil. HW, Oct.
      26, 1895.
1176 Simons, A. M. Social forces in American history.
      HM, May 1912, ec.
1177 Smalley, G. W. London letters. HM, Mar. 1891,
      es.

1178   Smith, F. H.   A vagabond gentleman.   HW, Nov. 30,
       1895.
1179   Smith, Gertrude.   The rousing of Mrs. Potter.   HW,
       Nov. 30, 1895.
       _____.   The Arabella and Araminta studies.   HW,
       Nov. 30, 1895.
1180   Smith, Goldwin.   The Civil War in America.   AM,
       Aug. 1866.
       _____.   Cowper.   AM, Sept. 1880.
1181   Smyth, A. H.   Bayard Taylor.   HW 40:294, Mar. 28,
       1896.
1182   Snider, D. J.   Homer in Chios.   HM, Jan. 1892, es.
1183   Snyder, Carl.   New conceptions in science.   HW,
       July 11, 1903; HM, Oct. 1903.
1184   Society verse.   Ed. by E. D. L. Pierson.   HM, Nov.
       1887, es.
1185   Solomons, Ikey.   Catherine, a story.   AM, Feb.
       1870.
1186   Stanton, H. B.   Random recollections.   HM, Sept.
       1887, es.
1187   Stedman, Edmund C.   The blameless prince.   AM,
       May 1869.
       _____.   Poems now first collected.   HW 42:174,
       Feb. 19, 1898.
       _____.   Poetical works.   AM, Jan. 1874.
       _____.   Poets of America.   HM, Mar. 1886, es.
1188   Stedman, Laura and Gould, G. M.   Life of Stedman.
       HM, Feb. 1911.
1189   Stephen, Leslie.   George Eliot.   HM, Nov. 1902, ec.
1190   Stetson, C. P.   In this our world.   HW 40:79, Jan.
       25, 1896.
1191   Stevens, O. C.   An idyl of the sun.   HM, Jan. 1892,
       es.
1192   Stevenson, Robert Louis.   The strange case of Dr.
       Jekyll and Mr. Hyde.   HM, May 1886, es.
1193   Stillman, William J.   Autobiography of a journalist.
       NAR 172:934-44, June 1901.
1194   Stockton, Frank.   Adventures of Captain Horn.   HW,
       Oct. 26, 1895.
       _____.   A story teller's pack.   HW 41:538, May
       29, 1897.
1195   Stoddard, C. W.   Exits and entrances.   HM, Dec.
       1903.
1196   Stoddard, Elizabeth.   Two men.   Nation 1:537-38,
       Oct. 26, 1865.
1197   Stowe, Harriet B.   Pink and white tyranny.   AM,
       Sept. 1871.

1198 Swinton, William. Masterpieces of English literature.
      AM, July 1880.
1199 Symonds, J.A. Renaissance in Italy. HM, Nov. 1887,
      es.

1200 Taine, Hippolyte. Art in Greece. AM, Feb. 1872.
      _____. Art in the Netherlands. AM, Mar. 1871.
      _____. History of English literature. Tr. by H.
      Van Laun. AM, Feb. 1872.
      _____. Notes on England. Tr. by W. F. Rae.
      AM, Aug. 1872.
      _____. Talks with Socrates about life. HM, May
      1887, es.
1201 Tarkington, Booth. The turmoil. HM, Apr. 1915,
      May 1915, ec.
1202 Taylor, Bayard. By-ways of Europe. AM, June
      1869.
      _____. The echo club. AM, Jan. 1877.
      _____. Home pastorals, ballads and lyrics. AM,
      Jan. 1876.
      _____. The masque of the gods. AM, June 1872.
      _____. The picture of St. John. AM, Jan. 1867.
      _____. The prophet. AM, Dec. 1874.
      _____. The story of Kennett. AM 17:775-78, June
      1866.
1203 Taylor, H.O. The medieval mind. HM, June 1912,
      ec.
1204 Taylor, Isaac. Origin of the Aryans. HM, Oct.
      1890, es.
1205 Taylor, Thomas. Our American cousin. HM, Mar.
      1916, ec.
1206 Tenney, E.P. Agatha and the shadow. HM, Apr.
      1887, es.
      _____. Constance of Arcadia. HM, Aug. 1886.
1207 Tennyson, Alfred Lord. Demeter. HM, Apr. 1890,
      es.
      _____. The Holy Grail and other poems. AM,
      Feb. 1870.
      _____. The last tournament. AM, Feb. 1872.
      _____. The lover's tale. AM, Aug. 1879.
1208 Thackeray, William M. Miscellanies. AM, Feb.
      1870.
1209 Thanet, Octave. Knitters in the sun. HM, Jan. 1888,
      Mar. 1888, es.
1210 Thaxter, Celia. Among the Isles of Shoals. AM,
      July 1873.
      _____. Poems. AM, Mar. 1872, Dec. 1874.

1211 Thomas, E.M. The inverted torch. HM, May 1891,
      es.
1212 Thompson, E.W. Old man Savarin. HW, Oct. 26,
      1895.
1213 Thompson, Maurice. Songs of fair weather. Inde-
      pendent 35:1249-50, Oct. 4, 1883.
      _____. The witchery of archery. AM, Aug. 1879.
1214 Thoreson, Magdalen. Old Olaf. AM, Nov. 1870.
1215 Tolstoy, Leo. Deux générations. HM, Feb. 1887,
      es.
      _____. La mort d'Ivan Illitch. HM, Feb. 1887,
      es.
      _____. The invaders. HM, Jan. 1888, es.
      _____. La puissance des ténèbres. HM, Mar.
      1888, es.
      _____. Que faire? HM, July 1887, es.
      _____. The Kreutzer sonata. HM, Oct. 1890, es.
      _____. The fruits of culture. HM, Apr. 1891, es.
1216 Toplady, A.M. Rock of ages. AM, Jan. 1879.
1217 Towle, G.M. Magellan. AM, Jan. 1880.
1218 Trescot, W.H. Memorial of the life of J. Johnston
      Pettigrew. AM, July 1871.
1219 Trevelyan, G.O. The American revolution. HM,
      Sept. 1904, ec; NAR, June 1908.
1220 Trollope, Adolphus. What I remember. HM, Apr.
      1888, es.
1221 Trollope, Anthony. Thackeray. AM, Aug. 1879.
1222 Trollope, Frances. Domestic manners of the Amer-
      icans. HM, Apr. 1888, Apr. 1913, ec.
1223 Trowbridge, J.T. The book of gold. AM, May 1878.
      _____. The emigrant's story. AM, Feb. 1875.
1224 Tuckerman, C.K. The Greeks of today. AM, Jan.
      1873.
1225 Turgenev, Ivan S. Dimitri Roudine. AM, Sept. 1873.
      _____. Liza. Tr. by W.R.S. Ralston. AM,
      Feb. 1873.
      _____. Smoke. Tr. by W.F. West. AM, Aug.
      1872.

1226 Underwood, F.H. Lord of himself. AM, Sept. 1874.

1227 Vachell, H.A. The Quinneys. HM, Mar. 1916, ec.
1228 Valdes, A.P. El cuarto poder. HM, Oct. 1888, es.
      _____. La alegria del Capitan Ribot. Lit, n.s.
      1:409-10, May 1899.
      _____. The joy of Captain Ribot. Tr. by Minna
      C. Smith. Lit, n.s. 1:409-10, May 12, 1899.

_____. Marta y Maria. HM, Apr. 1886, es;
HM, Nov. 1886, es.
_____. Reverita. HM, Nov. 1886, es.
_____. Jose. HM, Nov. 1886, es.
_____. I Malavoglio. HM, Nov. 1886, es.
_____. Maximina. HM, Jan. 1888, es.
_____. Scum. HM, Feb. 1891, es; HM, Apr.
1891, es.
1229 Valera, Juan. Dona Luz. HM, Nov. 1886, es.
_____. Pepita Ximeniz. HM, Nov. 1886, es.
1230 Veblen, Thorstein. Theory of the leisure class. Lit,
n. s. 1:361-62, 385-86, Apr. 28, May 5, 1899.
1231 Ventura, L. D. and Shovitch, S. Misfits and rem-
nants. HM, Nov. 1886, es.
1232 Verga, Giovanni. The house by the medlar tree.
HM, Oct. 1890.
1233 Villard, O. G. John Brown, 1800-1859. NAR 193:
26-34, Jan. 1911.
1234 Vosmaer, C. Works of William Unger. AM, Dec.
1877.

1235 Wallace, A. R. Man's place in the universe. HM,
Mar. 1904, ec.
1236 Ward, C. O. History of the ancient working people.
HM, Oct. 1889, es.
1237 Ward, Mrs. Humphry. The Coryston family. HM,
Jan. 1914, ec.
_____. Eleanor. NAR 173:134-44, July 1901;
HM, Feb. 1901, ec.
_____. Robert Elsmere. HM, Nov. 1888, es.
_____. Lady Rose's daughter. HW, Feb. 21,
1903.
1238 Ward, J. H. The life and letters of James Gates
Percival. AM, Jan. 1867.
1239 Ward, M. A. Dante. HM, Nov. 1887, es.
1240 Waring, G. E. The bride of the Rhine. AM, Apr.
1878.
_____. Tyral and the skirt of the Alps. AM,
Jan. 1880.
_____. Whip and spur. AM, July 1875.
1241 Warner, C. D. Backlog studies. AM, Apr. 1873.
_____. Baddeck and that sort of thing. AM,
June 1874.
_____. Being a boy. AM, Dec. 1877.
_____. In the wilderness. AM, Sept. 1878.
_____. A little journey in the world. HM, Feb.
1890, es.

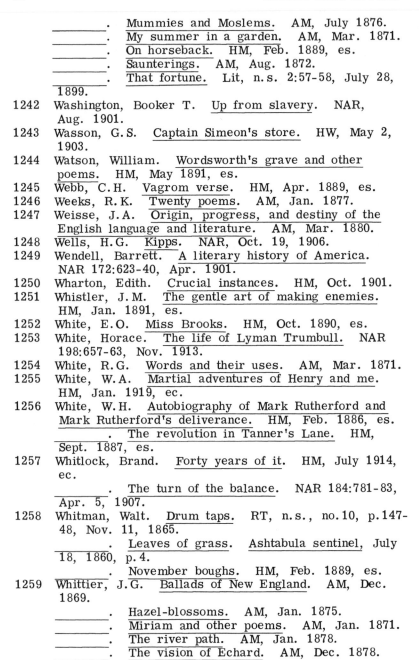

_____. Mummies and Moslems. AM, July 1876.
_____. My summer in a garden. AM, Mar. 1871.
_____. On horseback. HM, Feb. 1889, es.
_____. Saunterings. AM, Aug. 1872.
_____. That fortune. Lit, n. s. 2:57-58, July 28,
1899.
1242 Washington, Booker T. Up from slavery. NAR,
Aug. 1901.
1243 Wasson, G. S. Captain Simeon's store. HW, May 2,
1903.
1244 Watson, William. Wordsworth's grave and other
poems. HM, May 1891, es.
1245 Webb, C. H. Vagrom verse. HM, Apr. 1889, es.
1246 Weeks, R. K. Twenty poems. AM, Jan. 1877.
1247 Weisse, J. A. Origin, progress, and destiny of the
English language and literature. AM, Mar. 1880.
1248 Wells, H. G. Kipps. NAR, Oct. 19, 1906.
1249 Wendell, Barrett. A literary history of America.
NAR 172:623-40, Apr. 1901.
1250 Wharton, Edith. Crucial instances. HM, Oct. 1901.
1251 Whistler, J. M. The gentle art of making enemies.
HM, Jan. 1891, es.
1252 White, E. O. Miss Brooks. HM, Oct. 1890, es.
1253 White, Horace. The life of Lyman Trumbull. NAR
198:657-63, Nov. 1913.
1254 White, R. G. Words and their uses. AM, Mar. 1871.
1255 White, W. A. Martial adventures of Henry and me.
HM, Jan. 1919, ec.
1256 White, W. H. Autobiography of Mark Rutherford and
Mark Rutherford's deliverance. HM, Feb. 1886, es.
_____. The revolution in Tanner's Lane. HM,
Sept. 1887, es.
1257 Whitlock, Brand. Forty years of it. HM, July 1914,
ec.
_____. The turn of the balance. NAR 184:781-83,
Apr. 5, 1907.
1258 Whitman, Walt. Drum taps. RT, n. s., no. 10, p. 147-
48, Nov. 11, 1865.
_____. Leaves of grass. Ashtabula sentinel, July
18, 1860, p. 4.
_____. November boughs. HM, Feb. 1889, es.
1259 Whittier, J. G. Ballads of New England. AM, Dec.
1869.
_____. Hazel-blossoms. AM, Jan. 1875.
_____. Miriam and other poems. AM, Jan. 1871.
_____. The river path. AM, Jan. 1878.
_____. The vision of Echard. AM, Dec. 1878.

1260   Whymper, Edward.   Scrambles among the Alps.   AM,
       Oct. 1872.
1261   Wiggins, Kate D.   The village watch-tower.   HW,
       Nov. 30, 1895.
1262   Wilcox, Marrion.   Gray, an Oldhaven romance.   HM,
       Apr. 1888, es.
1263   Wilkeson, Frank.   Recollections of a private.   HM,
       Aug. 1887, es.
1264   Wilkins, M. E.   A humble romance.   HM, Sept. 1887,
       es.
       _____. A New England nun.   HM, June 1891, es.
       _____. The people of our neighborhood.   Lit,
       Dec. 31, 1898.
1265   Williams, J. L.   Remating time.   HM, Sept. 1916, ec.
       _____. The stolen story and other newspaper
       stories.   Lit, n. s. 1:457-58, May 26, 1899.
1266   Wilson, J. G.   Themes and variations.   HM, Apr.
       1890, es.
1267   Wilson, H. L.   Ruggles of red cap.   HM, June 1918,
       ec.
       _____. Somewhere in red cap.   HM, Jan. 1919,
       ec.
1268   Wilson, R. B.   Life and love.   HM, Sept. 1888, es.
1269   Winter, William.   Thistledown.   AM, July 1878.
1270   Wister, Owen.   Red men and white.   HW, Nov. 30,
       1895.
1271   Wood, Margaret.   A village tragedy.   HM, May 1889,
       es.
1272   Woods, K. T.   Six little rebels.   AM, Jan. 1880.
1273   Woolman, John.   Journal.   AM, Aug. 1871.
1274   Woolson, C. F.   Baedecker's handbooks for travelers.
       AM, June 1875.
       _____. Castle nowhere.   AM, June 1875; HM,
       Feb. 1887, es.
       _____. East angels.   HM, Aug. 1886, es.
1275   Wyatt, Edith.   Every one his own way.   HM, Oct.
       1901, ec.
1276   Wyckoff, W. A.   The workers, the East.   Lit 3:528-
       29, Dec. 3, 1898.
       _____. The workers, the West.   Lit 3:528-29,
       Dec. 3, 1898.
1277   Wyman, L. C.   Poverty grass.   HM, Feb. 1887, es.

1278   Yriarte, Charles.   Venice.   AM, Jan. 1880.

1279   Zangwill, Israel.   The children of the ghetto.   HW
       39:508, June 1, 1895.

1280   Zola, Emile. La terre. HM, Mar. 1888, es.

COLLECTIONS (Containing Book Reviews)

1281   Howells, William D. Criticism and fiction and other
       essays. Ed. with introduction and notes by Clara
       M. Kirk and Rudolf Kirk. N.Y., New York Univer-
       sity Press, 1959. 413p.
1282   Howells, William D. European and American masters.
       Edited with introduction by Clara and Rudolf Kirk.
       N.Y., Collier Books, 1963. 225p.
1283   Howells, William D. Discovery of a genius: William
       Dean Howells and Henry James. Compiled and edited
       by Albert Mordell. N.Y., Twayne, 1961. 207p.

BOOKS REVIEWED IN BOOKS

1284   Bjornson, Bjornstjerne. Arne, The happy boy, The
       fisher-maiden. In European and American masters.
       1963. p.33-39.
          Also in Criticism and fiction. 1959. p.104-09.
1285   Cable, George W. Bonaventure. In Discovery of a
       genius. 1961. p.129-30.
1286   De Forest, William. Miss Ravenel's conversion from
       secession to loyalty. In European and American
       masters. 1963. p.141-45.
          Also in Criticism and fiction. 1959. p.209-12.
1287   Eggleston, Edward. The Hoosier schoolmaster. In
       European and American masters. 1963. p.158-60.
          Also in Criticism and fiction. 1959. p.224-26.
1288   _____. The circuit rider: a tale of the heroic
       age. In European and American masters. 1963.
       p.160-62.
          Also in Criticism and fiction. 1959. p.226-28.
1289   Galdos, B. Perez. Dona Perfecta. In European and
       American masters. 1963. p.63-68.
1290   Hardy, Thomas. Jude the obscure. In European and
       American masters. 1963. p.79-82.
          Also in Criticism and fiction. 1959. p.150-53.
1291   Hay, John. The breadwinners: a social study. In
       Criticism and fiction. 1959. p.240-45.
1292   James, Henry. French poets and novelists. In Dis-
       covery of a genius. 1961. p.81-84.
1293   _____. Hawthorne. In Criticism and fiction.
       1959. p.232-36.

Also in Discovery of a genius. 1961. p. 92-97.
Included in European and American masters. 1963.
p. 166-70.

1294   . Daisy Miller. In Discovery of a genius.
1961. p. 180-91.

1295   . The passionate pilgrim and other tales.
In Discovery of a genius. 1961. p. 63-74.

1296   . Princess Cassamassima. In Discovery of
a genius. 1961. p. 123-25.

1297   . The reverberator. In Discovery of a
genius. 1961. p. 130.

1298   . The soft side. In Discovery of a genius.
1961. p. 177-79.

1299   . Stories reprinted in The Aspern papers
and A London life. In Discovery of a genius. 1961.
p. 126-28.

1300   . Terminations. In Discovery of a genius.
1961. p. 170-72.

1301   . The tragic muse. In Discovery of a genius. 1961. p. 165-68.

1302   . Transatlantic sketches. In Discovery of
a genius. 1961. p. 75-80.

1303 Nordau, Max. Degeneration. In European and American masters. 1963. p. 88-92.
Also in Criticism and fiction. 1959. p. 159-63.

1304 Norris, Frank. McTeague. In European and American masters. 1963. p. 216-18.

1305 Turgenev, Ivan S. Dimitri Roudine. In European
and American masters. 1963. p. 42-46.
Also in Criticism and fiction. 1959. p. 112-16.

1306 Valdes, Armando P. The fourth estate. In Discovery of a genius. 1961. p. 131-32.

1307   . Marta y Maria. In European and American
masters. 1963. p. 55-58.
Included in Criticism and fiction. 1959. p. 125-27.

1308   . Scum. In European and American masters.
1963. p. 58-59.
Also in Criticism and fiction. 1959. p. 128-29.

1309 Veblen, Thorstein. Theory of the leisure class. In
Criticism and fiction. 1959. p. 339-41.

1310 Wendell, Barrett. A literary history of America. In
Criticism and fiction. 1959. p. 315-32.

1311 Wilkins, Mary E. Portion of labor. In Criticism
and fiction. 1959. p. 342-44.

1312 Zola, Emile. La terre. In European and American
masters. 1963. p. 85-88.
Also in Criticism and fiction. 1959. p. 157-59.

DRAMA CRITICISM

GENERAL

1313 "Edward Harrigan's comedies." In Moses, Montrose
J. and Brown, John M. The American theatre as
seen by its critics, 1752-1934. N.Y., Norton, 1934.
p. 132-35.
1314 "Henrik Ibsen." North American review 183:1-14,
July 1906.
1315 "Ibsenism." In Howells, William D. European and
American masters. Edited by Clara M. Kirk and
Rudolf Kirk. N.Y., Collier Books, 1963. p. 74-76.
Appeared originally in Harper's weekly, Apr. 27,
1895.
1316 "The new poetic drama." North American review
172:794-800, May 1901.
1317 "The new taste in theatricals." Atlantic monthly 23:
635-44, May 1869.
1318 "On reading plays of Mr. Henry Arthur Jones."
North American review 186:205-12, Oct. 1907.
1319 "The play and the problem." Harper's weekly 39:294,
Mar. 30, 1895.
1320 "The plays of Eugene Brieux." North American review 201:402-11, Mar. 1915.
1321 "A question of propriety." In Howells, William D.
European and American masters. Edited by Clara
M. Kirk and Rudolf Kirk. N.Y., Collier Books,
1963. p. 71-74.
Contains a review of a performance of Ibsen's
Ghosts in 1899. Appeared originally in Literature,
July 7, 1899.

INDIVIDUAL PLAYS (Arranged by Author)

The following abbreviations are used for periodicals which
are frequently cited:

AM	Atlantic monthly
HM	Harper's monthly
HW	Harper's weekly

Lit   Literature
NAR   North American review

1322 Ade, George. The county chairman. HW, Jan. 16,
      1904.
      _____. Doc Horne. Lit, n.s. 2:249, Sept. 22,
      1899.
1323 Aeschylus. Agamemnon. HM, Oct. 1906, p. 795-96.
1324 Barrie, James. The admiral Crichton. HW, Jan.
      23, 1904, Feb. 24, 1906.
      _____. Little Mary. HW, Feb. 24, 1906, p. 272.
      _____. Peter Pan. HW, Feb. 24, 1906, p. 272.
      _____. The twelve pound look. HM, May 1913.
1325 Belasco, David and De Mille, H.C. The charity ball.
      HM, June 1890, p. 156.
1325a Björnson, Bjornstjerne. Sigurd Slembe. Tr. by
      W. M. Payne. HM, Feb. 1889, p. 490.
1326 Bennett, E.A. and Knoblauch, Edward. Milestones.
      HM, May 1913, p. 959-60.
1327 Ceconi, Teobaldo. Le commedie. NAR, Oct. 1864,
      p. 397-400.
1328 Clemens, Samuel L. Pudd'nhead Wilson. HW, Dec.
      28, 1895.
1329 Cohan, George M. Broadway Jones. HM, May 1913,
      p. 959.
      _____. Hit-the-trail Holliday. HM, Mar. 1916,
      p. 635-36.
1330 Cohan, George M. and Biggers, E.D. Seven keys to
      Baldpate. HM, Mar. 1914, p. 636-37.
1331 Craigie, P.R. Journeys end in lovers' meeting. HW,
      Dec. 28, 1895.
1332 Craven, H.T. The needful. Nation 1:570-71, Nov.
      2, 1865.
1333 Critchett, R.C. Lady Huntsworth's experiment. NAR,
      Mar. 1901.
1334 Dostoievsky, Feodor M. Rodion the student. HW,
      Dec. 28, 1895.
1335 Doyle, Conan. Story of Waterloo. HW, Dec. 28,
      1895.
1336 Ferrari, Paolo. Opere drammatiche. NAR, Oct.
      1864.
1337 Fitch, Clyde. Beau Brummel. HM, Aug. 1891,
      p. 477.
      _____. The climbers. NAR, Mar. 1901. p. 475.
      _____. Her own way. HW, Jan. 16, 1904.
      _____. Glad of it. HW, Jan. 16, 1904.
      _____. Runaway colt. HW, Dec. 28, 1895.

1338 Fyles, Franklin. The governor of Kentucky. HW 40:
      126, Feb. 8, 1896.
1339 Giacometti, Paolo. Teatro salto. NAR, Oct. 1864.
1340 Gillette, William. Secret service. HW, Jan. 30,
      1897, Dec. 4, 1897; HM, Mar. 1916, p. 637.
1341 Gordon, Jacob. The Kreutzer sonata. Tr. by
      Langdon Mitchell. HW, Nov. 24, 1906.
1342 Grant, Robert. Unleavened bread. NAR, Mar. 1901,
      p. 475.
1343 Harrigan, Edward. Dan's tribulations. HM, July
      1886, p. 316.
      _____. The leather patch. HM, July 1886,
      p. 316.
      _____. Marty Malone. HW, Oct. 10, 1896,
      p. 997.
      _____. Waddy Googan. HM, July 1889, p. 316.
1344 Herne, J. A. Rev. Griffith Davenport. Lit, n. s.
      1:265-66, Mar. 31, 1899.
      _____. Drifting apart. HM, June 1890, p. 154.
      _____. Margaret Fleming. HM, Aug. 1891, p. 478.
      _____. Sag Harbor. NAR, Mar. 1901, p. 471-74.
1345 Hobart, G. U. and Ferber, Edna. Our Mrs. McChes-
      ney. HM, Mar. 1916, p. 635.
1346 Howard, Bronson. Shenandoah. HM, June 1890,
      p. 155.
1347 Hoyt, C. H. A midnight bell. HM, July 1889, p. 318-
      19.
      _____. The rag baby. HM, July 1889, p. 318-19.
      _____. The tin soldier. HM, July 1889, p. 318-19.
      _____. A hole in the ground. HM, July 1889,
      p. 318-19.
      _____. The brass monkey. HM, July 1889,
      p. 318-19.
1348 Hutton, Lawrence. Curiosities of the American stage.
      HM, Mar. 1891, p. 643.
1349 Ibsen, Henrik. The enemy of the people. HW 39:
      390, Apr. 27, 1895.
      _____. Ghosts. HM, May 1888, es; Lit, n. s.
      1:529-30, June 16, 1899; Lit, n. s. 1:609, July 7,
      1899.
      _____. The pillars of society. HM, May 1888.
      _____. Letters. Tr. by J. N. Laurik and Mary
      Morison. HM, May 1906.
1350 Jefferson, Joseph. Autobiography. HM, Mar. 1891,
      p. 643.
1351 Jones, Arthur. The middleman. HM, Aug. 1891,
      p. 478.

        . Judah. HM, Aug. 1891, p.478.
1352 Jones, H.A. Mrs. Dane's defence. NAR, Mar. 1901.
        . The hypocrites. HW, Nov. 24, 1906.
        . The case of rebellious Susan. HW, Mar.
30, 1895, p.294.
        . The masqueraders. HW, Mar. 30, 1895.
        . Whitewashing Julia. HW, Jan. 16, 1904.
1353 Kemble, Fanny A. Journal. HM, Feb. 1914, p.474-
75.
1354 Kline, Charles. Maggie Pepper. HM, May 1913,
p. 959.
1355 Locke, Edward. The case of Becky. HM, May 1913,
p. 959.
        . Years of indiscretion. HM, May 1913,
p. 960.
1356 Entry omitted.
1357 Maeterlinck, Maurice. The intruder. HM, Jan.
1892, p.320.
1358 Marshall, Robert. A royal family. NAR, Mar. 1901,
p. 478.
1359 Matthews, Brander. The development of the drama.
HW 48:160-62, Jan. 30, 1904.
1360 Offenbach, Jacques. [La belle Hélène.] In Howells,
William D. Suburban sketches. N.Y., Houghton
Mifflin, 1901. p. 220-40.
1361 Ongaro, Francesco dall'. Stornelli italiani. NAR,
Jan. 1868, p. 26-42.
        . Fantasie drammatiche e liriche. NAR,
Jan. 1868, p. 26-42.
        . Florilegio drammatico. NAR, Oct. 1864.
        . Intorno alla natura e all'ufficio dell'arte
drammatica. NAR, Oct. 1864, p.401.
1362 Parker, L.N. Disraeli. HM, May 1913, p.961.
1363 Pinero, Arthur Wing. Benefit of the doubt. HW 40:
126, Feb. 8, 1896.
        . The gay Lord Quex. NAR, Mar. 1901.
        . The hobby horse. HW, Jan. 30, 1897.
        . The notorious Mrs. Ebbsmith. HW 40:
30-31, Jan. 11, 1896.
1364 Shakespeare. Hamlet. HW 39:892, Sept. 28, 1895.
1365 Shaw, George B. Arms and the man. HW 39:294,
Mar. 30, 1895.
        . Androcles and the lion. HM, Mar. 1914,
p. 637.
        . Fanny's first play. HM, May 1913, p. 958.
        . Major Barbara. HM, Mar. 1916, p. 637.

1366 Stoddard, Lorimer. Napoleon. HW, Dec. 28, 1895.
1367 Tennyson, Alfred. Harold. AM, Feb. 1877, p. 242-
      43.
      _____. Queen Mary. AM, Aug. 1875, p. 240-41.
1368 Thomas, Augustus. Arizona. NAR, Mar. 1901,
      p. 472-4.
      _____. The other girl. HW, Jan. 16, 1904.
1369 Wilde, Oscar. An ideal husband. HW, Mar. 30,
      1895, p. 294.
1370 Zangwill, Israel. Merely Mary Ann. HW, Jan. 23,
      1904.

SPEECHES

1371 [Address]. In Proceedings of the American Academy of Arts and Letters and of the National Institute of Arts and Letters, no. 3:7, 1915.

1372 [Address]. In Gould Memorial Home and Schools, Rome. Meeting of the Boston Ladies Association, Feb. 28, 1879. Boston, Beacon Press, 1879? p. 17-20.

1373 Address at the celebration of the one hundredth anniversary of the birth of Henry Wadsworth Longfellow, Sanders Theatre, Feb. 27, 1907. Cambridge, Mass., Cambridge Historical Society, 1907.
Reprint of the Cambridge Historical Society Publications II, Proceedings Oct. 23, 1906--Oct. 22, 1907.

1374 "Address of W. D. Howells." American Academy proceedings 2:7, Sept. 1, 1915.

1375 "Atlantic and its contributors." In Reed, T. B. Modern eloquence. N. Y., Modern Eloquence Corp., 1923. vol. 2, p. 244.

1376 "Atlantic dinner." Boston transcript 47:1, Dec. 17, 1874.

1377 "The Atlantic dinner, honors to Whittier." Boston transcript 50:1, 3, Dec. 18, 1877.

1378 "In memory of Mark Twain." In Reed, T. B. Modern eloquence. vol. 5, p. 224.

1379 "Mark Twain's seventieth birthday." Harper's weekly 49:1884-85, Dec. 23, 1905.

1380 "Mr. Howells on Mr. Bellamy." Critic ns29:391, June 11, 1898.
A portion of a speech given June 7 at the Social Reform Club.

1381 "New York letter." Literary world 17:152, May 1, 1886.
A speech given at the Authors' Club reception.

1382 "Opening address of the president, William Dean Howells." American Academy proceedings 1:5-8, June 10, 1910.

1383 Opening address. In Proceedings of the American Academy of Arts and Letters and of the National

Institute of Arts and Letters [in memory of Samuel
L. Clemens, Carnegie Hall, Nov. 30, 1910] no. 3:5-6,
1910-11.
1384   "Spanish prisoners of war." In Blackstone, H. Best
orations of today. enl. ed. N.Y., Hinds and Noble,
1926. p. 78.
1385   [Speech]. In Mark Twain's birthday; report of the
celebration of the sixty-seventh thereof at the Metropolitan Club, N.Y., Nov. 28, 1902. N.Y., Privately
printed, 1903. p. 2-4.
1386   "A tribute to William Dean Howells; souvenir of a
dinner given to the eminent author in celebration of
his seventy-fifth birthday." Harper's weekly 66:27-
34, Mar. 9, 1912.
       Contains a speech which Howells gave on this oc-
       casion. The speech is on p. 28-29. The speech
       is also included in Howells, William D. Criticism
       and fiction and other essays. Ed. by C.M. Kirk
       and Rudolf Kirk. N.Y., New York University
       Press, 1959. p. 366-74.
1387   "William Dean Howells at the dinner to Samuel L.
Clemens, Nov. 10, 1900." In After dinner speeches
at the Lotos Club. Arranged by John Elderkin and
others. N.Y., Privately printed, 1901. p. 394-96.
       The speech is also in Harper's weekly 44:1205,
       Dec. 15, 1900.

AUTOBIOGRAPHY AND REMINISCENCE

1388 "An autobiographical view of the 'Weekly'." Harper's
weekly 51:19-20, Jan. 5, 1907.
1389 "The bookcase at home." In My literary passions.
N.Y., Harper, 1895. p.1-9.
1390 A boy's town described for Harper's young people.
N.Y., Harper, 1890. 247p.
First published in Harper's young people, Apr. 8,
1890 through Aug. 26.
1391 "Certain preferences and experiences." In My literary
passions. N.Y., Harper, 1895. p.234-42.
1392 "The country printer." Scribner's magazine 13:539-58,
May 1893. In Howells, William D. Criticism and fiction and other essays. Edited by Clara and Rudolf
Kirk. N.Y., New York University Press, 1959.
p.290-98.
Also in Howells, William D. Impressions and experiences. N.Y., Harper, 1896. p.3-34. The
Plimpton Press in Norwood, Mass. printed the
essay as a separate in 1916.
1393 "Editor's easy chair." Harper's monthly 135:730-34,
Oct. 1917.
1394 "Eighty years and after." Harper's monthly 140:21-
28, Dec. 1919.
Published also as a pamphlet in 1919 by Harper.
1395 "In an old-time state capital." Harper's monthly
129:593-603, 740-51, 921-30, Sept.-Nov. 1914.
The article is about Columbus, Ohio. Much of
this essay appears in Years of my youth (1916).
1395a Letters home. N.Y. and London, Harper, 1903.
299p.
Appeared first in Metropolitan, Apr.-Sept. 1903.
1396 "Lighter fancies." In My literary passions. N.Y.,
Harper, 1895. p.44-47.
1397 Literary friends and acquaintance; a personal retrospect of American authorship. N.Y., Harper, 1900.
288p.
1398 "Men and letters, on coming back." Atlantic monthly
78:562-65, Oct. 1896.
1399 "Mr. Howells's paper." In Criticism and fiction and

other essays. Edited by Clara and Rudolf Kirk.
N.Y., New York University Press, 1959. p.377-84.
Also in The house of Harper. N.Y., 1912. p.319-
27.

1400 My year in a log cabin. N.Y., Harper, 1893. 62p.
First published in Youth's companion 60:213-15,
May 12, 1887.

1401 New Leaf Mills, a chronicle. New York and London,
Harper, 1913. 154p.

1402 "A non-literary episode." In My literary passions.
N.Y., Harper, 1895. p.124-28.

1403 "An old Venetian friend." Harper's monthly 138:634-
40, Apr. 1919.

1404 "Overland to Venice." Harper's monthly 137:837-45,
Nov. 1918.

1405 "Recollections of an Atlantic editorship." In Howells,
William D. European and American masters. Edited
by Clara and Rudolf Kirk. N.Y., Collier Books,
1963. p.117-38.

1406 "The story of the author's life." In The Howells story
book. Edited by Mary E. Burt and Mildred Howells.
N.Y., Scribner's, 1900. p.142-61.

1407 "The turning point of my life." Harper's bazaar 44:
165-66, Mar. 1910.
Also in Howells, William D. Criticism and fiction
and other essays. Edited by Clara and Rudolf
Kirk. N.Y., New York University Press, 1959.
p.353-62.

1408 Years of my youth. New York and London, Harper,
1916. 239p.
Most of the volume is a reprint of pages from
My year in a log cabin, Impressions and experiences, and "In an old-time state capital."

1409 "Young contributors and editors." Youth's companion
75:245, 267-68, May 9, 23, 1901.

1410 "A young Venetian friend." Harper's monthly 138:
827-33, May 1919.

INTERVIEWS

1410a Boyesen, Hjalmar H. "Mr. Howells interviewed by
        Prof. Boyesen." Review of reviews 8:90, July 1893.
1411 Brooks, Van Wyck. "Mr. Howells at work at seventy-
        two." World's work 18:11547.
1412 Brooks, Walter. "A talk with Mr. Howells." Author
        1:103-05, July 15, 1889.
1413 Calhoun, A.R. "William Dean Howells talks on liter-
        ature." Philadelphia press, Feb. 25, 1894, p. 24.
1414 Crane, Stephen. "Fears realists must wait; an in-
        teresting talk with William Dean Howells." New York
        times, Oct. 28, 1894, p. 20.
1415 Crawford, T.C. "Mr. Howells, his carer(sic), his
        present work, and his literary opinions." New York
        tribune, June 26, 1892, p. 14.
1416 Dreiser, Theodore. "How he climbed fame's ladder;
        William Dean Howells tells the story of his long
        struggle for success, and his ultimate triumph."
        Success, Apr. 1898, p. 5-6.
1417 _____. "The real Howells." Ainslee's 5:137-42,
        Mar. 1900.
        Also in Americana 37:274-82, Apr. 1943.
1418 E.J.C. "Howells at Nahant." Boston advertiser,
        Sept. 20, 1888, p. 5.
1419 Howells' meeting Miss Murfree." Literary news
        7:122, Apr. 1886.
1420 Johnson, Clifton. "Sense and sentiment." Outlook
        51:304-05, Feb. 23, 1895.
1421 _____. "The writer and the rest of the world."
        Outlook 49:580-82, Mar. 31, 1894.
1422 Kilmer, Joyce. "War stops literature." New York
        times, Nov. 29, 1914, section 5, p. 8.
1423 Marshall, Edward. "A great American writer."
        Philadelphia press, Apr. 15, 1894, p. 27.
1424 "Mr. Howells on realism; a talk with the novelist.
        Rider Haggard, a countercurrent--a Russian Shake-
        speare." New York tribune, July 10, 1887, p. 12.
        Interview mentions Hardy, Tolstoi, Turgenieff,
        Björnson, and Zola. In part reprinted in Critic
        ns8:32, July 16, 1887.
1424a "Mr. Howells interviewed." Critic 21(n. s. 18):36,

July 16, 1892.
Contains a sketch of Howells from the Tribune.
1425 "Mr. Howells beaming on 75th birthday." New York
      sun, Mar. 3, 1912, p. 10.
1426 "Mr. Howells's plans." Boston transcript, Jan. 1,
      1892, p. 6.
1427 "Mr. Howells's work." Literary news 7:155, May
      1886.
1428 "Mr. Howells's trip abroad; he gives some of his
      impressions in an entertaining chat." New York
      tribune, Nov. 10, 1897, p. 6.
1429 "New York letter." Literary world, April 17, 1886,
      p. 135.
      First appeared in Mail and express.
1430 "Poetry, war, and Mr. Howells." Literary digest
      18:607-08, May 27, 1899.
1431 "Politics but a good thing; William Dean Howells's
      views on the women's movement to aid Dr. Park-
      hurst." New York times, Oct. 13, 1894, p. 9.
1432 "The rambler." Bookbuyer 14:558-59, July 1897.
      Reprinted as "Mr. Howells, his own critic."
      Literary news 18:313, Oct. 1897.
1433 "Real conversations; a dialogue between William Dean
      Howells and Hjalmar Hjorth Boyesen." McClure's
      1:3-11, June 1893.
      A portion is reprinted in Bookman(London) 4:79-81,
      June 1893.
1434 Rood, Henry. "William Dean Howells at 75, talks of
      old literary New York." New York times, Feb. 25,
      1912, sec. 5, p. 4.
1435 Smith, Franklin. "An hour with Mr. Howells."
      Frank Leslie's magazine 74:118-19, Mar. 17, 1892.
1436 Van Westrum, A. Schade. "Mr. Howells on love and
      literature." Lamp 28:26-31, Feb. 1904.
1437 Wagstaff, W. de. "The personality of Mr. Howells; a
      study at close range." Book news monthly 26:739-41,
      June 1908.
1438 Walsh, W. S. "William Dean Howells believes in the
      future." New York herald, Dec. 30, 1900, p. 13.
1439 Wedmore, Frederick. "To Millicent, from America."
      Temple bar 77:241, June 1886.
         Includes comments on Björnson, Murfree, Hardy,
         Zola, and W. S. Gilbert. Appears also in Critic
         ns6:10, July 3, 1886.
1440 "William Dean Howells, a literary optimist." New
      York times, June 26, 1908, sec. 5, p. 5.
1441 "William Dean Howells at work." Current literature
      23:402-03, May 1898.

TRANSLATIONS BY HOWELLS

COLLECTION

1442 Longfellow, Henry W. The poets and poetry of
Europe. New ed., rev. and enl. Boston, Houghton
Mifflin, 1896.

INDIVIDUAL TITLES

1443 "The cardinals" (tr. from Dall'Ongaro). In The poets
and poetry of Europe. 1896. p. 884.
1444 "Chapter from Lazarillo de Tormes by Diego Hurtado
de Mendoza." Ashtabula sentinel 24:1, Nov. 15, 1855.
1445 "The decoration" (tr. from Dall'Ongaro). In The poets
and poetry of Europe. 1896. p. 884.
1446 "Don Pedro II, emperor of Brazil." Casket 2:121-24,
Aug. 1853.
1447 "The duchess" (tr. from Carrer). In The poets and
poetry of Europe. 1896. p. 877.
1448 "The Dutch mother, translated for the Sentinel from
the Spanish of Jacinto de Solas y Quiroga." Ashtabula
sentinel, Aug. 16, 23, 1855, p. 1.
1449 "The fair prisoner to the swallow" (tr. from Tommasso
Grossi). In The poets and poetry of Europe. 1896.
p. 873.
   Also in Commonwealth 2:1, Oct. 9, 1863.
1450 "The fisher-maiden" (tr. from the German of Heine).
In Piatt, John J. and Howells, William D. Poems of
two friends. Columbus, Ohio, Follett, Foster, 1860.
p. 128.
   First printed as "The fishermaid" in the Ashtabula
sentinel 27:103, Apr. 1, 1858.
1451 "A fragment, Heine" (tr. from the German of Heine).
Ashtabula sentinel 26:7, Nov. 26, 1857.
1452 "From an hour of my youth" (tr. from Aleardi). In
The poets and poetry of Europe. 1896. p. 881.
1453 "From Monte Circello" (tr. from Aleardi). In The
poets and poetry of Europe. 1896. p. 882.
1454 "From the Courrier des États-Unis." Ashtabula
sentinel 27:241, Aug. 5, 1858.

1455 "From the primal histories" (tr. from Aleardi).   In
      The poets and poetry of Europe.   1896.   p. 881.
1456 "The Germans in Italy."   Ohio state journal 22:2,
      Apr. 27, 1859.
1457 "I am a pilgrim swallow, and I roam" (tr. from
      Carrer).   In The poets and poetry of Europe.   1896.
      p. 878.
1458 "The imperial egg" (tr. from Dall'Ongaro).   In The
      poets and poetry of Europe.   1896.   p. 885.
1459 "The Lombard woman" (tr. from Dall'Ongaro).   In
      The poets and poetry of Europe.   1896.   p. 884.
1460 "The midnight ride" (tr. from Prati).   In The Poets
      and poetry of Europe.   1896.   p. 879.
1461 "The modern Danaides" (tr. from Courrier des Etats-
      Unis).   Ohio state journal 22:2, Jan. 14, 1859.
1462 "Morceaux" (tr. from the Spanish).   Ohio state journal,
      Mar. 4, 1859.   p. 1.
1463 Muller, Adalbert.   Venice.   Her art treasures and
      historical associations.   A guide to the city and
      neighboring islands.   Tr. from the 2d German edi-
      tion by William Dean Howells.   Venice, Münster, 1864.
1464 "Nanna" (tr. from Carcano).   In The poets and poetry
      of Europe.   1896.   p. 883.
1465 "Ode on superstition" (tr. from Vincenzo Monti).   In
      Benét, William R. and Cousins, Norman.   Poetry
      of freedom.   N. Y., Modern Library, 1948.   p. 626.
1466 "On the likeness of a beautiful woman carven upon
      her tomb" (tr. from Leopardi).   In Poets and poetry
      of Europe.   1896.   p. 872.
1467 "Original miscellany, Love through a keyhole, Felicity
      compared, A gastronome" (tr. from the Spanish).
      Ashtabula sentinel, June 7, 1855, p. 1.
1468 "The paper readers" (from the German).   Ashtabula
      sentinel 26:6, Aug. 27, 1857.
1469 "The perilous charity" (tr. from the Courrier des
      Etats-Unis).   Ohio state weekly journal 48:1, Mar.
      15, 1859.
1470 "Pio Nono" (tr. from Dall'Ongaro).   In The poets
      and poetry of Europe.   1896.   p. 884.
1471 "The poisoned bouquet--a story of the Italian opera,
      from the Courrier des Etats-Unis."   Ohio state
      journal 19:1, Nov. 29, 1855.
      Also in the Ashtabula sentinel, Jan. 17, 1856.
1472 "The ring of the last doge" (tr. from Dall'Ongaro).
      In The poets and poetry of Europe.   1896.   p. 885.
1473 "Romantic marriage."   Ohio state journal 22:2, Jan.
      18, 1859.

1474 "The royal road to music." Ohio state journal 23:2,
      Sept. 23, 1859.
1475 "Royer's verses." Ohio state journal 22:2, Jan. 18,
      1859.
1476 "Saint Ambrose" (tr. from Giusti). In The poets and
      poetry of Europe. 1896. p. 876.
1477 Samson, a tragedy in five acts. By Ippolito T. d'Aste.
      Tr. by W. D. Howells with the English and Italian
      words as performed by Signor Salvini, during his
      farewell American tour under the direction of Mr.
      A. M. Palmer. N. Y., Charles D. Koppel, 1889. 51p.
1478 "The shepherd" (from the German of Uhland). In
      Piatt, John J. and Howells, William D. Poems of two
      friends. Columbus, Ohio, Follett, Foster, 1860.
      p. 102.
1479 "The sister" (tr. from Dall'Ongaro). In The poets
      and poetry of Europe. 1896. p. 884.
1480 "Some Italian epigrams." Commonwealth 2:1, Jan.
      22, 1864.
      Translation of epigrams by Giuseppe Capparoggo
      and Clementino Vannetti.
1481 [Spanish proverbs translated]. Ohio state journal,
      Jan. 31, 1859.
      Unsigned.
1482 "The throstle" (from the German of Heine). In Piatt,
      John J. and Howells, William D. Poems of two
      friends. Columbus, Ohio, Follett, Foster, 1860.
      p. 94.
1483 "To my songs" (tr. from Dall'Ongaro). In The poets
      and poetry of Europe. 1896. p. 885.
1484 "To Sylvia" (tr. from Leopardi). In The poets and
      poetry of Europe. 1896. p. 872.
1485 "An unfortunate state of things." Ohio state journal
      22:2, Jan. 18, 1859.
1486 "The violets" (from the German of Lenau). In Piatt,
      John J. and Howells, William D. Poems of two
      friends. Columbus, Ohio, Follett, Foster, 1860.
      p. 109.
1487 "When will you dream you Germans" (tr. of Barbarossa
      of Giovanni B. Niccolini). In Benét, William R. and
      Cousins, Norman, eds. The poetry of freedom.
      N. Y., Modern Library, 1948. p. 627.
1488 "The white flag on the lagoon bridge of Venice" (tr.
      from the Italian of Fusinato). In Poems of places.
      Ed. by Henry W. Longfellow. Boston, Osgood,
      1877. vol. 3, p. 195-97.

1489 "Willing or loath" (tr. from Dall'Ongaro). In The
      poets and poetry of Europe. 1896.   p. 885.
1490 "The woman of Leghorn" (tr. from Dall'Ongaro).   In
      The poets and poetry of Europe. 1896.   p. 884.
1491 "Yorick's love" (adapted and translated from the
      Spanish of Estabenez). In Howells, William Dean.
      Complete plays. Edited by Walter J. Meserve.
      N.Y., New York University Press, 1960.   p. 115-39.
1492 No entry.

LETTERS

MAIN COLLECTIONS

1493 Life in letters of William Dean Howells. Edited by
     Mildred Howells. Garden City, N.Y., Doubleday,
     Doran, 1928. 2v.
        Some of the letters appeared in Bookman, May,
        June, Aug., and Oct. 1928. A review is in Book-
        man(London) 76:266, Aug. 1929.
1494 "The ante-room to fame; letters of William Dean
     Howells, 1856-1867." Edited by Herbert S. Gorman.
     Bookman 67:258-66, May 1928.
1495 "Howells and 'The Atlantic'; letters of William Dean
     Howells, 1870-1880." Edited by Herbert S. Gorman.
     Bookman 67:392-400, June 1928.
1496 "A decade of change; letters of William Dean Howells
     1880-1889." Edited by Herbert S. Gorman. Book-
     man 67:667-76, Aug. 1928.
1496a "The dean; letters of William Dean Howells 1890-
      1920." Edited by Herbert S. Gorman. Bookman
      68:188-203, Oct. 1928.
1497 "The letters of Howells to Higginson." Bibliophile
     Society, 27th annual report, 1929, p.17-56.
        Contains an introduction by George S. Hellman.
1498 Austin, James. Fields of the Atlantic monthly: letters
     to an editor 1861-1870. San Marino, Calif., Hunting-
     ton Library, 1953. 445p.
        Contains 16 Howells letters from the Fields collec-
        tion at the Huntington Library. They are located
        on pages 139-63.
1499 Mark Twain-Howells letters; the correspondence of
     Samuel L. Clemens and William D. Howells 1872-1910.
     Edited by Henry Nash Smith and William M. Gibson
     with the assistance of Frederick Anderson. Cam-
     bridge, Mass., Belknap Press, Harvard, 1960. 2v.
1500 Selected Mark Twain-Howells letters 1872-1910. Edited
     by Frederick Anderson, William M. Gibson, and
     Henry Nash Smith. Cambridge, Belknap Press, Har-
     vard University, 1967. 453p.
        Contains two letters not in the two-volume edition
        published in 1960.

1501 Mark Twain's letters. Arranged with comment by
      Albert Bigelow Paine. N.Y., Harper, 1917. 2v.
      Howells's letters are located here and there in the
      two volumes.
1502 Ekstrom, Kjell. "The Cable-Howells correspondence."
      Studia neophilologica 22:48-61, 1950.
1503 The letters of Henry James. Edited by Percy Lub-
      bock. London, Macmillan, 1920. 2v.
      Howells's letters are scattered throughout the two
      volumes.

      PERIODICAL ARTICLES (Containing Letters)

1504 Arms, George. " 'Ever devotedly yours': the Whit-
      lock-Howells correspondence." Journal of the Rutgers
      University Library 10:1-19, Dec. 1946.
1505 Ayers, Robert W. "William Dean Howells and Stephen
      Crane: some unpublished letters." American litera-
      ture 28:469-77, Jan. 1957.
1506 Cady, Edwin H. "Armando Palacio Valdes writes to
      William Dean Howells." Symposium 2:19-37, May
      1948.
1507 Carter, Paul. "A Howells' letter." New England
      quarterly 28:93-96, Mar. 1955.
      About The rise of Silas Lapham.
1508 Cary, Richard. "William Dean Howells to Thomas
      Sergeant Perry." Colby Library quarterly 7:157-
      215, Dec. 1968.
      Contains excerpts from the collection of 125
      Howells letters to Perry in Colby College, Water-
      ville, Maine.
1509 Conti, Giuseppe G. "Una lettera inedita di W. D.
      Howells." Studi Americani(Roma) 10:437-41. 1964.
      Contains a letter written to Guglielmo Ferrero,
      Apr. 1, 1908.
1510 Coyle, Leo P., ed. "Howells' campaign biography of
      Rutherford B. Hayes: a series of letters." Ohio
      historical quarterly 66:391-406, Oct. 1957.
1511 Crowder, Richard. "American nestor: six unpub-
      lished letters from Howells to Ade." Bucknell re-
      view 7:144-49, 1958.
1512 Downey, Jean. "Atlantic friends: Howells and Cooke."
      American notes and queries 1:132-33, May 1963.
      Contains letter by Rose Terry Cooke(1827-1892),
      a New England local colorist, to Howells and a
      reply from Howells.

1513 _____. "Three unpublished letters: Howells-
Cooke." American literature 32:463-65, Jan. 1961.
1514 Duffy, Charles. "An unpublished letter: Stedman to
Howells." American literature 30:369-70, Nov. 1958.
1515 Hamlin, Arthur T. "The Howells collection." Harvard library notes 3:147-53, 1938.
_____ Contains a descriptive account of letters addressed
to William Dean Howells now in Harvard Library.
1516 Kirk, Clara and Kirk, Rudolf. "Letters to an 'en-
chanted guest': William Dean Howells to Edmund
Gosse." Journal of the Rutgers University Library
22:1-25, June 1959.
1517 _____ and _____. "Two Howells letters." Journal
of the Rutgers University Library 21:1-7, Dec. 1957.
1518 Marston, F. C., Jr. "An early Howells letter."
American literature 18:163-65, May 1946.
_____ The letter is addressed to his brother Joseph,
Apr. 10, 1857.
1519 "New Letter of Paul Hamilton Hayne (to William Dean
Howells)." Edited by J. Delancey Lawrence. American literature 5:368-70, Jan. 1934.
1520 "A novel and two letters." Journal of the Rutgers
University Library 8:9-13, 1944.
_____ Contains manuscript letters relative to A woman's
reason.
1521 Schiffman, Joseph. "Mutual indebtedness: unpublished
letters of Edward Bellamy to William Dean Howells."
Harvard University bulletin 10:363-74, Autumn 1958.
1522 Shuman, R. Baird. "The Howells-Lowell correspondence: a new item." American literature 31:338-40,
Nov. 1959.
1523 Stronks, James B. "An early autobiographical letter
by William Dean Howells." New England quarterly
33:240-42, June 1960.
1524 Ward, John W. "Another Howells anarchist letter."
American literature 22:489-90, 1951.
_____ Contains a very short letter to Francis Fisher
Browne (1843-1913), poet and editor of the Dial.
1525 Wilson, Howard A. "William Dean Howells's unpublished letters about the Haymarket affair." Illinois
State historical society journal 56:5-19, Spring 1963.
1526 Woodress, James. "The Lowell-Howells friendship:
some unpublished letters." New England quarterly
26:523-28, Dec. 1953.

OTHER NON-FICTION AND EDITED WORKS

BOOKS

1527 Cervantes Saavedra, Miguel de. Don Quixote. Edited
by William Dean Howells with an introduction by
Mildred Howells. N.Y., Harper, 1923.
Howells abridged Charles Jervas's translation
(1742).

1528 Choice autobiographies. Edited, and with critical and
biographical essays, by William Dean Howells. Boston, Osgood, 1877-78. 6v.
Published in the "Little classic" style at $1.25 a
volume. According to an ad in the Houghton Mifflin edition of Venetian life (1895) eight volumes
were published. The autobiographies are about
Edward Gibbon, Carlo Goldoni, Edward Lord
Herbert and Thomas Ellwood, Jean Francois Marmontel, Vittorio Alfieri, and Frederica Sophia
Wilhelmina

1529 Clemens, Samuel L. Mark Twain's Library of humor.
N.Y., Harper, 1906. 4v.: vol.1, Men and things;
vol.2, Women and things; vol.3, The primrose way;
vol.4, A little nonsense.
Howells was one of the associate editors. See
Blodgett, Harold. "A note on Mark Twain's Li-
brary of humor." American literature 10:78-80,
Mar. 1938.

1530 The great modern American stories; an anthology.
Compiled and edited with an introduction by William
Dean Howells. N.Y., Boni and Liveright, 1920. 432p.

1531 Harper's novelettes. Edited by William Dean Howells
and Henry Mills Alden.
The novelettes were published in 1906 and 1907.
Howells wrote the introductions. For the titles
see entries 682-88 in this bibliography.

1532 The Howells story book. Edited by Mary E. Burt and
Mildred Howells. N.Y., Scribner's, 1900. 161p.

1533 Imaginary interviews. N.Y., Harper, 1910. 359p.
Most of the volume is taken from the "Editor's
easy chair" in Harper's monthly.

1534 Immortality and Sir Oliver Lodge.   Harper, n. d.
      (Pamphlet).
          First printed as "Editor's easy chair" in Harper's
          monthly 135:884-85, Nov. 1917.
1535 Impressions and experiences.   N. Y. , Harper, 1896.
      281p.
1536 Jubilee Days.   An illustrated daily record of the hu-
      morous features of the world's peace jubilee. Boston,
      Osgood, 1872.
          Howells and Thomas Bailey Aldrich wrote every-
          thing in it according to Gibson and Arms's Bib-
          liography of William Dean Howells, p. 23.
537   Letters of an Altrurian traveller 1893-1894; a facsimile
      reproduction.   With an introduction by Clara M. Kirk
      and Rudolf Kirk.   Gainesville, Fla. , Scholars' Fac-
      similes and Reprints, 1961.   127p.
          A reprint of eleven essays which first appeared in
          the Cosmopolitan, Nov. 1892-Sept. 1894.
1538 Library of universal adventure by sea and land, in-
      cluding original narratives and authentic stories of
      personal prowess and peril in all the waters and re-
      gions of the globe from the year 79 A. D. to the year
      1888 A. D.   Compiled and edited by William Dean
      Howells and Thomas Sergeant Perry.   N. Y. , Harper,
      1888.   1023p.
          T. S. Perry comments on this compilation in the
          New York Sun, Feb. 25, 1917, sec. 5, p. 10.
1539 Literature and life; studies.   N. Y. and London, Harper,
      1902.   322p.
1540 A little girl among the old masters.   With introduction
      and comment by W. D. Howells.   Boston, Osgood,
      1884.   3-65 numbered leaves.
          The book has drawings by Mildred Howells.
1541 Merwin, C. B.   Three years in Chili.   By a Lady of
      Ohio.   Columbus, Ohio, Follett, Foster, 1861.
          Howells edited and rewrote it.   The book appeared
          also under the title Chili through American spec-
          tacles.   N. Y. , John Bradburn, n. d.
1542 Sketch of the life and character of Rutherford B.
      Hayes ... Also a biographical sketch of William A.
      Wheeler.   N. Y. , Hurd and Houghton, 1876.   196p.
          Leo P. Coyle edited a series of letters relating
          to Howells's campaign biography of Rutherford B.
          Hayes.   The letters are in the Ohio historical
          quarterly 66:39-406, Oct. 1957.
1543 Stories of Ohio.   N. Y. , American Book Co. , 1897.
      287p.

1544 Winifred Howells. n. p. , n. d. 1891. 26p.
1545 Howells, William D. and Hayes, J. L. Lives and
      speeches of Abraham Lincoln and Hannibal Hamlin.
      Columbus, Ohio, Follett, Foster, 1860. 170p.
      Howells's life of Lincoln is on pages 19-94. See
      B. P. Thomas, "A unique biography of Lincoln."
      Bulletin of the Lincoln Association 35:3-8, June
      1934.
1546 North American review, Oct. 1872.
      This one issue was edited by Howells.

INDIVIDUAL ARTICLES

1547 "Aesthetic New York fifty-odd years ago." In Litera-
      ture and life... 1902. p. 222-27.
      Also in Literature ns2:105-06, Aug. 11, 1899.
1548 "American literary centres." Literature 2:649-51,
      704-06, June 4, 18, 1898.
      Also in Literature and life... 1902. p. 173-86.
1549 "Among the ruins." Atlantic monthly 31:97-101, Jan.
      1873.
1550 "Anglo-American copyright." North American review
      146:78, Jan. 1888.
1551 "Anticipative history." Harper's weekly 46:986, July
      26, 1902.
1552 "Anti-Lecompton meeting at Columbus." Cincinnati
      gazette 68:1, Feb. 22, 1858.
1553 "An anxious inquiry." Harper's weekly 46:651, May
      24, 1902.
1554 "The appeal to women." Harper's weekly 46:1506-07,
      Oct. 18, 1902.
1555 "The archangelic censorship." North American re-
      view 200:559-65, Oct. 1914.
1556 "Are the Americans Bible readers?" Literature ns1:
      585-86, June 30, 1899.
1557 "Are we a plutocracy?" North American review 158:
      185-96, Feb. 1894.
1558 "Arms and the men." Literature ns1:433-34, May 19,
      1899.
1559 "Around the council table, another correction." Au-
      thors League of America bulletin 4:11, May 1916.
1560 "The art of the adsmith." In Literature and life...
      1902. p. 265-72.
1561 "The artesian well at Columbus." Cincinnati gazette
      67:1, Jan. 14, 1858.
1562 "At a dime museum." In Literature and life... 1902.
      p. 193-201.

Taken from "Life and letters" in Harper's weekly
40:415, Apr. 25, 1896.

1563 "At the American artists." Harper's weekly 39:318,
Apr. 6, 1895.

1564 "Bars Ford party from war zone, answers to invita-
tions." New York times, Dec. 2, 1915, p. 2.

1565 "The beach at Rockaway." In Literature and life...
1902. p. 161-72.
Taken from "Life and letters" in Harper's weekly
40:870, 894, Sept. 5, 1896.

1566 "Beauties of mythology." Casket 2:154-55, Sept. 1853.

1567 "Bitters." Ohio state journal 23:2, Nov. 18, 1859.

1568 "Blackwood for October." Ashtabula sentinel 26:4,
July 16, 1857.

1569 "Blackwood's magazine." Ashtabula sentinel 26:3,
Nov. 12, 1857.

1570 "Carl Schurz 1829-1906." Harper's weekly 50:728,
May 26, 1906.

1571 "A circus in the suburbs." In Literature and life...
1902. p. 125-31.
Taken from "Life and letters" in Harper's weekly
40:774, Aug. 8, 1896.

1572 "Circuses and shows." In The Howells story book.
1900. p. 96-115.

1573 "The closing of the hotel." In Impressions and experiences. 1896. p. 140-65.

1574 "The coming translation of Dante." Round table 3:305-
06, May 19, 1866.

1575 "Concerning a counsel of imperfection." Literature
ns1:289-90, Apr. 7, 1899.

1576 "Confessions of a summer colonist." Atlantic monthly
82:742-50, Dec. 1898.

1577 "A counsel of consolation." see "In the house of
mourning." [entry no. 1614]

1578 "The day we celebrate." Ohio state journal 23:2,
July 4, 1859.

1579 "Destiny of the letter R in America." Literature
ns1:25-26, Jan. 17, 1899.

1580 "The Dial." Ohio state journal 23:2, Feb. 15, 1860.

1581 "The disadvantages of heroism." Harper's weekly
46:457, Apr. 12, 1902.

1582 "The discomforts of New York and their remedies."
New York times 15:4, Oct. 18, 1865.

1583 "Diversions of the higher journalist, a change in the
insular attitude." Harper's weekly 47:997, June 13,
1903.

1584 "Diversions of the higher journalist, decay of American manners." Harper's weekly 47:1256, Aug. 1, 1903.

1585   "Diversions of the higher journalist, an eye for an
       eye." Harper's weekly 47:1696, Oct. 24, 1903.
1586   "Diversions of the higher journalist, wanted, a name."
       Harper's weekly 47:1508, Sept. 19, 1903.
1587   "Diversions of the higher journalist, the livable sort
       of city." Harper's weekly 47:1936, Dec. 5, 1903.
1588   "Diversions of the higher journalist, a new evil."
       Harper's weekly 47:1580, Oct. 3, 1903.
1589   "Diversions of the higher journalist, reversible prov-
       erbs." Harper's weekly 47:1472, Sept. 12, 1903.
1590   "Diversions of the higher journalist, a scientific city."
       Harper's weekly 47:1220, July 25, 1903.
1591   "Diversions of the higher journalist, the serial story
       and its shrinkage." Harper's weekly 47:2090, Dec.
       26, 1903.
1592   "Diversions of the higher journalist, world-power
       weather." Harper's weekly 47:1055, June 20, 1903.
1593   "An east side ramble." In Impressions and experi-
       ences. 1896. p. 94-110.
1594   "The editorial convention at Tiffin." Ohio state jour-
       nal 23:2, Jan. 21, 1860.
1595   "An embarrassing situation." Harper's weekly 47:
       916, May 30, 1903.
1596   "Entertaining on thirty-five hundred a year." Harper's
       weekly 47:691, Apr. 25, 1903.
1597   "Equality as the basis of good society." Century
       magazine 51(ns29) 63-67, Nov. 1895.
1598   "Esthetic reporting--the French propagandists." New
       York times 105:4, Sept. 28, 1865.
1599   "Evidences of civilization." Harper's weekly 46:1405-
       06, Oct. 4, 1902.
1600   "Execution by electricity." Harper's weekly 32:23,
       Jan. 14, 1888.
1601   "An exemplary citizen." North American review 173:
       280-88, Aug. 1901.
1602   "An experience." Harper's monthly 131:940-42, Nov.
       1915.
1603   "Fantasies and superstitions." In The Howells story
       book. 1900. p. 116-27.
1604   "A fatal ignorance of liberty." Harper's weekly 46:
       325, Mar. 15, 1902.
1605   "Garfield." Atlantic monthly 48:707-09, Nov. 1881.
1606   "George William Curtis." Harper's weekly 36:868,
       870, Sept. 10, 1892.
1607   "Glimpses of Central Park." In Impressions and ex-
       periences. 1896. p. 224-44.
1608   "Good resolutions." Harper's weekly 47:20, Jan. 3,
       1903.

1609 "The grand old name of gentleman." Harper's weekly
      46:389, Mar. 29, 1902.
1610 "Henry Mills Alden: in memoriam." Harper's month-
      ly 140:133-36, Dec. 1919.
1611 "The horse show." In Literature and life... 1902.
      p. 206-15.
          Appears also in "Life and letters" in Harper's
          weekly 40:1171, Nov. 28, 1896.
1612 No entry.
1613 "In the country, birds and things." Ohio state jour-
      nal 23:1, June 11, 1859.
          Signed "Chispa."
1614 "In the house of mourning." Harper's bazaar 43:
      360-63, Apr. 1909.
          Included under the title of "A counsel of consola-
          tion" in In after days; thoughts on the future life.
          By William Dean Howells and others. N. Y.,
          Harper, 1910. p. 3-16.
1615 "The Irish executions." Nation 102:541, May 18,
      1916.
1616 "Italian brigandage." North American review 101:
      162-89, July 1865.
1617 "An Italian view of humor." North American review
      173:567-76, 709-20, Oct. -Nov. 1901.
1618 "John Fiske." Harper's weekly 45:732, July 20, 1901.
1619 "Jubilee days." In Suburban sketches. N. Y.,
      Houghton, 1901. p. 195-219.
          Also in Atlantic monthly 24:245-54, Aug. 1869.
1620 "The late Horatio S. Noyes." Newton journal, Aug.
      18, 1883, p. 2.
1621 "The latest royal scandal." Harper's weekly 47:61,
      Jan. 10, 1903.
1622 "The limitations of irony." Harper's weekly 46:133,
      Feb. 1, 1902.
1623 "Literary outlawry." Literature ns2:81-82, Aug. 4,
      1899.
1624 "A little about jokes." Ashtabula sentinel, Mar. 1,
      1855, p. 1.
1625 "The magazines for November." Ashtabula sentinel
      24:4, Oct. 25, 1855.
1626 "Manners and customs." In The Howells story book.
      1900. p. 55-72.
1627 "Marriage among the Italian priesthood." New York
      times, Oct. 19, 1865, p. 4.
          Attribution made by Gibson and Arms in their
          Bibliography of William Dean Howells.

1628 "A marvellous boy." Ohio state journal 22:2, Apr.
      11, 1859.
1629 "Memorabilia of the Chicago convention." In Howells,
      William D. Lives and speeches of Abraham Lincoln
      and Hannibal Hamlin. Ohio, Follett, Foster, 1860.
      p. 99-111.
1630 "The midnight platoon." In Literature and life...
      1902. p. 154-60.
      Appears also in "Life and letters" in Harper's
      weekly 39:416-17, May 4, 1895.
1631 "The military convention at Columbus." Cincinnati
      gazette 68:1, Jan. 20, 21, 1858. Signed Chispa.
1632 "Millionaires." Harper's monthly 104:500-04, Feb.
      1902.
1633 "The modern American mood." Harper's monthly 95:
      199-204, July 1897.
1634 "The mulberries in Pay's garden." In The Hesperian
      tree; an annual of the Ohio Valley 1900. Ed. by
      John James Piatt. Cincinnati, Ohio, George C. Shaw,
      1900. p. 431-36.
      Issued also as a pamphlet in 1906 by the Western
      Literary Press.
1635 "My first friend in Cambridge." In "The City and the
      sea" with other Cambridge contributions in aid of the
      Hospital Fund. Compiled by Helen L. Reed. Cam-
      bridge, John Wilson and Son, University Press, 1881.
      p. 73-78.
1636 "The nature of boys." In The Howells story book.
      1900. p. 128-41.
1637 "The nature of liberty." Forum 20:401-09, Dec. 1895.
1638 "The new phase of the labor problem." Harper's
      weekly 46:521, Apr. 26, 1902.
1639 "New York, the loneliest city in the world." New
      York herald, Feb. 10, 1901, p. 1.
1640 "New York Saturday press issue of Sept. 1860."
      Harper's monthly 112:633-37, Mar. 1906.
1641 "New York streets." In Impressions and experiences.
      1896. p. 181-207.
1642 "The next president." Atlantic monthly 21:628-32,
      May 1868.
1643 "A novelist on art." Literary digest 20:662-63, June
      2, 1900.
1644 "On coming back." Atlantic monthly 78:562-65, Oct.
      1896.
1645 "One branch of native industry that needs protection."
      Nation 1:774-75, Dec. 21, 1865.
1646 "Our consuls in China and elsewhere." Nation 1:551-
      52, Nov. 2, 1865.

1647 "Our daily speech." Harper's bazaar 40:930-34, Oct. 1906.

1648 "Our Italian assimilators." Harper's weekly 53:28, Apr. 10, 1909.

1649 "Our real grievance with England." Literature ns2: 297, Oct. 6, 1899.

1650 "Our Spanish prisoners at Portsmouth." Harper's weekly 42:826-27, Aug. 20, 1898.
Also in Literature and life... 1902. p.141-53.

1651 "A painful subject." Harper's weekly 48:48, Jan. 9, 1904.

1652 "Part of which I was." North American review 201: 135-41, Jan. 1915.

1653 "The passing of the beard." Harper's weekly 47:102, Jan. 17, 1903.

1654 "The peacemakers at Portsmouth." Harper's weekly 49:1225, 1244, Aug. 26, 1905.

1655 "A personal question." Harper's weekly 47:388-89, Mar. 7, 1903.

1656 "Pets." In The Howells story book. 1900. p. 96-115.

1657 "Philippine casuistry." Harper's weekly 46:715, June 7, 1902.

1658 "Ping-pong and popular fiction." Harper's weekly 46:779, June 21, 1902.

1659 "Police report." In Impressions and experiences. 1896. p. 35-69.

1660 "Politics." Atlantic monthly 30:127-28, July 1872.

1661 "Politics of American authors." In his Literature and life... 1902. p. 290-97.
Also in Literature 3:41-42, July 16, 1898.

1662 "The premature preference of the Rev. Dr. Bagnall." Harper's weekly 46:293, Mar. 8, 1902.

1663 "The problem of the summer." In his Literature and life... 1902. p. 216-21.
Appeared also in "Life and letters" in Harper's weekly 40:678, June 11, 1896.

1664 "Proposed purchase of Venetia." New York times 105:4, Sept. 29, 1865.

1665 "The psychology of plagiarism." In his Literature and life... 1902. p. 273-77.
Also in Literature n.s. 2:129-30, Aug. 18, 1899.

1666 "Public billing and cooing." Harper's weekly 47:956, June 6, 1903.

1667 "Question of monuments." Atlantic monthly 17:646-49, May 1866.

1668 "Race patriotism." Harper's weekly 46:585, May 10, 1902.

1669 "Ralph Keeler." Atlantic monthly 33:366-67, Mar.
       1874.
1670 "Reading for a grandfather." Harper's bazaar 37:
       1153-57, Dec. 1903.
1671 "The Republican Party. What will they do now?"
       Ashtabula sentinel 26:4, Nov. 19, 1857.
1672 "The revival of mosaic painting in Venice." Boston
       advertiser 101:2, May 2, 1863.
           Also in Ashtabula sentinel 32:1, May 13, 1863.
1673 "Sawdust in the arena." In Literature and life...
       1902. p.187-92.
           Appeared first in "Life and letters" in Harper's
           weekly 40:966, Oct. 3, 1896.
1674 "A she hamlet." In Literature and life... 1902.
       p.132-40.
           First published in the "Editor's easy chair" in
           Harper's monthly 102:640-43, Mar. 1901.
1675 "Some considerations for monarchical countries."
       Harper's weekly 46:617, May 17, 1902.
1676 "Some modest misgivings." Harper's weekly 46:946,
       July 19, 1902.
1677 "Some traits of a good brisk day." Balloon post,
       Apr. 1871, no.2, p.3.
1678 "Some unpalatable suggestions." North American re-
       view 188:254-61, Aug. 1908.
1679 "Spanish-Italian amity." New York times 15:4, Sept.
       23, 1865.
1680 "Spoiling the rod and sparing the child." Harper's
       weekly 48:232, Feb. 13, 1904.
1681 "Spring birds and spring thoughts." Ohio state weekly
       journal 49:4, Apr. 26, 1859. Unsigned.
1682 "Staccato notes of a vanished summer." Literature,
       Oct. 13--Nov. 10, 1899.
           Also in Literature and life... 1902. p.253-64.
1683 "The standard household-effect company." In Litera-
       ture and life... 1902. p.240-52.
           Appeared in "Life and letters" in Harper's weekly
           39:628, 653, July 6-13, 1895.
1684 "The state house warming at Columbus." Cincinnati
       gazette 65:1, Jan. 8, 1857.
1685 "State manslaughter." Harper's weekly 48:196, 198,
       Feb. 6, 1904.
1686 "Storage." In Literature and life... 1902. p.298-
       308.
           Appeared first in "Editor's easy chair" in Harper's
           monthly 104:162-66, Dec. 1901.

1687 "A subscription theater." Literature ns1:313-14, Apr. 14, 1899.
1688 "A suggestion from the Boer War." Harper's weekly 46:747, June 14, 1902.
1689 "Superfluous partings." Harper's weekly 46:864, July 5, 1902.
1690 "Tainted money." Harper's weekly 47:468, Mar. 21, 1903.
1691 "The threatening aspect of the servant problem." Harper's weekly 46:1754, Nov. 22, 1902.
1692 "To the Jews a stumbling block and to the Greeks foolishness." Harper's weekly 47:189, Jan. 31, 1903.
1693 "Tribulations of a cheerful giver." Century magazine 50(ns28):181-85, 417-21.
       Also in his Impressions and experiences. 1896. p. 111-39.
1694 "True, I talk of dreams." Harper's monthly 90:836, May 1895.
1695 "The turning of the dove." Harper's weekly 46:165, Feb. 8, 1902.
1696 "The unreality of reality." Harper's weekly 47:229, Feb. 7, 1903.
1697 "The vulgarity of wealth." Harper's weekly 46:2021-22, Dec. 27, 1902.
1698 "War movements in Ohio (from our own correspondent), Columbus, Ohio." New York world 1:6, May 15, 1861.
1699 "War as seen by famous authors." New York times, Dec. 2, 1917, section 2, p. 8.
1700 "Was there nothing to arbitrate?" Harper's weekly 32:286, Apr. 21, 1888.
1701 "The what and the how in art." In Literature and life... 1902. p. 284-89.
       Appeared in "Life and letters" in Harper's weekly 40:270, Mar. 21, 1896.
1702 "What shall we do with our sympathies." Harper's weekly 48:321, Feb. 27, 1904.
1703 "What should girls read." Harper's bazaar 36:956-60, Nov. 1902.
1704 "Who are our brethren?" Century magazine 51(ns29):932-36, Apr. 1896.
1705 "Why?" North American review 201:676-82, May 1915.
1706 "Wild flowers of the asphalt." In Literature and life... 1902. p. 89-94.
       Appeared in "Life and letters" in Harper's weekly 41:706, July 17, 1897.

1707 "Without our special wonder." Harper's weekly 46:
      811, June 28, 1902.
1708 "Woman's limitations in burlesque." Harper's weekly
      46:1465, Oct. 11, 1902.
1709 "Worries of a winter walk." Harper's weekly 41:338-
      39, Apr. 3, 1897.
1710 "The worst of being poor." Harper's weekly 46:261,
      Mar. 1, 1902.

      BRIEF NOTES, STATEMENTS, MISCELLANEOUS

1711 [Anecdote.] In Anecdotes of the hour by famous men
      as told by Winston Churchill, Jack London and about
      100 notable men. N. Y., Hearst's International Li-
      brary, 1914. p. 127.
1712 The booklovers reading club handbook to accompany
      the reading course entitled Florence in art and litera-
      ture; talks and lectures by Preston Stearns, and Wil-
      liam Goodyear, and Lewis F. Pilcher. Editorial notes
      by Charlotte Brewster Jordan. Phila., The Book-
      lovers Library, 1901. 124p.
           William Dean Howells helped to select the books
           for the course. He also compiled the list of sup-
           plementary books on p. 113-24.
1713 Griswold, W. M. A descriptive list of books for the
      young. Cambridge, Mass., 1895.
           Includes a four-page insertion by W. D. Howells.
           Page 2 has an extract from Harper's magazine
           84:479-80, Feb. 1892.
1714 [Brief statement.] In Towne, Charles H. For
      France.... Garden City, N. Y., Doubleday, Page,
      1917. p. 11.
1715 [Contribution.] In Mylene, Alice R., ed. Advice to
      young authors to write or not to write. Boston,
      Morning Star Publishing House, 1891. p. 40-41.
1716 [Contribution.] In King Albert's book. A tribute to
      the Belgian King and people from representative men
      and women throughout the world. Edited by Hall
      Caine. N. Y., Hearst's International Library Co.,
      1914; i. e. 1915. p. 112.
1717 "Contribution." In Sixty American opinions on the
      war. London, T. Fisher Unwin, 1915. p. 90-91.
1718 "A daily paper of the past." Bazaar daily, Dec. 13,
      1916. p. 27.
           William D. Howells was a contributing editor of
           the Bazaar daily.

1719 "Gossip." Ashtabula sentinel, Mar. 13, 1856, p. 2.
1720 "Editorial table talk." Ashtabula sentinel, Mar. 20,
        1856, p. 2.
1721 "From Ohio (from our own correspondent) Columbus,
        Apr. 16." New York world 1:3, Apr. 22, 1861.
        About Ohio's reaction to the war.
1722 "From Ohio (from our own correspondent)" New York
        world 1:3, May 21, 1861.
        About war matters.
1723 "From Ohio (from our own correspondent)" New York
        world 2:4, July 17, 1861.
        About military activity in Columbus.
1724 "From Ohio (from our own correspondent), Columbus,
        June 5." New York world 1:8, June 10, 1861.
        About the military situation in Ohio and Washington.
1725 "The incredible cruelty of the Teutons." In The World
        War utterances concerning its issues and conduct by
        members of the American Academy of Arts and Let-
        ters. N.Y., American Academy of Arts and Letters,
        1919. p. 20-21.
1726 "Letter from Columbus." Cincinnati gazette, Jan. 4,
        1858 through Apr. 13, 1858.
        Signed Chispa. Written by the author, and by the
        father when the son was ill. According to A bib-
        liography of William Dean Howells by Gibson and
        Arms, 64 letters were written. See also Marston's
        dissertation, p. 144. Some information is also
        found in Years of my youth. N.Y., Harper, 1916.
        p. 143-44. Some of the letters begin simply with
        "From Columbus."
1727 "Letters from Columbus." Cleveland herald, Spring
        1858.
        Signed "Gemug." At the end of the legislative ses-
        sion the pseudonym changed to "Enough." The
        correspondence is almost the same as that in the
        Cincinnati gazette.
1728 "Columbus correspondence." Ashtabula sentinel, Jan.
        7, 14, 21, and Feb. 18, 1858.
        Signed "W." Unsigned items appeared Feb. 25
        and Mar. 4, 1858.
1729 "Letters from the country I. June 30, 1860." Ohio
        state weekly journal 50:1, July 10, 1860.
1730 "Local affairs." Ohio state weekly journal 49:3,
        July 12, Aug. 30, Sept. 6, 1859.
1731 "Mr. Howells's response." In The Atlantic monthly
        supplement. The Holmes breakfast... Boston, Feb.
        1880, p. 6-7.

1732 [Note.] In 50th anniversary of the founding of the
      Tribune, celebrated Apr. 10, 1891 at the Metropolitan
      Opera House, N.Y. N.Y., The Tribune, 1891. p.26.
1733 [Note.] In The art autograph, May 1880. N.Y., Art
      Interchange, 1880. p.6.
1734 [Note.] In Walt Whitman as man, poet and friend.
      Collected by Charles N. Elliott. Boston, Gorham
      Press, 1915. p.117.
1735 "News and humors of the mail." Cincinnati gazette
      65:1, May 4, 1857.
1736 "News and humors of the mail." Ashtabula sentinel,
      Jan. 7, 1859, p.1.
1737 "News and humors of the mails." Ohio state journal,
      Jan. 1 through Dec. 24, 1859.
          A column which appeared on p.1 through Oct. 11
          and on p.2 from Oct. 14. Howells began the
          column on Nov. 22, 1858. See A bibliography of
          William Dean Howells by Gibson and Arms, p.80-
          81.
1738 "Notices of magazines." Ashtabula sentinel 24:4,
      June 28, July 12, Aug. 2, 1955.
1739 "Our emended edition of Shakespeare." Ashtabula
      sentinel 23:2, Aug. 24, 1854.
          Contains 35 lines of dialog between Pistol, Nym,
          and Bardolph describing the heat in diction à la
          Shakespeare.
1740 "Our state exchange." "Local affairs." Ohio state
      journal 22:2, Dec. 7, 1858.
1740a "The reviews." Ashtabula sentinel, Feb. 28,
      1856, p.4.
1741 [Statement on vivisection.] The report of the Amer-
      ican Humane Association on vivisection and dissection
      in schools. Chicago, The American Humane Associa-
      tion, 1895. p.38-39.
          His statement is in the section of the report that
          has the heading "Extracts from replies to the
          second circular."
1742 [Statement on woman suffrage.] In The book-lover's
      almanac for 1895. N.Y., Duprat, 1894. p.47.
1743 [Statement.] In Study and stimulants. Edited by
      A. Arthur Reade. Manchester, Abel Heywood, 1883.
      p.71.
          The statement is dated Mar. 2, 1882.
1744 [Statement.] In What American authors think about
      international copyright. N.Y., American Copyright
      League, 1888. p.6.

1745   "To a great editor." In Henry Alden's 70th birthday;
       souvenir of its celebration. N.Y., Harper, 1906.
       p. 1812.
1746   "Consular report, Mar. 31, 1864." In Executive
       documents printed by order of the House of Represent-
       atives during the 2d session of the 38th Congress,
       1864-65. vol. 11, p. 462-67.
1747   "Consular report, Sept. 30, 1862." In Executive
       documents printed by order of the House of Repre-
       sentatives during the 3d session of the 37th Congress,
       1862-63. vol. 12, p. 376-80.
1748   "Consular report, Oct. 5, 1863." In Executive docu-
       ments printed by the order of the House of Repre-
       sentatives during the first session of the 38th Con-
       gress, 1863-64. vol. 10, p. 360-62.
1749   "Consular statement." In Executive documents printed
       by the order of the House of Representatives during
       the first session of the thirty-ninth Congress, 1865-
       66.   vol. 10, p. 355-56.

BOOKS

1750 Bennett, George N. William Dean Howells; the development of a novelist. Norman, University of Oklahoma
Press, 1959. 220p.

1751 Brooks, Van Wyck. Howells: his life and world.
N.Y., Dutton, 1959. 296p.

1752 Cady, Edwin H. The road to realism; the early years,
1837-1885, of William Dean Howells. Syracuse,
N.Y., Syracuse University Press, 1956. 283p.

1753 _____. The realist at war; the mature years, 1885-
1920. Syracuse, N.Y., Syracuse University Press,
1958. 299p.

1754 _____ and Frazier, David L., eds. The war of the
critics over William Dean Howells. Evanston, Illinois, Row, Peterson, 1962. 244p.

1755 Carrington, George C., Jr. The immense complex
drama; the world and art of the Howells novel.
Columbus, Ohio State University Press, 1966. 245p.

1756 Carter, Everett. Howells and the age of realism.
Phila., Lippincott, 1954. 307p.

1757 Cooke, Delmar G. William Dean Howells; a critical
study. N.Y., Dutton, 1922. 279p.

1758 Dean, James L. Howells' travels toward art. Al-
buquerque, University of New Mexico, 1970. 145p.

1759 Eble, Kenneth E., ed. Howells, a century of criticism. Dallas, Texas, Southern Methodist University
Press, 1962. 247p.

1760 Firkins, Oscar W. William Dean Howells; a study.
Cambridge, Harvard University Press, 1924. 356p.

1761 Fryckstedt, Olov W. In quest of America; a study of
Howells' early development as a novelist. Cambridge,
Harvard University Press, 1958. 287p.

1761a Gibson, William M. William Dean Howells. Minneapolis, University of Minnesota, 1967. 48p. (University of Minnesota pamphlets on American writers,
no. 63.)

1762 Harvey, Alexander. William Dean Howells; a study
of the achievement of a literary artist. N.Y.,
Huebsch, 1917. 267p.

1762a Hough, Robert L. The quiet rebel: William Dean
      Howells as social commentator. Lincoln, University
      of Nebraska Press, 1959. 137p.
1763 Keenan, Randall H. Howells' The rise of Silas Lap-
      ham. N.Y., Monarch Press, 1965. 95p. (Monarch
      notes and study guides.)
1764 Kirk, Clara M. William Dean Howells and art in his
      time. New Brunswick, N.J., Rutgers University
      Press, 1965. 336p.
1765 _____. William Dean Howells, traveler from
      Altruria. New Brunswick, N.J., Rutgers University
      Press, 1962.
1766 _____ and Kirk, Rudolf. William Dean Howells.
      N.Y., Twayne, 1962. 223p.
1767 McMurray, William J. The literary realism of Wil-
      liam Dean Howells. With a preface by Harry T.
      Moore. Carbondale, Southern Illinois University
      Press, 1967. 147p. (Crosscurrents: modern cri-
      tiques.)
1767a Lynn, Kenneth S. William Dean Howells: An Amer-
      ican life. N.Y., Harcourt, Brace Jovanovich, 1971.
      372p.
1768 Vanderbilt, Kermit. The achievement of William
      Dean Howells; a reinterpretation. Princeton, N.J.,
      Princeton University Press, 1968. 226p.
1769 Wagenknecht, Edward C. William Dean Howells; the
      friendly eye. N.Y., Oxford University Press, 1969.
      340p.
1770 Walts, Robert W. William Dean Howells' The rise
      of Silas Lapham; a study guide. Bound Brook, N.J.,
      Shelley Publishing Co., 1963. 80p. (Shelley's study
      guides.)
1771 Woodress, James L., Jr. Howells and Italy. Dur-
      ham, N.C., Duke University Press, 1952. 223p.

ESSAYS (in Books and Periodicals)

1772 Aaron, Daniel. "William Dean Howells: the gentle-
      man from Alturria." In his Men of good hope; a
      story of American progressives. N.Y., Oxford,
      1951. p.172-207.
1773 Abel, Darrel, ed. "'Howells or James?': an essay
      of Henry Blake Fuller." Modern fiction studies
      3:159-64, Summer 1957.
1774 Adams, Hazard. "Criteria of criticism in literature."
      Journal of asethetics and art criticism 21:31-35,
      Fall 1962.

1775   Adrian, Arthur A. "Augustus Hoppin to William Dean
       Howells." New England quarterly 24:84-89, Mar.
       1951.
1776   Ahnebrink, Lars. "W. D. Howells and Criticism and
       fiction." In his The beginnings of naturalism in
       American fiction... 1891-1903. Uppsala, A.B.
       Lundeqvistska Bokhandeln, 1950. p.129-35.
1777   Alden, Henry M. "Editor's study. "Harper's month-
       ly 134:903-04, May 1917.
            An article about Howells's 80th birthday.
1778   . "William Dean Howells." Bookman 49:
       549-54, July 1919.
1779   . "William Dean Howells: recollections of
       a fellow-worker." Book news monthly, June 1908,
       p.729-31.
1780   Amacher, Anne W. "The genteel primitivist and the
       semi-tragic octoroon." New England quarterly 29:
       216-27, June 1956.
1781   "America's foremost living man of letters." Current
       literature 52:461-63, Apr. 1912.
1782   "American literature in England." Blackwood 133:
       148-61, Jan. 1883.
            Also in Eble, K.E., ed. Howells, a century of
       criticism. 1962. p.19-33.
1782a Andersen, Kenneth. "Mark Twain, W.D. Howells,
       and Henry James: three agnostics in search of salva-
       tion." Mark Twain journal 15:13-16, Winter 1970.
1783   Anderson, Quentin. "William Dean Howells." In his
       The American Henry James. New Brunswick, N.J.,
       Rutgers University Press, 1957. passim.
1784   Anicetti, Luigi. "William Dean Howells, console a
       Venezia, 1861-65." Nuova rivista storica 41:87-106,
       Jan.-Apr. 1957.
1785   Anthony, Mother Mary. "Howells' A modern instance."
       Explicator 20, item 20.
1786   Arms, George W. "Further inquiry into Howells's
       socialism." Science and society, Spring 1939, p.245-
       48.
1787   . "Howells' New York novel: comedy and
       belief." New England quarterly 21:313-25, Sept.
       1948.
1788   . "Introduction." In Howells, William D.
       A hazard of new fortunes. N.Y., Dutton, 1952.
       p.vii-xviii.
1789   . "Introduction." In Howells, William D.
       The rise of Silas Lapham. N.Y., Rinehart, 1949.
       p.v-xvi.

1790 _____. "Howells' A hazard of new fortunes." Explicator 1:14, Nov. 1942.

1791 _____. "Howells' English travel books: problems in technique." Publications of the Modern Language Association 82:104-16, Mar. 1967.

1792 _____. "The literary background of Howells's social criticism." American literature 14:260-76, Nov. 1942.

1793 _____ and Gibson, William M., eds. "Five interviews with William Dean Howells." Americana 37:no.2, Apr. 1943.

1794 _____ and _____. "Silas Lapham, Daisy Miller, and the Jews." New England quarterly 16:118-22, Mar. 1943.

1795 _____ and Wasserstrom, William. "That psychological stain and a rejoinder." New England quarterly 33:243-45, June 1960.

1796 Arvin, Newton. "Usableness of Howells." New republic 91:227-28, June 30, 1937.

1797 Atherton, Gertrude. "Why is American literature bourgeois?" North American review 178:771-81, May 1904.

1798 "Authors who are a present delight: William Dean Howells." Journal of education 65:311-12, Mar. 21, 1907.

1799 Ayscough, John. "Of some Americans." Catholic world 116:41-55, Oct. 1922.

1800 Badger, G.H. "Howells as an interpreter of American life." International review 14:380, May-June 1883.

1801 Baldwin, Charles C. "William Dean Howells." In his Men who make our novels. rev. ed. N.Y., Dodd, Mead, 1924. p.272-81.

1802 Baldwin, Marilyn A. "Introduction." In Howells, William Dean. My Mark Twain. Baton Rouge, La., Louisiana State University, 1967. p.ix-xviii.

1803 Bass, Altha S. "The social consciousness of William Dean Howells." New republic 26:192-94, Apr. 13, 1921.

1804 Baumes, J.R. "William Dean Howells and the scholastic epoch in novel writing." Baptist quarterly review 5:340-53, 1885.

1805 Baxter, Annette K. "Caste and class: Howells' Boston and Wharton's New York." Midwest quarterly 4:353-61, July 1963.

1806 _____. "Archetypes of American innocence: Lydia
      Blood and Daisy Miller." In Cohen, Hennig, ed. The
      American experience. N.Y., Houghton, 1968. p.148-
      56.
          Appeared originally in American quarterly 5:31-38,
          Spring 1953.
1807 Baxter, Sylvester. "Howells's Boston." New England
      magazine ns 9:129-52, Oct. 1893.
1808 Becker, George J. "William Dean Howells: the
      awakening of conscience." College English 19:283-91,
      Apr. 1958.
1809 Behrens, Ralph. "Howells' A hazard of new fortunes."
      Explicator 18:item 52.
1810 Belcher, Hannah G. "Howells' opinions on the reli-
      gious conflicts of his age as exhibited in magazine
      articles." American literature 15:262-78, Nov. 1943.
          Also in Eble, K.E. Howells, a century of criti-
          cism. 1962. p.203-18.
1811 Berces, Francis A. "Mimesis, morality and The
      rise of Silas Lapham." American quarterly 22:190-
      202, Summer 1970.
1812 Berthoff, Warner. [William Dean Howells]. In his
      The ferment of realism: American literature 1884-
      1919. N.Y., Free Press, 1965. passim.
1813 Berti, Luigi. "Saggio su William Dean Howells."
      Inventorio 5:49-62, Jan.-Sept. 1953.
1814 Betts, William W., Jr. "The relations of William
      Dean Howells to German life and letters." In Anglo-
      German and American-German crosscurrents. Chapel
      Hill, University of North Carolina, 1957. p.189-239.
1815 Bishop, William H. "Mr. Howells in Beacon St.,
      Boston." Critic 9:259-60, Nov. 27, 1886.
1816 Black, Alexander. "The king in white." In his
      American husbands and other alternatives. Indianapo-
      lis, Ind., Bobbs, 1925. p.173-82.
1817 Blanc, Therese. "William Dean Howells." In her
      Les nouveaux romanciers américains. Paris, C.
      Levy, 1885. p.7-70.
1818 Boardman, Arthur. "Social point of view in the
      novels of William Dean Howells." American litera-
      ture 39:42-59, Mar. 1967.
1819 Botero Restrepo, Hernan. "La redencion de Silas
      Lapham." Arco 9:422-24, July 1967.
1820 Bowman, Sylvia E. "Introduction." In Howells,
      William D. Discovery of a genius: William Dean
      Howells and Henry James. Comp. and ed. by Albert
      Mordell. N.Y., Twayne, 1961. p.7-25.

1821 Boyd, E. "Readers and writers." Independent 114:
      20, Jan. 3, 1925.
1822 Boyesen, Hjalmar H. "Mister Howells and his work."
      Cosmopolitan 12:502-03, Feb. 1892.
1823 No entry.
1824 Braly, Earl B. "William Dean Howells, author and
      journalist." Journalism quarterly 32:456-62, Fall
      1955.
1825 Brenner, Jack. "Howells and Ade." American litera-
      ture 38:198-207, May 1966.
1826 Briggs, Austin, Jr. [William Dean Howells]. In his
      The novels of Harold Frederic. Ithaca, Cornell Uni-
      versity Press, 1969. p. 60-61, 104-06, and passim.
1827 Brockway, Wallace. "Afterword." In Howells, Wil-
      liam D. A modern instance. N.Y., New American
      Library, 1964. p. 422-30.
1828 Brooks, Van Wyck. "Howells." In his Chilmark
      miscellany. N.Y., Dutton, 1948. p. 231-45.
1829 _____. "Howells in New York." In his New Eng-
      land: Indian summer, 1865-1915. N.Y., Dutton,
      1940. p. 373-94.
1830 _____. "Howells in Venice." In his The dream of
      Arcadia. N.Y., Dutton, 1958. p. 145-54.
1831 _____. "Introduction." In Howells, William D.
      A hazard of new fortunes. N.Y., Bantam Books,
      1960. p. v-xii.
1832 No entry.
1833 No entry.
1834 Bryan, James E. "The chronology of Silas Lapham."
      American notes and queries 4:56. 1965.
1835 Budd, Louis J. "Howells' 'blistering and cauterizing'."
      Ohio State archeological and historical quarterly 62:
      334-47, Oct. 1953.
1836 _____. "Howells, the Atlantic monthly and repub-
      licanism." American literature 24:139-56, May 1952.
1837 _____. "The naming of Altruria, Calif." Western
      folklore 10:169, Apr. 1951.
1838 _____. "Twain, Howells, and the Boston nihilists."
      New England quarterly 32:351-71, Sept. 1959.
1839 _____. [William Dean Howells]. In his Mark
      Twain: social philosopher. Bloomington, Indiana
      University Press, 1962. passim.
1840 _____. "William Dean Howells' debt to Tolstoi."
      American Slavic and East European review 9:292-301.
      1950.

1841   Bunnell, A. H. "Celebrities of old Western Reserve;
       birthplace of William Dean Howells, Joshua Giddings
       and B. F. Wade described by a native." State service
       3:17-20, Nov. 1919 (not verified).

1842   Cady, Edwin H. "Howells in 1948." University of
       Kansas City review 15:83-91, Winter 1948.
1843   _____. "The Howells nobody knows." Mad River
       review 1:3-25, Winter 1964-65.
1844   _____. "Howells and Twain: the world in mid-
       western eyes." Ball State Teachers College forum
       3:3-8, Winter 1962-63.
1845   _____. "Introduction." In Howells, William The
       rise of Silas Lapham. Boston, Houghton Mifflin,
       1957. p. v-xviii.
1846   _____. "Introduction." In Howells, William D.
       The shadow of a dream and An imperative duty.
       N. Y., Twayne, 1962. p. 7-15.
1847   _____. "The neuroticism of William Dean Howells."
       Publications of the Modern Language Association 61:
       229-38, Mar. 1946.
1848   _____. "A note on Howells and 'the smiling aspects
       of life'." American literature 17:175-78, May 1945.
1849   _____. "William Dean Howells and the Ashtabula
       sentinel." Ohio archeological and historical quarterly
       53:39-51, Jan. -Mar. 1944.
1850   Cahan, Abraham. "The talent and personality of
       William Dean Howells; the renowned American author
       who died this week." Tr. by Curt Leviant from the
       Yiddish of the Jewish daily forward, May 16, 1920.
       Included in the appendix to Rudolf and Clara Kirk's
       article "Abraham Cahan and William Dean Howells:
       The story of a friendship." American Jewish histor-
       ical quarterly 52:25-57, Sept. 1962.
1851   Cargill, Oscar. "Henry James's moral policeman:
       William Dean Howells." American literature 29:
       371-98, Jan. 1958.
1852   Carter, Everett. "Introduction." In Howells, William
       D. The rise of Silas Lapham. N. Y., Harper, 1958.
       p. v-xiv.
1853   _____. "The palpitating divan." English journal
       39:237-42, May 1950.
1854   _____. "Taine and American realism." Revue de
       littérature comparée 26:357-64, July 1952.
1855   _____. "William Dean Howells' theory of critical
       realism." English literary history 16:151-66, June
       1949.

1856 Carter, Paul J., Jr. "The influence of William Dean
      Howells upon Mark Twain's social satire." Univer-
      sity of Colorado studies, series in language and
      literature, no. 4, p. 93-100. 1953.
1857 Cary, Elizabeth L. "William Dean Howells: a point
      of view." Lamp 29:597-604, Jan. 1905.
1858 Cecil, L. Moffitt. "William Dean Howells and the
      South." Mississippi quarterly 20:13-24, Winter 1966-
      67.
1859 Cecioni, Cesare G. "Introduction." In Howells,
      William D. Le fortune di Silas Lapham. Rome,
      Opere Nuove, 1962.
1860 _____. "La prima esperienza italiana di W. D.
      Howells." Siculorum gymnasium 18:93-119, Jan-June
      1965.
1861 Celebrating the 80th birthday of William Dean Howells."
      Current opinion 62:278, Apr. 1917.
1862 Chamberlayne, E. S. "Howells' philosophy and The
      son of Royal Langbrith." Poet-lore 16:144.
1863 Chase, Richard. "The vacation of the Kelwyns."
      In his The American novel and its tradition. Garden
      City, Doubleday Anchor Books, 1957. p. 177-84.
1864 Chislett, William, Jr. "Some critics of William Dean
      Howells." In his Moderns and near-moderns; essays
      on Henry James, Stockton, Shaw, and others. N. Y.,
      Grafton Press, 1928. p. 112-15.
1865 Chubb, Edwin W. "Howells calls on Emerson, and
      describes Longfellow." In his Stories of authors,
      British and American. new ed. N. Y., Macmillan,
      1926. p. 284-89.
1866 Clark, Harry H. "Introduction." In Howells, Wil-
      liam D. The rise of Silas Lapham. N. Y., Modern
      Library, 1951. p. v-xix.
1867 _____. "The role of science in the thought of Wil-
      liam Dean Howells." Transactions of the Wisconsin
      Academy of Science, Arts, and Letters 42:263-303.
      1953.
1868 Clarkson, Helen W. "Our debt to Mr. Howells."
      Harper's weekly 56:6, Mar. 9, 1912.
1869 Clemens, Cyril. "Howells and the age of realism."
      Hobbies 60:106-07, May 1955.
1870 Clemens, Samuel L. "William Dean Howells." In
      his What is man? and other essays. N. Y., Harper,
      1917. p. 228-39.
          Also in Eble, K. E., ed. Howells, a century of
      criticism. 1962. p. 78-87.

1871 Coanda, Richard. "Howells' The rise of Silas Lap-
      ham." Explicator 22, item 6, Nov. 1963.
1872 Coard, Robert L. "When women were women with
      ess." Georgia review 14:385-88, Winter 1960.
1873 Cobley, W. D. "William Dean Howells: 1837-1920."
      Manchester quarterly 51:93-120. 1925.
1874 Colby, F. M. "Curiosities of literary controversy."
      Bookman 28:124-26, Oct. 1908.
1875 "Collapse of the Howells realism in the light of
      Freudian romanticism." Current opinion 63:270-71,
      Oct. 1917.
1876 "Columbia honors Mr. Howells." Harper's weekly
      49:956, July 1, 1905.
1877 Commager, Henry S. "The business of America."
      Senior scholastic 58:18-19, Feb. 7, 1951.
1878 _____. "Introduction." In Howells, William D.
      The rise of Silas Lapham. N. Y., Printed for the
      members of the Limited Editions Club, 1961. p. v-
      xiii.
1879 _____. "Introduction." In Howells, William D.
      Selected writings. Edited by H. S. Commager. N. Y.,
      Random House, 1950. p. vii-xvii.
1880 _____. "Literature of revolt." In his American
      mind. New Haven, Yale, 1950. p. 247-76.
1881 _____. "Return to Howells." Spectator (London)
      180:642-43, May 28, 1948.
1882 Conti, Giuseppi G. "Le due ascese di Silas Lapham."
      Studi Americani 12:137-67. 1966.
1883 Cooke, Delmar G. "The humanity of William Dean
      Howells." Texas review 6:6-25, Oct. 1920.
1884 Cooper, J. A. "Bellamy and Howells." Canadian
      magazine 9:344-46, Aug. 1897.
1885 Cooperman, Stanley. "Utopian realism: the futurist
      novels of Bellamy and Howells." College English
      24:464-67, Mar. 1963.
1886 Cowie, Alexander. "William Dean Howells (1837-
      1920)" In his Rise of the American novel. N. Y.,
      American Book Company, 1948. p. 653-701.
1887 Coyle, Leo P. "Mark Twain and William Dean
      Howells." Georgia review 10:302-11, Fall 1956.
1888 [Critical studies of Howells and James]. Kolos'ra,
      no. 4, p. 267-73.
1889 Cronkhite, G. Ferris. "Howells turns to the inner
      life." New England quarterly 30:474-85, Dec. 1957.
1890 Cumpiano, Marion W. "The dark side of Their
      wedding journey." American literature 40:472-86,
      Jan. 1969.

1891 Dawes, Anna L. "The moral purpose in Howells's novels." Andover review 11:23-36, Jan. 1889.
1892 Dean, Clarence L. "Mr. Howells's female characters." Dial (Chicago) 3:106-07, Oct. 1882.
1893 De Mille, George E. "Howells." In his Literary criticism in America; a preliminary survey. N. Y., Dial, 1931. p.182-205.
1894 _____. "The infallible dean; a study of William Dean Howells as a prophet of realism." Sewanee review 36:148-56, Apr. 1928.
1895 De Mott, Benjamin. "Afterword." In A hazard of new fortunes. N. Y., New American Library, 1965. p.433-41.
1896 Dietrichson, Jan W. "The image of money in the works of William Dean Howells." In his The image of money in the American novel of the gilded age. N. Y., Humanities Press, 1969. p.166-314.
1897 Diplomaticus. "Portrayer of the commonplace." Westminster review 178:597-608, Dec. 1912.
1898 Dixon, James M. "The ideals of William Dean Howells." Personalist 2:35-46, Jan. 1921.
1899 Dove, John R. "Howells' irrational heroines." University of Texas studies in English 35:64-80. 1956.
1900 Dowling, Joseph A. "W. D. Howells' literary reputation in England, 1882-1897." Dalhousie review 45:277-88, Autumn 1965.
1901 Duffy, Charles. "Mark Twain writes to Howells." Mark Twain quarterly 8:4, Summer-Fall 1948.
1902 Duffy, Myrtle M. "Twain in Howells' A modern instance." American quarterly 16:612-14, Winter 1964.

1903 "The earlier and later work of Mr. Howells." Lippincott 30:604-08, Dec. 1882.
1904 Eble, Kenneth E. "Howells' kisses." American quarterly 9:441-47, Winter 1957.
1905 _____. "The western ideals of William Dean Howells." Western humanities review 11:331-38, Autumn 1957.
1906 Edel, Leon. "William Dean Howells." In his Henry James; the middle years 1882-1895. Phila., Lippincott, 1962. passim.
1907 _____. "William Dean Howells." In his Henry James; the conquest of London, 1870-1881. Phila., Lippincott, 1962. passim.
1908 Edwards, Herbert. "The dramatization of The rise of Silas Lapham." New England quarterly 30:235-43, June 1957.

1909   _____. "Howells and Herne." American literature
        22:432-41, Jan. 1951.
            James A. Herne (1839-1901) was a dramatist.
1910   _____. "Howells and the controversy over realism
        in American fiction." American literature 3:237-48,
        Nov. 1931.
1911   Ekstrom, William F. "The equalitarian principle in
        the fiction of William Dean Howells." American
        literature 24:40-50, Mar. 1952.
1912   Elkins, Kimball C. "Eliot, Howells, and the courses
        of graduate instruction 1869-1871." Harvard library
        bulletin 10:141-46, Winter 1956.
1913   Ellis, James. "William Dean Howells and the family
        home." College Language Association journal (Morgan
        State College) 8:240-45, Mar. 1965.
1914   Erskine, John. "William Dean Howells." Bookman
        51:385-89, June 1920.
1915   Evanoff, Alexander. "William Dean Howells' economic
        chance-world in A hazard of new fortunes: an Amer-
        ican classic reviewed." Discourse 6:382-88, Winter
        1962-63.

1916   Falk, Robert P. "The eighties: Howells: maturity
        in fiction." In his The Victorian mode in American
        fiction, 1865-1885. Lansing, Michigan State Univer-
        sity, 1965. p.121-38.
1917   _____. "William Dean Howells: the romance of
        real life." In his The Victorian mode in American
        fiction 1865-1885. Lansing, Michigan State Univer-
        sity, 1965. p.43-53.
            About A modern instance and The rise of Silas
            Lapham.
1918   Fawcett, Waldon. "Mr. Howells and his brother."
        Critic 35:1026-28, Nov. 1899.
1919   Fertig, Walter L. "Maurice Thompson and A modern
        instance." American literature 38:103-111, Mar.
        1966.
1920   Firkins, Oscar W. "Howells always found the right
        word." Christian science monitor 37:6, Jan. 22,
        1945.
            Contains an excerpt from his William Dean Howells:
            a study.
1921   _____. "Last of the mountaineers." Saturday re-
        view of literature 5:774-75, Mar. 16, 1929.
            Also in his Selected essays. Minneapolis, Univer-
            sity of Minnesota Press, 1933. p.94-108.

1922 _____. "William Dean Howells." In Dictionary of American biography. N.Y., Scribner, 1932. v. 5, p. 306-11.

1923 _____. "William Dean Howells." Sewanee review 29:171-76, Apr. 1921.

1924 Fiske, Horace S. "The rise of Silas Lapham." In his Provincial types in American literature. Chatauqua, N.Y., Chatauqua Press, 1907. p. 11-42.

1925 Fitch, George H. "Howells, first of living American novelists." In his Great spiritual writers of America. San Francisco, P. Elder, 1916. p. 127-35.

1926 Follett, Helen T. and Follett, Wilson. "Contemporary novelists." Atlantic monthly 119:362-72, Mar. 1917.

1927 _____ and _____. "William Dean Howells." In their Some modern novelists; appreciations and estimates. N.Y., Holt, 1918. p. 99-123.

1928 Foner, Philip S. "William Dean Howells." In his Mark Twain, social critic. N.Y., International Publishers, 1958. passim.

1929 Ford, Thomas W. "Howells and the American Negro." Texas studies in literature and language 5:530-37, Autumn 1963.

1929a Fortenberry, George. "The unnamed critic in William Dean Howells' Heroines of fiction." Mark Twain journal 16:7-8, Winter 1971-72.

1930 Foster, Richard. "The contemporaneity of Howells." New England quarterly 32:54-78, Mar. 1959.

1931 Fox, Arnold B. "Howells as a religious critic." New England quarterly 25:199-216, June 1952.

1932 _____. "Howells' doctrine of complicity." Modern language quarterly 13:56-60, Mar. 1952.

1933 Franklin, Viola P. "Lowell's appreciation of Howells." Methodist review 84:112-15, Jan. 1902.

1934 Frazier, David L. "Time and the theme of Indian summer." Arizona quarterly 16:260-67, Autumn 1960.

1935 _____. "Their wedding journey and Howells' fictional craft." New England quarterly 42:323-49, Sept. 1969.

1936 Fréchette, A.H. "William Dean Howells." Canadian bookman 2:9-12, July 1920.

1937 Frederick, John T. "William Dean Howells." In his The darkened sky; nineteenth century American novelists and religion. Notre Dame, Ind., University of Notre Dame, 1969. p. 177-228.

1938 Free, William J. "Howells' 'Editha' and pragmatic belief." Studies in short fiction 3:285-92, Spring 1966.

142   William Dean Howells

1939 Fryckstedt, Olov W. "Howells and Conway in Venice."
      Studia neophilologica 30:165-74, 1958.
1940 Gargano, James W. "A modern instance: the twin
      evils of society." Texas studies in literature and
      language 4:399-407, Autumn 1962.
1941 Garland, Hamlin. "Howells." In Macy, John A.,
      ed. American writers on American literature, by
      thirty-seven contemporary writers. N.Y., Liveright,
      1931. p. 285-97.
1942 _____. "Meetings with Howells." Bookman 45:1-7,
      Mar. 1917.
1943 _____. "Mr. Howells' latest novels." New Eng-
      land magazine n. s. 2:244-50, May 1890.
      Also in Eble, K. E., ed. Howells, a century of
      criticism. 1962. p. 54-59.
1944 _____. "Sanity in fiction." North American re-
      view 176:336-48, Mar. 1903.
1945 _____. "William Dean Howells, master craftsman."
      Art world 1:410-12, Mar. 1917.
1946 _____. "Roadside meetings of a literary nomad."
      Bookman 70:246-50, Nov. 1929.
      Also in his Roadside meetings. N. Y., Macmillan,
      1930. p. 55-64.
1947 Garvin, Harry R. "Howells, Venice, and the Amer-
      ican novel." Annali Istituto Universitario Orientale,
      Napoli, Sezione Germanica 5:249-61. 1962.
1948 Geismar, Maxwell. "William Dean Howells." In his
      Henry James and the Jacobites. Boston, Houghton
      Mifflin, 1963. passim.
1949 "Genial wisdom of eighty." Nation 104:261-62, Mar.
      8, 1917.
1950 Gettman, R. A. "Turgenev in England and America."
      University of Illinois studies in language and litera-
      ture 27:51-63. 1941.
1951 Getzels, Jacob W. "William Dean Howells and so-
      cialism." Science and society 2:376-86, Summer 1938.
1952 Giannone, Richard. "Howells' A foregone conclusion:
      theme and structure." College Language Association
      journal (Morgan State College) 6:216-20, Mar. 1963.
1953 Gibson, William M. "Introduction." In Howells,
      William D. Indian summer. N.Y., Dutton, 1951.
      p. vii-xix.
1954 _____. "Introduction." In Howells, William D.
      A modern instance. Boston, Houghton Mifflin, 1957.
      p. v-xviii.
1955 _____. "Material and form in Howells's first
      novels." American literature 19:158-66, May 1947.

1956 _____. "Mark Twain and Howells: anti-imperi-
alists." New England quarterly 20:435-70, Dec.
1947.
1957 _____. "William Dean Howells." In Encyclopaedia
Britannica. 1965. 11:796-97.
1958 _____. "William Dean Howells." In Six American
novelists of the nineteenth century. Edited by Richard
Foster. Minneapolis, University of Minnesota Press,
1968. p. 155-90.
1959 Gifford, Henry. "W. D. Howells: his moral conserva-
tism." Kenyon review 20:124-33, Winter 1958.
1960 Gilder, Jeannette L. "Howells and some of his
friends." Critic 38:165-68, Feb. 1901.
1961 Gilenson, B. A. [W. D. Howells and L. N. Tolstoi]
Uchenye Zapiski Gori Kovskogo universiteta 1963,
t. 60. L. N. Tolstoi. Stat'i i materialy, vyp. 5,
p. 282-95.
1962 Gohdes, Clarence. "Realism for the middle class:
William Dean Howells." In Quinn, Arthur H., ed.
Literature of the American people.... N. Y., Appleton, 1951. p. 665-80.
1963 Goldfarb, Clare R. "From complicity to Altruria:
the use of Tolstoy in Howells." University review
(Kansas City, Mo.) 32:311-17, Summer 1966.
1964 _____. "William Dean Howells' The minister's
charge: a study of psychological perception."
Markham review 2:1-4, 1969.
1965 Goodman, Henry. "Brave voice of conscience." Social studies 27:87-91, Feb. 1936.
1966 Gorlier, Claudio. "William Dean Howells e le
definizioni del realismo." Studi Americani, no. 2,
p. 83-125. 1956.
1967 Gosse, Edmund. "Passing of William Dean Howells."
Living age 306:98-100, July 10, 1920.
1968 _____. "William Dean Howells." In his Silhouettes.
London, Heinemann, 1925. p. 193-99.
1969 Gottesman, Ronald and Nordloh, David J. "The
quest for perfection or, surprises in the consumma-
tion of Their wedding journey." Center for Editions
of American Authors newsletter (Modern Language
Association) 1:12-13.
1970 Graham, Kenneth. ["William Dean Howells."] In
his English criticism of the English novel 1865-1900.
Oxford, Clarendon Press, 1965. p. 49-56 and
passim.
1971 Grant, Robert. "William Dean Howells 1837-1920."
In Howe, Mark A. De Wolfe, ed. Later years of

the Saturday Club, 1870-1920. Boston, Houghton Mifflin, 1927. p. 69-77.

1972 Grattan, C. Hartley. "Howells, ten years after." American mercury 20:42-50, May 1930.

1973 Grey, Rowland. "William Dean Howells: the last." Fortnightly review 115:154-63, Jan. 1921.

1974 Griswold, Hattie T. "William Dean Howells." In her Personal sketches of recent authors. Chicago, McClurg, 1898. p. 209.

1975 Gullason, Thomas A. "New light on the Cranes-Howells relationship." New England quarterly 30: 389-92, Sept. 1957.

1976 Hackett, Francis. "William Dean Howells." In his Horizons; a book of criticism. N. Y., Huebsch, 1918. p. 21-30.

1977 Haight, Gordon S. "Realism defined: William Dean Howells." In Spiller, Robert E., and others, eds. Literary history of the United States. N. Y., Macmillan, 1948. v. 2, p. 878-98.

1978 Hall, Vernon, Jr. "William Dean Howells." In his A short history of literary criticism. N. Y., New York University Press, 1963. p. 113-17.

1979 Harlow, Virginia. "William Dean Howells and Thomas Sergeant Perry." Boston Public Library bulletin 1:135-50, Oct. 1949.

1980 Harper, Joseph H. [William Dean Howells.] In his The house of Harper. N. Y., Harper, 1912. p. 318-30, and passim.

1981 _____ . ["William Dean Howells."] In his I remember. N. Y., Harper, 1934. p. 149-58.

1982 Hart, John E. "The commonplace as heroic in The rise of Silas Lapham." Modern fiction studies 8: 375-83, Winter 1962-63.

1983 Hartman, Lee F. "Mr. Howells and the logic of love." Harper's weekly 49:871, June 17, 1905.

1984 Hartwick, Harry. "Sweetness and light." In his Foreground of American fiction. N. Y., American Book Co., 1934. p. 315-40.

1985 Harvey, Alexander. "William Dean Howells." In Howells, William D. A hazard of new fortunes. N. Y., Boni and Liveright, 1889. p. ix-xiv.

1986 Hatcher, Harlan H. ["William Dean Howells."] In his Creating the modern American novel. N. Y., Farrar and Rinehart, 1935. p. 14-15.

1987 Hazard, Lucy L. "Howells a hundred years later." Mills quarterly 20:167-72, Feb. 1938.

1988 Hedges, Elaine R. "César Birotteau and The rise of Silas Lapham: a study in parallels." Nineteenth century fiction 17:163-74, Sept. 1962.
    César Birotteau was written by Balzac.

1989   . "Howells on a Hawthornesque theme." Texas studies in literature and language 3:129-43, Spring 1961.
    About The shadow of a dream.

1990 Herford, Oliver. "Celebrities I have not met." American mercury 75:95, Mar. 1913.
    A satiric poem.

1991 Hicks, Granville. "Battlefield." In his Great tradition; an interpretation of American literature since the Civil War. rev. ed. N.Y., Macmillan, 1935. p. 68-99.

1992   . "Fame at the end was fickle." Saturday review 50:83-84, Apr. 22, 1967.

1993   . "A grasping imagination." Sewanee review 59:505-17, July 1951.

1994 Hill, Hamlin. "William Dean Howells." In his Mark Twain and Elisha Bliss. Columbia, University of Missouri Press, 1964. passim.

1995 Hillquit, Morris. "William Dean Howells." In his Loose leaves from a busy life. N.Y., Macmillan, 1934. p. 115-16.

1996 Hind, Charles L. "William Dean Howells." In his Authors and I. N.Y., John Lane, 1921. p. 157-60.

1997 Hinton, Richard J. "The Howells family." The Voice (New York), July 15, 1897, p. 6.

1998 Hirsch, David H. "William Dean Howells and Daisy Miller." English language notes 1:123-28, Dec. 1963.

1999 Hoffman, Frederic J. "Henry James, William Dean Howells, and the art of fiction." In his The modern novel in America 1900-1950. Chicago, Regnery, 1951. p. 1-27.

1999a "The honor of meeting." Spectator 105:898-99, Nov. 26, 1910.

2000 Hough, Robert L. "William Dean Howells and The rise of Silas Lapham." In Stegner, Wallace, ed. The American novel from James Fenimore Cooper to William Faulkner. N.Y., Basic Books, 1965. p. 73-85.

2001 "Howells and relics of feudalism." Spectator 98:450-51, Mar. 23, 1907.
    Contains a review of Certain delightful English towns.

2002 "Howells and the future; a new study of our greatest
      realistic novelist." Current opinion 78:306-07, Mar.
      1925.
          This article is an essay on O.W. Firkins's Wil-
          liam Dean Howells: a study.
2003 "Howells as a victim of the 'dead hand' in American
      fiction." Current opinion 54:411, May 1913.
2004 "Howells, at eighty, receives notable tributes as the
      dean of American letters." Current opinion 62:357,
      May 1917.
2005 "Howells at his summer home." Harper's weekly
      46:929-30, July 19, 1902.
          Contains several pictures of the author. One of
          them shows Howells standing on the bluff in front
          of his country house at Kittery Point, Maine.
2006 "Howells, octogenarian." Outlook 115:454, Mar. 14,
      1917.

2007 "In honor of Mr. Howells; some of the memorable
      happenings at last week's birthday dinner to the Dean
      of American Letters." Harper's weekly 56:28-34,
      Mar. 9, 1912.
2008 Izzo, Carlo. "Dall'Arnaldo da Brescia di G.B.
      Niccolini a The Waste land di T.S. Eliot per il
      tramite di W.D. Howells." In Studi in onore di
      Lorenzo Bianchi. Bologna, Zanichelli, 1960. p.103-
      14.

2009 James, Henry. "Literary recollections." North
      American review 195:558-62, Apr. 1912.
2010 _____. "William Dean Howells." In Wilson,
      Edmund, ed. Shock of recognition.... N.Y., Double-
      day, 1943. p.570-79.
          Also in Harper's weekly 30:394-95, June 19, 1886.
2011 Jones, Howard M. "Introduction." In Howells, Wil-
      liam D. A traveler from Altruria. N.Y., Sagamore
      Press, 1957. p.v-vii.
2012 _____. "A study of Howells." Freeman 7:163,
      Apr. 25, 1923.
          Contains a review of Delmar G. Cooke's William
          Dean Howells; a critical study.
2013 Jones, M. "Balzac aux Etats-Unis." Revue de
      littérature comparée 24:232-33, Apr. 1950.
2014 Josephson, Matthew. "Those who stayed." In his
      Portrait of the artist as American. N.Y., Harcourt,
      Brace, 1930. p.161-66.

2015 Kar, Annette see Annette K. Baxter. [nos. 1805-06]
2016 Kazin, Alfred. "Howells, a late portrait." Antioch
      review 1:216-33, Summer 1941.
2017 Kehler, Harold. "Howells' 'Editha'." Explicator
      19: item 41. 1961.
2018 Kelley, C. P. "The early development of Henry
      James." University of Illinois studies in language
      and literature 15:73-80 and passim. 1930.
2019 Kindilien, Carlin T. ["William Dean Howells."] In
      his American poetry in the eighteen nineties. Provi-
      dence, R. I., Brown University Press, 1956. p.151-
      53.
2020 Kirk, Clara M. " 'The brighter side' of fiction--
      according to Howells and James." College English
      24:463-64, Mar. 1963.
2021 _____. "Niagara revisited." Columbia library
      columns 7:4-12, Feb. 1958.
2022 _____. "Reality and actuality in the March family
      narratives of W. D. Howells." Publications of the
      Modern Language Association 74:137-52, Mar. 1959.
2023 _____. "Toward a theory of art: a dialogue
      between W. D. Howells and C. E. Norton." New
      England quarterly 36:291-319, Summer 1963.
2024 _____ and Kirk, Rudolf. "Howells and the Church
      of the Carpenter." New England quarterly 32:185-
      206, June 1959.
2025 _____ and _____. "Howells in caricature." Journal
      of the Rutgers University Library 21:69-70, June
      1958.
2026 _____ and _____. "Introduction." In Howells,
      William D. European and American masters. rev.
      ed. N. Y., Collier Books, 1963.
2027 _____ and _____. "Introduction." In their William
      Dean Howells, representative selections. N. Y.,
      American Book Co., 1950. p.xv-clxvii.
2028 _____ and _____. "Introduction." In their William
      Dean Howells; representative selections. rev. ed.
      N. Y., Hill and Wang, 1961. p.xv-clxvii.
      Both the 1950 and the 1961 edition contain bibliog-
      raphy and notes by Clara and Rudolf Kirk.
2029 _____ and _____. "Introduction." In Howells,
      William D. Criticism and fiction, and other essays.
      Edited with introduction and notes by Clara and
      Rudolf Kirk. N. Y., New York University Press,
      1959. p.13-16.
2030 _____ and _____. "Introduction." In Howells,
      William D. Letters of an Altrurian traveller, 1893-
      94. Gainesville, Fla., Scholars' Facsimile and

Reprints, 1961. p. v-xii.

2031 _____ and _____. "William Dean Howells, George William Curtis, and the Haymarket affair." American literature 40:487-98, Jan. 1969.

2032 _____ and _____, eds. " 'The Howells family' by Richard J. Hinton." Journal of the Rutgers University Library 14:14-23, Dec. 1950.
Contains an article reprinted from The voice, July 15, 1897, a New York temperance newspaper. Richard J. Hinton and Howells were friends.

2033 Kirk, Rudolf and Kirk, Clara. "Abraham Cahan and William Dean Howells: the story of a friendship." American Jewish historical quarterly 52:25-57, Sept. 1962.

2034 _____ and _____. "Howells' guidebook to Venice." American literature 33:221-24, May 1961.

2035 _____ and _____. "Niagara revisited by William Dean Howells: the story of its publication and suppression." In Essays in literary history presented to J. Milton French. New Brunswick, N.J., Rutgers University Press, 1960. p. 177-95.

2036 _____ and _____. "William Dean Howells." In Collier's Encyclopedia. N.Y., Crowell Collier and Macmillan, 1966. v. 12, p. 332-33.

2037 _____ and _____. "Introduction." In Howells, William D. The rise of Silas Lapham. N.Y., Collier Books, 1962. p. 5-11.

2038 Kono, Yotaro. "The Victorian realists in the United States: Henry James and William Dean Howells." In Maekawa Shunichi, Kyoju Kanreki Kinen-ronbunshu. Tokyo, Eihosha, 1968.

2039 Kraus, W. Keith. "The convenience of fatalism: thematic unity in William Dean Howell's [sic] A hazard of new fortunes." English record 18:33-36, Oct. 1967.

2040 Kummer, George. "Introduction." In Taneyhill, Richard H. and Bennett, R. King. The leatherwood god, 1869-70: a source of William Dean Howells' novel of the same name, in two versions. Gainesville, Fla., Scholars Facsimiles and Reprints, 1965. p. vii-xv.

2041 Lappin, Henry. "Passing of William Dean Howells." Catholic world 111:445-53, July 1920.

2042 Lawrence, C.E. "William Dean Howells." Bookman (London) 52:88-91, June 1917.

2043 _____. "William Dean Howells as a novelist." Living age 294:173-77, July 21, 1917.

2044 Lee, Gerald S. "Mr. Howells on the platform."
Critic 35:1029-30, Nov. 1899.
2045 Lessing, O.E. "William Dean Howells." Das
literarische Echo 15: columns 155-61, Nov. 1, 1912.
2046 Linneman, William R. "Satires of American realism,
1880-1900." American literature 34:80-93, Mar.
1962.
2047 Linson, Corwin K. ["William Dean Howells."] In
her My Stephen Crane. Syracuse, N.Y., Syracuse
University Press, 1958. passim.
2048 "Lowell and Howells." Harper's weekly 46:101, Jan.
25, 1902.
2049 Lutwack, Leonard I. "The New England hierarchy."
New England quarterly 28:164-85, June 1955.
2050   . "William Dean Howells and the 'Editor's
study'." American literature 24:195-207, May 1952.
2051 Lydenberg, John and Cady, Edwin H. "Essay review: the Howells revival: rounds two and three."
New England quarterly 32:394-407, Sept. 1959.

2052 Mabie, Hamilton W. "The story of Mr. Howells'
career." Book news monthly, June 1908, p.333-34.
2053   . "A presentation address at the Boston
meeting of the Academy and Institute of Arts and
Letters." Outlook 111:786-87, Dec. 1, 1915.
2054 McCabe, Lida R. "Literary and social recollections
of William Dean Howells." Lippincott 40:547-52,
Oct. 1887.
2055   . "One never can tell." Outlook 59:131-32,
May 14, 1898.
An essay about Poems of two friends by John J.
Piatt and William Dean Howells.
2056 McMahon, Helen. "Howells." In her Criticism of
fiction; a study of trends in the Atlantic monthly
1857-1898. N.Y., Bookman Associates, 1952.
passim.
2057 McMurray, William J. "The concept of complicity
in Howells' fiction." New England quarterly 35:489-
95, Dec. 1962.
2058   . "Point of view in Howells's The landlord
at Lion's head." American literature 34:207-14, May
1962.
2059 Macy, John A. "Howells." In his Spirit of American literature. Garden City, N.Y., Doubleday,
Page, 1913. p.278-95.
2060 Maksimov, N. [Foreword to The sketches "American women"] Trud, no. 8 (1895), p.358-66.

2061   Malone, Clifton. "The realism of William Dean
       Howells." Quarterly bulletin of the Oklahoma Bap-
       tist University 34:3-22, Feb. 1949.
2062   Manierre, William R. "The rise of Silas Lapham:
       retrospective discussion as dramatic technique."
       College English 23:357-61, Feb. 1962.
2063   Marden, Orison S. "How William Dean Howells
       worked to secure a foothold." In his How they suc-
       ceeded. Boston, Lothrop, 1901. p. 171-84.
2064   Martin, Edward S. "W. D. Howells." Harper's
       monthly 141:265-66, July 1920.
2065   Mathews, James W. "The heroines of Hawthorne and
       Howells." Tennessee studies in literature 7:37-46.
       1962.
2066   Matthews, Brander. "American character in Amer-
       ican fiction." Munsey's 49:794-98, Aug. 1913.
2067   _____. "Bret Harte and Mr. Howells as drama-
       tists." In Moses, Montrose J. and Brown, John
       M., eds. American theatre as seen by its critics,
       1752-1934. N. Y., Norton, 1934. p. 147-48.
2068   _____. "Mr. Howells as a critic." Forum 32:
       629-38, Jan. 1902.
2069   Matthiessen, F. O. "Monument to Howells." In his
       Responsibilities of the critic.... N. Y., Oxford, 1952.
       p. 97-100.
       Appeared also in New republic 58:284-85, Apr. 24,
       1929.
2070   Maxwell, Perriton. "Howells, the editor." Book
       news monthly, June 1908, p. 735-38.
2071   Mead, C. David. "Introduction." In Howells, Wil-
       liam Dean. The rise of Silas Lapham. N. Y.,
       Dodd, Mead, 1964. p. v-x.
2072   Medrano, Higinio J. "William Dean Howells." Cuba
       contemporanea 23:252-56, July 1920.
2073   Mencken, Henry L. "The dean." In his Prejudices.
       1st series. N. Y., Knopf, 1919. p. 52-58.
       Also in Eble, K. E., ed. Howells a century of
       criticism. 1962. p. 94-98. First printed, in
       part, in the Smart set, Jan. 1917, p. 266-68.
2074   Meserole, Harrison T. "The Dean in person:
       Howells' lecture tour." Western humanities review
       10:337-47, Autumn 1956.
2075   Meserve, Walter J. "Colonel Sellers as a scientist:
       a play by S. L. Clemens and W. D. Howells." Mod-
       ern drama 1:151-56, Dec. 1958.
2076   _____. "An edition of William Dean Howells'

plays." Bulletin of the Mississippi Valley American
Studies Association 1:15-17, Fall 1957.
2077 _____. "Introduction." In Howells, William
Dean. Complete plays. Edited by Walter J.
Meserve.... N. Y., New York University Press,
1960. p. xv-xxxiii.
2078 _____. "Truth, morality and Swedenborg in
Howells' theory of realism." New England quarterly
27:252-57, June 1954.
2079 Michaud, Regis. "Henry James, Edith Wharton,
William Dean Howells and American society on
parade." In his American novel today; a social and
psychological study. Boston, Little, Brown, 1928.
p. 47-70.
2080 Millgate, Michael. "The emotional commitment of
William Dean Howells." Neophilologus 44:48-54,
1960.
2081 _____. "William Dean Howells." In his American social fiction: James to Cozzens. N. Y.,
Barnes and Noble, 1964. p. 18-37.
2082 "Mr. Howells as a critic." Nation 51:111-12, Aug.
7, 1890.
2083 "Mr. Howells in England." Literary digest 65:37,
June 19, 1920.
2084 "Mr. Howells in England." Spectator 95:810, Nov.
18, 1905.
2085 "Mr. Howells on rag-babies." Bookman 35:451-52,
July 1912.
2086 "Mr. Howells's 'Americanisms'" Critic 25:193,
Sept. 22, 1894.
2087 "Mr. Howells's literary creed." Atlantic monthly
68:566-69, Oct. 1891.
2088 "Mr. Howells' novels." Westminster review 122:
347-75, Oct. 1884.
2089 "Mr. Howells' socialism." American fabian 4:1-2,
Feb. 1898.
2090 "Mr. Maurice Thompson on Mr. Howells." Literary
world 18:281, Sept. 3, 1887.
2091 Mitchell, Robert E. "Aesthetic values as depicted
in the fiction of William Dean Howells." In Petit,
Herbert H., ed. Essays and studies in language and
literature. Pittsburgh, Duquesne University Press,
1964. p. 207-18.
2092 Monroe, Harriet E. "Talk between Senator Ingalls
and William Dean Howells." Lippincott 39:128-32,
Jan. 1887.
2093 Moore, Harry T. "Afterword." In Howells, William

D. The rise of Silas Lapham. N.Y., New American
Library of World Literature, 1963.

2094 Morby, Edwin S. "William Dean Howells and Spain."
Hispanic review 14:187-212, July 1946.

2095 Mordell, Albert. "William Dean Howells and the classics." Stratford monthly n.s. 2:199-205, Sept. 1924.

2096 Morgan, Howard W. "The realist as reformer." In
his American writers in rebellion from Mark Twain
to Dreiser. N.Y., Hill and Wang, 1965. p.37-75.

2097 Morris, Lloyd. "Conscience in the parlor." American scholar 18:407-16, Autumn 1949.

2098 _____ . "The melancholy of the masters." In his
Postscript to yesterday. N.Y., Random House, 1947.
p. 89-106.

2099 Mowbray, J.P. "Mr. Howells's réchauffé." Critic
42:21-26, Jan. 1903.
Contains an essay on Literature and life by William
Dean Howells.

2100 Muirhead, James F. "Howells and Trollope." Living
age 308:304-09, Jan. 29, 1921.

2101 Munford, Howard M. "The disciple proves independent:
Howells and Lowell." Publications of the Modern
Language Association 74:484-87, Sept. 1959.

2102 _____ . "Introduction." In Howells, William D.
The rise of Silas Lapham. N.Y., Oxford, 1948.

2103 Murray, Donald M. "Henry B. Fuller, friend of
Howells." South Atlantic quarterly 52:431-44, July
1953.

2104 "New tributes to the irrepressible youth and vitality of
William Dean Howells." Current opinion 60:352, May
1916.

2105 Noble, David W. "William Dean Howells: the discovery of society." Midwest quarterly 3:149-62, Apr.
1962.

2106 Norris, Frank. ["William Dean Howells."] In his
The responsibilities of the novelist. London, Grant
Richards, 1903. p.3-10, 196, 213-20.

2107 [On the translation of the novel A guest [sic] from
Altruria] Vestnik Evropy, no.1 (1895), p.212-13.

2108 "Novel writing as a science." Catholic world 42:274-
80, Nov. 1885.

2109 Orcutt, William D. "Friends through the pen." In
his Quest of the perfect book; reminiscences and reflections of a bookman. Boston, Little, Brown, 1926.
p.183-89.

2110 _____. "Italian dividends." In his Celebrities
off parade. Chicago, Willett, 1935. p. 86-132.
2111 Orr, A. (Mrs. Sutherland) "International novelists
and Mr. Howells." Contemporary review 37:741-65,
May 1880.
Also in Littell's living age 145:599-615, June 5,
1880.

2112 Parker, Henry T. "Mr. Howells and the realistic
movement." Harvard monthly 5:145-49, Jan. 1888.
2113 Parks, Edd W. "A realist avoids reality: William
Dean Howells and the Civil War years." South
Atlantic quarterly 52:93-97, Jan. 1953.
2114 _____. "Howells and the gentle reader." South
Atlantic quarterly 50:239-47, Apr. 1951.
2115 Parrington, Vernon L. "Sheldon and Howells:
Christian dreamers." In his American dreams.
Providence, R.I., Brown University, 1947. p. 166-
75.
2116 _____. "William Dean Howells and the realism
of the commonplace." In his Main currents in
American thought. N.Y., Harcourt, Brace, 1930.
vol. 3, p. 241-53.
2117 Pattee, Fred L. "Following the Civil War." In
The development of the American short story. N.Y.,
Harper, 1923. p. 208-11.
2118 _____. "The classical reaction." In his A history
of American literature since 1870. N.Y., Century,
1915. p. 197-217.
2119 Payne, Alma J. "The family in the utopia of William Dean Howells." Georgia review 15:217-29,
Summer 1961.
2120 _____. "William Dean Howells and the independent
woman." Midwest review 5:44-52, 1963.
2121 Pearce, Roy H. "Adams, Howells and their associates." Virginia quarterly review 35:149-53, Winter
1959.
2122 Peck, Harry T. "Living critics: William Dean
Howells." Bookman 4:529-41, Feb. 1897.
2122a _____. "William Dean Howells." In his The
personal equation. N.Y., Harper, 1898. p. 3-52.
2123 Pennell, Joseph. "Adventures with an illustrator:
with Howells in Italy." Century magazine 104:135-
41, May 1922.
2124 Perkins, George. "Howells and Hawthorne." Nineteenth century fiction 15:259-62, Dec. 1960.

2125   Perry, Thomas S. "His friends greet William Dean
       Howells at eighty." New York Sun, Feb. 25, 1917,
       section 5, p.10.
2126   _____. "William Dean Howells." Century maga-
       zine 23:680-85, Mar. 1882.
2127   Persons, Stow. "The origins of the gentry: William
       Dean Howells." In Essays on history and literature.
       Ed. by Robert H. Bremmer. Columbus, Ohio State
       University Press, 1966. p.115-18.
2128   Phelps, William L. "An appreciation." North Amer-
       ican review 212:17-20, July 1920.
2129   _____. "William Dean Howells." Yale review
       ns10:99-109, Oct. 1920.
       Appears in Spanish translation in Inter-America
       4:281-86, Jan. 1921.
2130   _____. "Howells." In his Howells, James, Bryant,
       and other essays. N.Y., Macmillan, 1924. p.156-
       80.
2131   _____. "William Dean Howells." In his Essays on
       modern novelists. N.Y., Macmillan, 1910. p.56-81.
2132   Pict, Douglas R. "William Dean Howells: realistic
       realist." Research studies of Washington State Uni-
       versity 35:92-94, Mar. 1967.
2133   Pizer, Donald. "Crane reports Garland on Howells."
       Modern language notes 70:37-39, Jan. 1955.
2134   _____. "The ethical unity of The rise of Silas Lap-
       ham." American literature 32:322-27, Nov. 1960.
2135   _____. "Evolutionary literary criticism and the
       defense of Howellsian realism." Journal of English
       and Germanic philology 61:296-304. 1962.
2136   _____. "The evolutionary foundation of W.D.
       Howells's Criticism and fiction." Philological quar-
       terly 40:91-103, Jan. 1961.
2137   Pratt, Cornelia. "William Dean Howells, some as-
       pects of his realistic novels." Critic 35:1021-25,
       Nov. 1899.
2138   Preston, Harriet W. "The Kenton; latest novels of
       Howells and James." Atlantic monthly 91:77, Jan.
       1903.
2139   Price, Robert. "Young Howells drafts a life for
       Lincoln." Ohio history 76:232-46. 1967.
2140   Pritchard, John P. "The realists: William Dean
       Howells." In his Criticism in America. Norman,
       University of Oklahoma, 1956. p.163-75.
2141   _____. "William Dean Howells." In his Return to
       the fountains.... Durham, Duke University, 1942.
       p.135-47.

2142 Quinn, Arthur H. "The art of William Dean Howells."
      Century 100:674-81, Sept. 1920.
2143 ————. "William Dean Howells and the approach to
      realism." In his A history of the American drama
      from the Civil War to the present day. N.Y., Ap-
      pleton-Century, 1943. vol. 1, p. 66-81.
2144 ————. "William Dean Howells and the establish-
      ment of realism." In his American fiction. N.Y.,
      Appleton-Century, 1936. p. 257-78.
2145 Quint, Howard H. ["William Dean Howells."] In his
      The forging of American socialism: origins of the
      modern movement. Columbia, University of South
      Carolina Press, 1953. p. 78, 80.

2146 Rankin, Daniel S. "William Dean Howells: 1837-1920."
      Commonweal 26:597-98, Oct. 22, 1937.
2147 Ratcliffe, S. K. "William Dean Howells." New states-
      man 15:195-96, May 22, 1920.
2148 Ratner, Marc L. "Howells and Boyesen: two views of
      realism." New England quarterly 35:376-90, Sept.
      1962.
          Hjalmar H. Boyesen (1848-1895) was a Norwegian
          novelist and educator.
2149 Reardon, Mark S. "My visit [in 1914] to William Dean
      Howells." Mark Twain quarterly 8:5, 11, Summer-
      Fall 1948.
2150 Reeves, John K. "The case of the dead-pan scholar."
      Prism; bulletin of the friends of the Skidmore College
      Library 1:[7-15] 1951.
2151 ————. "Introduction." In Howells, William Dean.
      Their wedding journey. Bloomington, Indiana Univer-
      sity Press, 1968. p. xiii-xxxiii.
2152 ————. "The limited realism of Howells' Their
      wedding journey." Publications of the Modern Lan-
      guage Association 77:617-28, Dec. 1962.
2153 ————. "The way of a realist; a study of Howells'
      use of the Saratoga scene." Publications of the Mod-
      ern Language Association 65:1035-52, Dec. 1950.
2154 Reid, Forrest. "William Dean Howells." Irish states-
      man 1:333-34, Sept. 27, 1919; 1:359-60, Oct. 4, 1919.
2155 Rein, David M. "Howells and the Cosmopolitan."
      American literature 21:49-55, Mar. 1949.
2156 "Reminiscences of an evening with Howells." North
      American review 212:1-16, July 1920.
          Contains an essay about a dinner given in honor of
          Howells's 75th birthday.

2157   Rhodes, James A. "William Dean Howells." In his
       Teenage hall of fame. Indianapolis, Bobbs-Merrill,
       1960. p. 23-25.
2158   Richardson, L. N. [Men of letters and the Hayes ad-
       ministration.] New England quarterly 15:117-27, Mar.
       1942.
2159   Ricus. "A suppressed novel of Mr. Howells." Book-
       man 32:201-03, Oct. 1910.
       The suppressed novel is Private theatricals, which
       appeared first in the Atlantic monthly and later was
       published as a book under the title of Mrs. Farrell.
2160   Rideing, William H. "William Dean Howells." In his
       Boyhood of living authors. N. Y., Crowell, 1887.
       p. 74-85.
2161   Robertson, John M. "Mr. Howells' novels." In his
       Essays towards a critical method. London, Fisher,
       1889. p. 149-99.
2162   Rood, Henry. "William Dean Howells; some notes of
       a literary acquaintance." Ladies' home journal 37:42,
       Sept. 1920.

2163   "The safe and sane genius of William Dean Howells."
       Current opinion 69:93-96, July 1920.
2164   Samokhvalor, N. [William Dean Howells and American
       critical realism] Uchenye Zapiski Krasnodarskogo
       pedagogicheskogo instituta. 1961. vyp 24. Russkaia
       i zarubezhnaia literatura. p. 146-94.
2165   Sanborn, Franklin B. "Literary recollections." North
       American review 195:562-66, Apr. 1912.
2166   Schneider, Robert W. "William Dean Howells, the
       mugwump rebellion." In his Five novelists of the
       progressive era. N. Y., Columbia University Press,
       1965. p. 19-59.
2167   Schwartz, Henry B. "The Americanism of William
       Dean Howells." Methodist review 101:226-32, Mar.
       1918.
2167a Seelye, John. "The rise of William Dean Howells."
       New republic 165:23-26, July 3, 1971.
2168   Seyersted, Per E. "Turgenev's interest in America,
       as seen in his contacts with H. H. Boyesen, W. D.
       Howells, and other American authors." Scando-
       Slavica (Copenhagen) 11:25-39, 1965.
2169   Sherman, Ellen. "To the use of edifying: Howells'
       lecture on the novel." Critic 34:319-20, Apr. 1899.
2170   Shriber, Michael. "Cognitive apparatus in Daisy
       Miller, The ambassadors, and two works by Howells;
       a comparative study of the epistemology of Henry
       James." Language sciences 2:207-25, 1969.

2171 Simon, Myron. "Howells on romantic fiction." Stud-
      ies in short fiction 2:241-46, Spring 1965.
2172 Sinclair, Robert B. "Howells in the Ohio valley."
      Saturday review of literature 28:22-23, Jan. 6, 1945.
2173 Sinnott, Joseph E. "The nabob and Silas Lapham."
      Harvard monthly 1:164-68, Jan. 1886.
2174 Sirluck, Ernest. "Howells' A modern instance."
      Manitoba arts review 10:66-72, Winter 1956.
2175 Smith, Bernard. "Howells, the genteel radical."
      Saturday review of literature 11:41-42, Aug. 11, 1934.
2176 Snell, George. "Howells' grasshopper." College Eng-
      lish 7:444-51, May 1946.
      This essay appeared in 1947 in George Snell's
      Shapers of American fiction 1798-1947.
2177 Sokoloff, B.A. "Printing and journalism in the novels
      of William Dean Howells." Transactions of the
      Wisconsin Academy of Sciences, Arts, and Letters
      46:165-78. 1957.
2178 _____. "William Dean Howells and the Ohio village:
      a study in environment and art." American quarterly
      11:58-75, Spring 1959.
2179 Solomon, Eric. "Howells, houses and realism."
      American literary realism 1:89-93, Fall 1968.
2179a Spangler, George. "Shadow of a dream; Howells'
      homosexual tragedy." American quarterly 23:110-19,
      Spring, 1971.
2180 Spiller, Robert E. "Literary rediscovery: Howells,
      Mark Twain." In his Cycle of American literature.
      N.Y., Macmillan, 1955. p.141-62.
2180a _____. "Father of modern American realism."
      Saturday review of literature 33:10-11, Sept. 2, 1950.
2181 Spinning, James M. [Notes, questions, topics for
      themes and suggestions for dramatization.] In Howells,
      William D. The rise of Silas Lapham. Boston,
      Houghton Mifflin, 1928.
2182 Sprague, Dew H.C. "William Dean Howells" In
      Webb, Mary G. and Edna L., eds. Famous living
      Americans. Greencastle, Ind., Charles Webb, 1915.
      p. 260-76.
2183 Springer, Haskell S. "The leatherwood god: from
      narrative to novel." Ohio history 74:191-202, Sum-
      mer 1965.
2184 Starke, Aubrey H. "William Dean Howells and Sidney
      Lanier." American literature 3:79-82, Mar. 1931.
2185 _____. "William Dean Howells refuses an inter-
      view." American literature 10:492-94, Jan. 1939.

2186 Steinmetz, Marion L. "Problems in connection with
      The rise of Silas Lapham." Exercise exchange 3:6-10,
      Feb. 1956.
2187 Stewart, George. "Howells." In his Evenings in the
      library.... St. John, N. B., R. A. H. Morrow, 1878.
      p. 194-223.
2188 Stoddard, Richard H., and others ["Howells."] In
      their Poets' homes. Boston, Lothrop, 1877. p. 119-
      38.
2189 Stronks, James. "A modern instance." American
      literary realism 1:87-89, Fall 1968.
2190 _____. "The Howells revival." Commonweal 71:
      445-47, Jan. 15, 1960.
2191 _____. "Paul Lawrence Dunbar and William Dean
      Howells." Ohio history quarterly 67:95-108, Apr.
      1958.
2192 _____. "The Boston seasons of Silas Lapham."
      Studies in the novel 1:60-66. 1969.
2193 _____. "William Dean Howells, Ed Howe, and
      The story of a country town." American literature
      29:473-78, Jan. 1958.
      Ed Howe wrote The story of a country town.
2194 Strunsky, Simeon. "About books, more or less."
      New York times, section 3, Feb. 24, 1924, p. 4.
2195 Sullivan, Sister Mary Petrus. "The function of setting
      in Howells's The landlord at lion's head." American
      literature 35:38-52, Mar. 1963.
2196 Sweeney, Gerard M. "The Medea Howells saw."
      American literature 42:83-89, Mar. 1970.
      About A modern instance and Franz Grillparzer's
      Medea.

2197 Tanner, Tony. "Introduction." In Howells, William
      D. A hazard of new fortunes. London, Oxford,
      1967. p. vii-xxxv.
2198 Tanselle, G. Thomas. "The architecture of The rise
      of Silas Lapham." American literature 37:430-57,
      Jan. 1966.
2199 Tarkington, Booth. "Introduction." In Howells,
      William D. The rise of Silas Lapham. Boston,
      Houghton Mifflin, 1937.
2200 _____. "Mr. Howells." Harper's monthly 141:
      346-50, Aug. 1920.
2201 Taylor, Gordon O. "The dual life: William Dean
      Howells." In his The passages of thought: psycho-
      logical representation in the American novel 1870-
      1900. N.Y., Oxford, 1969. p. 85-109.

2202 Taylor, Walter F. "On the origin of Howells's interest in economic reform." American literature 2:3-14, Mar. 1930.

2203 _____. [William Dean Howells.] In his The economic novel in America. Chapel Hill, University of North Carolina, 1942. p. 214-81.

2204 _____. "William Dean Howells and the economic novel." American literature 4:103-13, May 1932.

2205 _____. "William Dean Howells, artist and American." Sewanee review 46:288-303, July 1938.

2206 _____. "Comedy, ethics, and economics: William Dean Howells." In his A history of American letters. N.Y., 1936. p. 295-303.

2207 Thayer, William R. "The new story-tellers and the doom of realism." Forum 18:470-80, Dec. 1894.

2208 Thomas, Edith M. "Mr. Howells's way of saying things." Putnam's magazine 4:443-47, July 1908.

2209 Thompson, Maurice. "The analyst, analyzed." Critic ns 6:19-22, July 10, 1886.

2210 Thorburn, Neil. "William Dean Howells as a literary model: the experience of Brand Whitlock." Northwest Ohio quarterly 39:22-36, Winter 1966-67. Brand Whitlock (1869-1934) was an Ohio novelist and politician.

2211 Ticknor, Caroline. "William Dean Howells." In her Glimpses of authors. Boston, Houghton Mifflin, 1922. p. 169-78.

2212 Timpe, Eugene F. "Howells and his German critics." Jahrbuch für Amerikastudien 11:256-59. 1966.

2213 Tomlinson, May. "Fiction and Mr. Howells." South Atlantic quarterly 20:360-67, Oct. 1921.

2214 Towers, Tom H. "Savagery and civilization: the moral dimensions of Howells's A boy's town. American literature 40:499-509, Jan. 1969.

2215 Towne, Charles H. "An acquaintance with Howells." In his Adventures in editing. N.Y., Appleton, 1926. p. 139-46.

2216 _____. "The kindly Howells." Touchstone 7:280-82, July 1920.

2217 Trent, William P. "Mr. Howells and romanticism." In his Authority of criticism, and other essays. N.Y., Scribner, 1899. p. 259-67.

2218 "Tribute to William Dean Howells." Harper's weekly 56:27-34, Mar. 9, 1912.

2219 Trilling, Lionel. "William Dean Howells and the roots of modern taste." Partisan review 18:516-36, Sept.-Oct. 1951.

Also in his The opposing self. N.Y., Viking Press,
1955. p.76-103.

2220 Trites, W.B. "William Dean Howells." Forum 49:
217-40, Feb. 1913.

2221 Turaj, Frank. "The social gospel in Howells' novels."
South Atlantic quarterly 66:449-64, Summer 1967.

2222 Twain, Mark. "William Dean Howells." Harper's
monthly 113:221-25, July 1906.

2223 Underwood, John C. "William Dean Howells and
Altruria." In his Literature and insurgency. N.Y.,
M. Kennerley, 1914. p.87-129.

2224 Utley, Frances L. "Howells' New York City ballad
seller." Journal of American folklore 70:361-62,
Oct.-Dec. 1957.

2225 Vanderbilt, Kermit. "Howells among the Brahmins:
why 'the bottom dropped out' during The rise of Silas
Lapham." New England quarterly 35:291-317, Sept.
1962.

2226 _____. "Howells and Norton: some frustrations
of the biographer." New England quarterly 37:84-89,
Mar. 1964.

2227 _____. "Marcia Gaylord's electra complex: a
footnote to sex in Howells." American literature 34:
365-74, Nov. 1962.

2228 _____. "The undiscovered country: Howells ver-
sion of American pastoral." American quarterly 17:
634-55, Winter 1965.

2229 _____. "William Dean Howells." In his Charles
Eliot Norton: apostle of culture in a democracy.
Cambridge, Belknap Press of Harvard University,
1959. p.150-58.

2230 _____. "The conscious realism of Howells' April
hopes." American literary realism 1870-1910, 3:53-
66, Winter 1970.

2231 Van Doren, Carl C. "Howells and realism." In his
American novel, 1789-1939. rev. ed. N.Y., Macmillan, 1940. p.115-36.

2232 _____. "Eulogium [Howells]." In his The roving
critic. N.Y., Knopf, 1923. p.69-80.

2233 _____. "The later novel: Howells." In the Cambridge history of American literature. N.Y., Putnam, 1921. p.66-85.

2234 Van Dyke, Henry. "A traveller from Altruria." In
his Camp-fires and guide-posts; a book of essays and
excursions. N.Y., Scribner, 1921. p.310-19.

2235   Van Nostrand, Albert D. "Fiction's flagging man of
commerce." English journal 48:1-11, Jan. 1959.
Compares The rise of Silas Lapham with John
Marquand's Point of no return.

2236   Van Westrum, A. Schade. "Mr. Howells and American
aristocracies." Bookman 25:67-73, Mar. 1907.
Contains a full-page picture of Howells sitting with
book in his hands from a photo by Zaida Ben-Yusuf.

2237   Vedder, Henry C. "William Dean Howells." In his
American writers to-day. N. Y., Silver, Burdett,
1894. p. 43-68.

2238   Vorse, M. H. "Overlooked phases of American life."
Critic 43:83-84, July 1903.

2239   Wagenknecht, Edward C. "The American mirror:
William Dean Howells." In his Cavalcade of the
American novel. N. Y., Holt, 1952. p. 127-44.

2240   Walton, Clyde C. "Introduction." In Howells, William
D. Life of Abraham Lincoln. Bloomington, Indiana
University Press, 1960. p. vii-x.

2241   Walts, Robert W. "A not-so-tame Howells." South
central bulletin 26:58-66.
An article about The shadow of a dream and An
imperative duty.

2242   Wasserstrom, William. "William Dean Howells: the
indelible stain." New England quarterly 32:486-95,
Dec. 1959.

2243   _____. "Howells' mansion and Thoreau's cabin."
College English 26:366-72, Feb. 1965.

2244   Weber, Carl J. "Thomas Hardy and his New England
editors." New England quarterly 15:681-99, Dec.
1942.

2245   Westbrook, Max. "The critical implications of Howells'
realism." University of Texas studies in English 36:
71-79. 1957.

2246   Westbrook, Perry D. [William Dean Howells.] In his
Mary Wilkins Freeman. N. Y., Twayne Publishers,
1967. passim.

2247   White, Morton and White, Lucia. "The ambivalent
urbanite: William Dean Howells." In their The in-
tellectual vs. the city: from Thomas Jefferson to
Frank Lloyd Wright. Cambridge, Mass., Harvard
University Press, 1962. p. 95-116.

2248   Whiteley, Mary N. "A visit to William Dean Howells."
Mark Twain quarterly 2:7, Fall 1937.

2249   Whitelock, William W. "The otherwise man." In his
The literary guillotine. N. Y., J. Lane, 1903. p. 238-
62.

2250 Whiting, Lillian. "William Dean Howells at home."
      Author 3:130-31, Sept. 15, 1891.
2251 Wilcox, Marrion. "Works of William Dean Howells."
      Harper's weekly 40:655-56, July 4, 1896.
2252 Wilkinson, William C. "William Dean Howells as man
      of letters." In his Some new literary valuations.
      N.Y., Funk and Wagnalls, 1909. p.11-73.
2253 "William Dean Howells." Saturday review of literature
      15:8, Mar. 13, 1937.
2254 "William Dean Howells." Nation 110:673, May 22,
      1920.
2255 "William Dean Howells." Chautauquan 48:267-69, Oct.
      1907.
2256 "William Dean Howells." Independent 72:533-34, Mar.
      7, 1912.
2257 "William Dean Howells." In Ohio authors and their
      books ... 1796-1950. Cleveland, World Publishing
      Co., 1962. p.319-22.
2258 "William Dean Howells." In National cyclopedia of
      American biography. N.Y., White, 1891. v.1,
      p.281.
2259 "William Dean Howells helped this young man write
      a play." Literary digest 65:56-58, June 19, 1920.
          Frank C. Drake was the young man.
2260 "William Dean Howells, printer, journalist, poet, and
      novelist." Literary digest 65:53-57, June 12, 1920.
2261 Williams, Stanley T. "William Dean Howells." In
      his Spanish background of American literature. N.Y.,
      Yale University Press, 1955. v.2, p.240-67.
2262 Wilson, Calvin D. and Fitzgerald, David B. "A day
      in Howells's 'Boy's town'." New England magazine
      n.s.36:289-97, May 1907.
2263 Wilson, Jack H. "Howells' use of George Eliot's
      Romola in April hopes." Publications of the Modern
      Language Association 84:1620-27, Oct. 1969.
2264 Winter, William. "Vagrant comrades." In his Old
      friends.... N.Y., Moffat, Yard, 1909. p.89-92.
2265 Wirzberger, Karl-Heinz. "The simple, the natural,
      and the honest: William Dean Howells als Kritiker
      und die Durchsetzung des realismus in der amerik-
      anischen Literatur des ausgehenden 19. Jahrunderts."
      Zeitschrift fur Anglistik und Amerikanistik (East
      Berlin) 9:5-48. 1961.
2266 Wister, Owen. "William Dean Howells." Atlantic
      monthly 160:704-13, Dec. 1937.
2267 "A woman's tribute to Mr. Howells." Literary digest
      44:485, Mar. 9, 1912.

2268   Woodress, James L. Jr. "Howells' Venetian priest."
        Modern language notes 66:266-67, Apr. 1951.
2269   Woolley, Celia P. "Mr. Howells again." New Eng-
        land magazine ns9:408-11, Dec. 1893.
2270   Wright, Conrad. "The sources of Mr. Howells's so-
        cialism." Science and society 2:514-17, Fall 1938.
2271   Wright, Nathalia. "The enigmatic past: Howells."
        In her American novelists in Italy, the discoverers:
        Allston to James. Phila., University of Pennsylvania
        Press, 1965. p.168-97.
2272   Wyatt, Edith F. "A national contribution." North
        American review 196:339-52, Sept. 1912.
        Also in her Great companions. N.Y., Appleton-
        Century, 1917. p.113-42.

2273   Young, Philip. "William Dean Howells." In Encyclo-
        pedia international. N.Y., Grolier, 1966. vol.9,
        p.21-22.

2274   Ziff, Larzer. "Literary hospitality: William Dean
        Howells." In his The American 1890's; the life and
        times of a lost generation. N.Y., Viking, 1966.
        p.24-49.

THESES AND DISSERTATIONS

2274a Adkins, Sue H. "Relationships between the sexes in
selected novels of William Dean Howells." Master's
thesis, Southwest Texas State College, 1967.
2275 Altenbernd, August L. "The influence of European
travel on the political and social outlook of Henry
Adams, William Dean Howells, and Mark Twain."
Ph. D. dissertation, Ohio State University, 1954. 290p.
2276 Arader, Harry F. "American novelists in Italy:
Hawthorne, Howells, James, and Crawford." Ph. D.
dissertation, University of Pennsylvania, 1953. 493p.
2277 Arms, George W. "The social criticism of William
Dean Howells." Ph. D. dissertation, New York University, 1939.
2278 Balcom, Lois. "The value of a comparative analysis
of an author's autobiographical and fictional writings
for interpretation of aspects of his personality; a study
based on selected works of William Dean Howells."
Ph. D. dissertation, New York University, 1955. 2v.
2279 Baldwin, Marilyn A. "An edition of W. D. Howells'
My Mark Twain: introduction and notes. Ph. D. dissertation, Rutgers University, 1963. 276p.
2280 Ballinger, Richard H. "A calendar of the William
Dean Howells collection in the Library of Harvard University." Ph. D. dissertation, Harvard University,
1953.
2281 Belcher, Hannah G. "William Dean Howells: a magazine writer (1860-1920)" Ph. D. dissertation, University of Michigan, 1942.
2282 Bennett, George N. "William Dean Howells: the
Boston years 1866-1888" Ph. D. dissertation, Yale
University, 1954.
2283 Blanche, Mary M. "Women in some representative
novels of William Dean Howells." M. A. thesis, St.
Louis University, 1950.
2284 Boardman, Arthur M. "Social status and morality
in the novels of William Dean Howells." Ph. D. dissertation, University of California, Berkeley, 1965.
185p.
2285 Boewe, Charles E. "Heredity in the writings of

Hawthorne, Holmes, and Howells." Ph. D. dissertation, University of Wisconsin, 1955.

2286 Brenni, Vito J. "William Dean Howells: A checklist of his poetry, 1852-1920." Master's thesis, State University College, New Paltz, 1970.

2287 Budd, Louis J. "William Dean Howells' relations with political parties." Ph. D. dissertation, University of Wisconsin, 1949.

2288 Burrows, David J. "Point-of-view in the novels of William Dean Howells." Ph. D. dissertation, New York University, 1964. 306p.

2289 Butler, Robert E. "William Dean Howells as editor of the Atlantic monthly." Ph. D. dissertation, Rutgers University, 1950.

2290 Carrington, George C., Jr. "William Dean Howells as a satirist." Ph. D. dissertation, Ohio State University, 1959. 330p.

2291 Carter, Everett. "William Dean Howells's theory of realism in fiction." Ph. D. dissertation, University of California at Los Angeles, 1947.

2292 Coholan, John F. "The portrayal of the moral world in the novels of William Dean Howells." Ph. D. dissertation, Notre Dame University, 1951.

2293 Cooke, Delmar G. "William Dean Howells: a critical study." Ph. D. dissertation, University of Illinois, 1917.

2294 Cumpiano, Marion W. "Howells' bridges: a study of literary techniques in the early novels exemplified by Their wedding journey and Indian summer." Ph. D. dissertation, Columbia University, 1969.

2294a Cuthbert, Martha M. "Criticism of fiction in the novels of William Dean Howells." Master's thesis, University of Tennessee, 1965.

2295 Daeschner, Naomi L. "The dramatic works of William Dean Howells." M. A. thesis, University of Kansas, 1934.

2296 Daniel, Maggie B. "A study of William Dean Howells attitude toward and criticism of the English and their literature." Ph. D. dissertation, University of Wisconsin, 1954.

2297 Dean, James L. "Howells' travel writing: theory and practice." Ph. D. dissertation, University of New Mexico, 1968. 208p.

2298 Dowling, Joseph A. "William Dean Howells and his relationship with the English: a study of opinion and literary reputation." Ph. D. dissertation, New York University, 1958. 323p.

2299   Dubé, Anthony. "William Dean Howells's theory and practice of drama." Ph.D. dissertation, Texas Technological College, 1967. 190p.

2300   Dykstra, Abraham J. "The utopian novels of Edward Bellamy and William Dean Howells." M.A. thesis, Ohio State University, 1962.

2301   Eberwine, Laura A. "The women of James and Howells, 1875-1885." M.A. thesis, Ohio State University, 1931.

2302   Eble, Kenneth E. "Character and conscience; a study of characterization and morality in the novels of William Dean Howells." Ph.D. dissertation, Columbia University, 1956.

2303   Edmondson, Elsie F.L. "The writer as hero in important American fiction since Howells." Ph.D. dissertation, University of Michigan, 1954.

2304   Ekstrom, William F. "The social idealism of William Morris and of William Dean Howells: a study of four utopian novels." Ph.D. dissertation, University of Illinois, 1947.

2305   Edelen, Dexter (Brother). "The moderate realism of William Dean Howells and of Newton Booth Tarkington." Ph.D. dissertation, St. John's University, 1955.

2306   Fischer, W.C., Jr. "The representation of mental processes in the early fiction of William Dean Howells and Henry James." Ph.D. dissertation, University of California, Berkeley, 1967.

2307   Fortenberry, George E. "The comic elements in the fiction of William Dean Howells." Ph.D. dissertation, University of Arkansas, 1967. 212p.

2308   Fox, Arnold B. "The progress of thought in William Dean Howells." Ph.D. dissertation, New York University, 1947.

2309   Fox, Harold D. "William Dean Howells: the literary theories in Criticism and fiction and their application in the novels of 1886 and 1887." Ph.D. dissertation, University of Southern California, 1969.

2310   Frazier, David L. "Love and self-realization in the fiction of William Dean Howells." Ph.D. dissertation, University of New Mexico, 1968. 192p.

2311   Fryckstedt, Olov W. "In quest of America: a study of Howells' early development as a novelist." Doctoral dissertation, University of Uppsala, Sweden, 1958. 287p.

2312   Gargano, James W. "William Dean Howells: his critical standards and their applications to his fiction." M.A. thesis, University of Buffalo, 1947.

2313 Garrow, Argyle S. "The short novels of William
      Dean Howells." Ph. D. dissertation, University of
      North Carolina, 1967. 243p.
2314 Getzel, J. W. "William Dean Howells: victim of
      transition." Master's thesis, Columbia University,
      1936.
2315 Goldfarb, Clare R. "Journey to Altruria: William
      Dean Howells's use of Tolstoy." Ph. D. dissertation,
      Indiana University, 1964. 233p.
2316 Gordon, Evelyn B. "The social consciousness of Wil-
      liam Dean Howells." M. A. thesis, Ohio State Uni-
      versity, 1936.
2317 Hamill, Elma G. and Hess, Kathleen G. "A dictionary
      of the characters in the novels of William Dean
      Howells." M. A. thesis, University of Kansas, 1928.
2318 Hanna, Willard A. "William Dean Howells." M. A.
      thesis, Ohio State University, 1937. 148 leaves.
2319 Hiatt, David F. "An edition of William Dean Howells's
      Literary friends and acquaintance, with an introduc-
      tion treating literary reminiscence as a genre." Ph. D.
      dissertation, University of New Mexico, 1960.
2320 Hirst, Anna B. "A test of realism." M. A. thesis,
      Ohio State University, 1900.
2321 Hiveley, Robert W. "The literary criteria of William
      Dean Howells as they are evident in his novels."
      M. A. thesis, University of Miami, 1954. 145p.
2322 Holzschlag, Phyllis-Joyce. "Howells's portraits of
      artists." Ph. D. dissertation, New York University,
      1964. 244p.
2323 Hough, Robert L., Jr. "William Dean Howells: so-
      cial commentator." Ph. D. dissertation, Stanford
      University, 1957. 242p.
2324 Hughey, Clare M. "An analysis of the characteriza-
      tions of women in the novels of William Dean Howells."
      M. A. thesis, Ohio State University, 1932. 78p.
2325 Iles, Robert L. "Limitations on individualism in the
      utopias of Bellamy and Howells." Master's thesis,
      Bowling Green State University, 1960.
2326 Joyce, Alice B. "The courtship theme in Howells'
      fiction." M. A. thesis, Ohio State University, 1960.
      68p.
2326a Karazincir, Tuge. "Henry Adams and William Dean
      Howells: two critics of the gilded age." Master's
      thesis, State University of New York at Buffalo, 1966.
2326b Knox, Nancy C. "The realist as short story writer:
      William Dean Howells." Ph. D. dissertation, Texas
      Christian University, 1970.

2327 Kolb, Harold M. "The illusion of life: American
      realism as a literary form in the writings of Mark
      Twain, Henry James and William Dean Howells in the
      mid-1880's." Ph. D. dissertation, Indiana University,
      1968. 211p.
2328 Konigsberger, Susanne. "Die Romantechnik von Wil-
      liam Dean Howells." Ph. D. dissertation, University
      of Berlin, 1933.
2329 Kreisel, Henry. "Aspects of modern realistic fiction
      in America." M. A. thesis, University of Toronto,
      1947. 117p.
2330 Krzyzanowski, Jerzy R. "Turgenev, Tolstoy and
      William Dean Howells: transitions in the development
      of a realist." Ph. D. dissertation, University of
      Michigan, 1965. 220p.
2331 Lauck, Ada B. "The influence of Tolstoy on William
      Dean Howells; a study particularly of ethical paral-
      lels." M. A. thesis, University of Iowa, 1925.
2332 Livingston, Audrey L. "A study of character and
      methods of characterization in a selection from the
      novels of William Dean Howells." M. A. thesis, Uni-
      versity of Toronto, 1959. 151p.
2333 Lowenherz, Robert J. "Mark Twain and William Dean
      Howells: a literary relationship." Ph. D. dissertation,
      New York University, 1954. 261p.
2333a Lynch, John E. "From narration to dramatic char-
      acterization: the impact of drama on Howells' literary
      development between 1870-1879." Master's thesis,
      San Diego State College, 1967.
2334 McBride, Sara. "Setting in the novels of William Dean
      Howells." M. A. thesis, University of Iowa, 1919.
2335 McCluskey, John E. "Realism and romance in the
      late Victorian period; literary criticism in England
      and America." Ph. D. dissertation, Michigan State
      University, 1968. 249p.
2336 McMurray, William J. "Intention and actuality in the
      fiction of William Dean Howells." Ph. D. disserta-
      tion, University of New Mexico, 1961. 254p.
2337 Malone, Clifton J. "The hitherto uncollected critical
      opinions of William Dean Howells." Ph. D. disserta-
      tion, University of Oklahoma, 1947.
2338 Mao, Nathan K. "William Dean Howells on evil."
      Ph. D. dissertation, University of Wisconsin, 1966.
      347p.
2339 Marshall, Carl L. "American critical attitudes toward
      the fiction of William Dean Howells." Ph. D. disserta-
      tion, Ohio State University, 1954. 279p.

2340   Marston, Frederic C., Jr. "The early life of William
       Dean Howells: a chronicle 1837-1871." Ph.D. dis-
       sertation, Brown University, 1944.
2341   Mathews, James W. "Hawthorne and Howells: the
       middle way in American fiction." Ph.D. dissertation,
       University of Tennessee, 1960. 301p.
2342   Mayer, Charles W. "Satire and humor in William
       Dean Howells' fiction." M.A. thesis, Ohio State Uni-
       versity, 1954. 88p.
2343   Miles, Elton R. "William Dean Howells: the impact
       of science." Ph.D. dissertation, University of Texas,
       1952.
2344   Miller, Charles T. "Howells's theory of the novel."
       Ph.D. dissertation, University of Chicago, 1947. 152p.
2345   Miller, Raymond A., Jr. "Representative tragic
       heroines in the work of Brown, Hawthorne, Howells,
       James, and Dreiser." Ph.D. dissertation, University
       of Wisconsin, 1957. 470p.
2346   Mills, Richard P. "Traveler to Altruria: Max East-
       man and the statesmen of the new order." M.A.
       thesis, Columbia University, 1967. 85p.
2347   Minkiel, Adam F., "William Dean Howells and the
       one-act play." M.A. thesis, St. John's University,
       1945. 37p.
2348   Mitchell, Mary. "A study of the early novels of Wil-
       liam Dean Howells." M.S. thesis, Columbia Univer-
       sity, 1964.
2349   Molaison, Woodrow J. "William Dean Howells and the
       doctrine of complicity." M.A. thesis, Auburn Uni-
       versity, 1961. 73p.
2349a Moldenhauer, Mary L. "An analysis of the biograph-
       ical basis for the political, economic, social and
       literary theories of William Dean Howells." Master's
       thesis, University of Omaha, 1966.
2350   Moore, Howard K. "William Dean Howells as a lit-
       erary critic." Ph.D. dissertation, Boston University,
       1950.
2351   Munford, Howard M. "The genesis and early develop-
       ment of the basic attitudes of William Dean Howells."
       Ph.D. dissertation, Harvard University, 1951.
2352   Munson, Nelson A. "A closer look at the realism of
       William Dean Howells." M.A. thesis, Washington
       University, 1951. 45p.
2352a Nelson, Bertil C. "Realist and romanticist: The
       paradox of William Dean Howells' social realism."
       Master's thesis, Southern Connecticut State College,
       1967.

2353 Nordloh, David J. "A critical edition of W. D. Howells'
      Years of my youth." Ph. D. dissertation, Indiana Uni-
      versity, 1969. 450p.
2354 Obrecht, Denise M. "William Dean Howells." Ph. D.
      dissertation, University of Paris, 1950.
2355 Patterson, Marjorie S. "William Dean Howells's re-
      lation to Spanish literature." M. A. thesis, University
      of Kansas, 1925.
2356 Pattison, Eugene H. "William Dean Howells' The
      leatherwood god: genesis, artistry, reception."
      Ph. D. dissertation, University of Michigan, 1963.
      305p.
2357 Payne, Alma J. "The American family: William Dean
      Howells." Ph. D. dissertation, Western Reserve Uni-
      versity, 1956. 429p.
2358 Perkins, George B., Jr. "The conflict between coun-
      try and city in the novels of William Dean Howells."
      Ph. D. dissertation, Cornell University, 1960. 148p.
2359 Pierson, Helen H. "Howells' passionate women."
      Master's thesis, Indiana University of Pennsylvania,
      1969. 78p.
2360 Reilly, Cyril A. "William Dean Howells: a critical
      study of A modern instance and Indian summer."
      Ph. D. dissertation, University of Notre Dame, 1954.
      322p.
2361 Rudolph, Edwin P. "A study of the evidences of the
      puritanism in the novels of William Dean Howells."
      M. A. thesis, Ohio State University, 1944.
2362 Schieber, Alois J. "Autobiographies of American
      novelists: Twain, Howells, James, Adams, and
      Garland." Ph. D. dissertation, University of Wiscon-
      sin, 1957.
2363 Schneider, Clarence E. "The serialized novels of
      William Dean Howells 1878-1890." Ph. D. disserta-
      tion, University of Southern California, 1957.
2364 Sharpe, D. R. "William Dean Howells theory of real-
      ism in prose fiction." M. A. thesis, University of
      North Carolina, 1944.
2364a Smith, Dorothy B. "Howells' attitude toward the
      middle west and middle western material." M. A.
      thesis, University of Chicago, 1929. 123p.
2364b Snook, Donald. "Humor in the early novels of Wil-
      liam Dean Howells." Master's thesis, Auburn Uni-
      versity, 1966.
2365 Sokoloff, Benjamin A. "William Dean Howells: the
      Ohio years in his novels." Ph. D. dissertation, Uni-
      versity of Illinois, 1956. 211p.

2366 Spencer, Anna R. "The realism of William Dean
      Howells." M.A. thesis, University of Kansas, 1917.
2367 Stanton, Elizabeth B. "William Dean Howells: a
      study of his literary theories and practices during his
      Atlantic monthly years 1866-1881." Ph.D. disserta-
      tion, Ohio State University, 1943.
2367a Steele, Sue. "The structure of the international mood
      novel as revealed in Nathaniel Hawthorne's The marble
      faun, Henry James' The portrait of a lady and William
      Dean Howells' Indian Summer." Master's thesis,
      Eastern Kentucky University, 1967.
2368 Stern, Jerome H. "William Dean Howells: the later
      phase." Ph.D. dissertation, University of North
      Carolina, 1967. 259p.
2369 Stiles, Marion L. "Travel in the life and writings of
      William Dean Howells." Ph.D. dissertation, Univer-
      sity of Texas, 1946.
2370 Stronks, James B. "The early midwestern realists
      and William Dean Howells." Ph.D. dissertation, Uni-
      versity of Chicago, 1956.
2371 Thomas, Jonathan. "Howells to the English: the con-
      tributions of William Dean Howells to the London
      periodical Literature." Ph.D. dissertation, Rutgers
      University, 1966. 397p.
2372 Titus, Catherine F. "Depiction of women in the novels
      of William Dean Howells." Ph.D. dissertation, Uni-
      versity of Missouri, 1955. 193p.
2373 Turner, Peggy. "William Dean Howells: dramatist."
      M.S. thesis, North Texas State College, 1954. 79p.
2374 Walts, Robert W. "William Dean Howells and the
      House of Harper." Ph.D. dissertation, Rutgers Uni-
      versity, 1954.
2375 Warlick, Henry C. "William Dean Howells interest in
      drama." M.A. thesis, University of North Carolina,
      1953.
2376 Weber, Eva. "The literary code of William Dean
      Howells." M.A. thesis, University of Iowa, 1923.
2377 Weisl, Reyna L. "Howells and England." M.A.
      thesis, Columbia University, 1955. 87p.
2378 White, Howard H. "The image of society in the novels
      of William Dean Howells." Ph.D. dissertation, Uni-
      versity of Minnesota, 1958. 243p.
2379 Wilson, Benjamin H., Jr. "Quiet realism: women
      writers in the William Dean Howells' tradition."
      Ph.D. dissertation, University of North Carolina,
      1965. 436p.

2380   Wilson, Jack H. "George Eliot in America, her vogue
        and influence, 1858-1900." Ph.D. dissertation, Uni-
        versity of North Carolina, 1965.
2381   Woodress, James L., Jr. "The Italian phase of Wil-
        liam Dean Howells." Ph.D. dissertation, Duke Uni-
        versity, 1950.
2382   Zuber, Lucy L. "William Dean Howells in Columbus
        1851-1852, 1857, 1858-1861." M.A. thesis, Ohio
        State University, 1954.   76p.

REVIEWS OF HOWELLS' BOOKS

2383 ALBANY DEPOT
   Harper's monthly 83: sup. 2, Nov. 1891
2384 ANNIE KILBURN
   Harper's monthly 83:162, sup. 4, June 1891
2385 APRIL HOPES
   Harper's monthly 83:486, sup. 3-4, Aug. 1891
2386 BETWEEN THE DARK AND THE DAYLIGHT
   Bookman 26:275, Nov. 1907
   Spectator 99:717, Nov. 9, 1907
2387 A BOY'S TOWN
   Harper's monthly 81:810 sup. 1-2, Oct. 1890
   Nation 51:385, Nov. 13, 1890
2388 CERTAIN DELIGHTFUL ENGLISH TOWNS
   Atheneum, April 13, 1907, p. 435
   London times 6:100, Mar. 29, 1907
   Spectator 98:450, Mar. 23, 1907
2389 CHRISTMAS EVERY DAY AND OTHER STORIES
   Harper's monthly 86:324, sup. 3, Jan. 1893
2390 COAST OF BOHEMIA
   Critic 25(n. s. 22):2, July 7, 1894
   Dial 15:340-41, Dec. 1, 1893
   Harper's monthly 88:326, sup. 3-4, Jan. 1894
   Nation 57:394-95, Nov. 23, 1893
2391 A COUNTERFEIT PRESENTIMENT
   Pennsylvania monthly 9:400
2392 CRITICISM AND FICTION
   Atheneum 98:223, Aug. 15, 1891
   Atlantic monthly 68:566-69, Oct. 1891
   Critic (ns16):13, July 11, 1891
   Dial 12:144, Sept. 1891
   Harper's monthly 83:486, sup. 2-3, Aug. 1891
   Nation 53:73, July 23, 1891
   Spectator 67:294-96, Aug. 29, 1891
2393 THE DAUGHTER OF THE STORAGE
   Boston transcript, July 1, 1916, p. 6
   Nation 102:622, June 8, 1916
   New York times 21:117, Apr. 2, 1916
   Publishers' weekly 89:1315, Apr. 15, 1916
   Spectator 117:20, July 1, 1916
   Springfield republican, Sept. 17, 1916, p. 15

2394 THE DAY OF THEIR WEDDING
        Bookman 3:258-60, May 1896
        Critic 28(ns25):307, May 2, 1896
        Dial 20:335, June 1, 1896
        Harper's monthly 92:490, sup. 1, Feb. 1896
2395 DR. BREEN'S PRACTICE
        Spectator 55:665
        America 3:187
        Dial (Chicago) 2:214
2396 EVENING DRESS
        Harper's monthly 87:810, sup. 3, Oct. 1893
2397 FAMILIAR SPANISH TRAVELS
        Bookman 38:387, Dec. 1913
        Nation 97:567, Dec. 11, 1913
        New York times book review 18:679, Nov. 30, 1913
2398 FEARFUL RESPONSIBILITY
        Dial (Chicago) 2:85
2399 FENNEL AND RUE
        Bookman 27:281, May 1908
        Nation 86:309, Apr. 2, 1908
        New York times book review 13:151, Mar. 21, 1908
        Review of reviews 37:760, June 1908
        Spectator 100:710, May 2, 1908
2400 A FOREGONE CONCLUSION
        North American review 120:207
2401 A HAZARD OF NEW FORTUNES
        Atlantic monthly 65:563-67, Apr. 1890
        Catholic world 51:119-22, Apr. 1890
        Critic ns13:13-14, Jan. 11, 1890
        Harper's monthly 80:313-14, Jan. 1890
        Nation 50:454, June 5, 1890
        Spectator 64:342-43, Mar. 8, 1890
        Westminster 134:89, July 1890
2402 HEROINES OF FICTION
        Dial 31:506-07, Dec. 16, 1901
        Nation 73:479
        Independent 53:3087-88
        Atheneum, Mar. 8, 1902, p. 301
        Living age 232:760-64, Mar. 22, 1902
2403 HITHER AND THITHER IN GERMANY
        Dial 68:666, May 1920
        Nation 110:661, May 15, 1920
        Springfield republican, Feb. 24, 1920, p. 6
2404 IMAGINARY INTERVIEWS
        Spectator 105:898, Nov. 26, 1910
2405 IMPERATIVE DUTY
        Atheneum 99:211, Feb. 13, 1892

2415 LONDON FILMS
        Bookman (London) 29:140, Dec. 1905
2416 MISS BELLARD'S INSPIRATION
        Atheneum, July 8, 1905, p. 41
        Bookman 21:610, Aug. 1905
        Critic 47:452, Nov. 1905
        Dial 39:115, Sept. 1, 1905
        Literary digest 31:187, Aug. 5, 1905
        London times 4:209, June 30, 1905
        Nation 81:101, Aug. 3, 1905
        Public opinion 39:283, Aug. 26, 1905
        Spectator 95:124, July 22, 1905
2417 MRS. FARRELL
        Boston transcript, Aug. 31, 1921, p. 7
        Independent 107:18, Oct. 1, 1921
        Literary review, Sept. 10, 1921, p. 3
        New York times book review, Sept. 4, 1921, p. 3
        Outlook 129:186, Oct. 5, 1921
        Springfield republican, Dec. 11, 1921, p. 11a
2418 A MODERN INSTANCE
        Atheneum 2:461
        Atlantic monthly 50:709
        America 5:74
        Saturday review 54:548
        Spectator 55:1658
2419 THE MOTHER AND THE FATHER
        Independent 67:1318, Dec. 9, 1909
        New York times book review 14:342, May 29, 1909
        Review of reviews 40:123, July 1909
2420 MY LITERARY PASSIONS
        Atlantic monthly 76:701-03, Nov. 1895
        Bookman 1:400-02, July 1895
        Critic 27(ns24):244, Oct. 19, 1895
        Dial 19:78, Aug. 1, 1895
        Harper's monthly 91:486
        Nation 61:156, Aug. 29, 1895
2421 MY MARK TWAIN
        Dial 49:238, Oct. 1, 1910
        Literary digest 41:553, Oct. 1, 1910
        Nation 91:395, Oct. 27, 1910
        New York times 15:557, Oct. 8, 1910
        Spectator 105:864, Nov. 19, 1910
2422 MY YEAR IN A LOG CABIN
        Harper's monthly 87:648, sup. 4, Sept. 1893
2423 NEW LEAF MILLS
        Atlantic monthly 112:701, Nov. 1913
        Boston transcript, Mar. 5, 1913, p. 22

Dial 54:463, June 1, 1913
Independent 74:1302, June 5, 1913
Nation 96:415, Apr. 24, 1913
New York sun, Mar. 1, 1913, p. 3
New York times 18:111, Mar. 2, 1913
Spectator 110:584, Apr. 5, 1913
Springfield republican, Mar. 27, 1913, p. 5

2424 A PAIR OF PATIENT LOVERS
Atheneum, Aug. 31, 1901, p. 282
Harper's monthly 95:832-51, Nov. 1897

2425 A PARTING AND A MEETING
Critic 28(ns25):405, June 6, 1896
Harper's monthly 93:324, sup. 3, July 1896

2426 PARTING FRIENDS
Independent 71:597, Sept. 14, 1911
New York times 16:520, Aug. 27, 1911

2427 POEMS OF TWO FRIENDS (WITH JOHN J. PIATT)
Outlook 59:131-32, May 14, 1898

2428 PREVIOUS ENGAGEMENT
Harper's monthly 94:818, sup. 1, Apr. 1897

2429 QUALITY OF MERCY
Atheneum 99:339, Mar. 12, 1892
Atlantic monthly 69:702-04, May 1892
Critic 20(ns17):262, May 7, 1892
Dial 13:102, Aug. 1892
Harper's monthly 85:162; sup. 2, 316-17, June 1892
Nation 55:33-34, July 14, 1892

2430 QUESTIONABLE SHAPES
Critic 43:374-75, Oct. 1903
Atheneum, July 11, 1903, p. 59
Independent 55:1932-33, Aug. 13, 1903

2431 RAGGED LADY
Academy 56:627
Atheneum 113:719, June 10, 1899
Bookman (London) 16:168, Sept. 1899
Dial 27:20-21, July 1, 1899
Harper's monthly 98:830, sup. 1, Apr. 1899
Spectator 82:647, May 6, 1899

2432 THE RISE OF SILAS LAPHAM
Andover review 4:417
Critic 7:224
Literary world (Boston) 16:299
Saturday review 60:517

2433 ROMAN HOLIDAYS AND OTHERS
Dial 45:409, Dec. 1, 1908
New York times 13:774, Dec. 12, 1908
Spectator 102:703-04, May 1909

2434 THE SEEN AND THE UNSEEN AT STRATFORD-ON-
      AVON
          Boston transcript, May 16, 1914
          Catholic world 100:550, Jan. 15, 1914
          Current opinion 57:51, July 1914
          Dial 56:470, June 1, 1914
          Nation 98:630, May 28, 1914
          New York times 19:225, May 10, 1914
          Outlook 108:281, Sept. 30, 1914
2435 SEVEN ENGLISH CITIES
          Dial 47:459, Dec. 1, 1909
          Spectator 104:151-52, Jan. 29, 1910
2436 THE SHADOW OF A DREAM
          Atheneum 95:828, June 28, 1890
          Critic 17(ns14):44, July 26, 1890
          Harper's monthly 81:324, sup. 1, July 1890
          Nation 51:252-53, Sept. 25, 1890
          Spectator 65:213-15, Aug. 16, 1890
2437 THE SON OF ROYAL LANGBRITH
          Bookman 20:372-74, Dec. 1904
          Critic 46:184, Feb. 1905
          Dial 37:310-11, Nov. 16, 1904
          Nation 79:419, Nov. 24, 1904
          Reader 5:130-31, Dec. 1904
          Spectator 94:22, Jan. 7, 1905
2438 STOPS OF VARIOUS QUILLS
          Bookman 2:525-27, Feb. 1896
          Harper's monthly 92:166, sup. 3, Dec. 1895
2439 THE STORY OF A PLAY
          Atheneum 112:252, Aug. 20, 1898
          Book buyer 17:146
          Bookman 7:515-17, Aug. 1898
          Dial 25:21, July 1, 1898
          Harper's monthly 97:496, sup. 1, Aug. 1898
          Nation 67:299, Oct. 20, 1898
          Spectator 81:22, July 2, 1898
2440 THEIR SILVER WEDDING JOURNEY
          Independent 52:257-58, Jan. 25, 1900
          Nation 70:245, Mar. 29, 1900
          Westminster 143:226-29, Feb. 1895
2441 THROUGH THE EYE OF THE NEEDLE
          Atheneum, June 29, 1907, p. 786
          Bookman 25:394, June 1907
          Independent 62:1207, May 23, 1907
          Literary digest 34:885, June 1, 1907
          London times 6:165, May 24, 1907

Springfield republican, Dec. 4, 1916, p. 6
Times literary supplement, Dec. 7, 1916, p. 585

2450 The Altrurian romances. Introduction and notes to the text by Clara and Rudolf Kirk. Text established by Scott Bennett. Bloomington, Indiana University Press, 1968. 494p. (A selected edition of W. D. Howells, v. 20.)
Contains A traveler from Altruria, Letters of an Altrurian traveller, and Through the eye of the needle.

2451 Annie Kilburn. With an introduction by William B. Cairns. N.Y., Harper, 1919. 331p. (Harper's modern classics.)

2452 Boy life; stories and readings selected from the works of William Dean Howells and arranged for supplementary reading in elementary schools by Percival Chubb. N.Y., Harper, 1909. (Harper's modern series of supplementary readers for the elementary schools.)

2452a A chance acquaintance. Introduction and notes to the text by Jonathan Thomas and David J. Nordloh. Text established by Ronald Gottesman, David J. Nordloh and Jonathan Thomas. Bloomington, Indiana University Press, 1971. 189p. (A selected edition of W. D. Howells, vol. 6.)

2453 Character and comment selected from the novels of William Dean Howells by Minnie Macoun. Boston, Houghton Mifflin, 1889. 162p.

2454 Christmas every day; a story told a child by W. D. Howells with illustrations and decorations by Harriet Roosevelt Richards. N.Y., Harper, 1908.

2455 The coast of Bohemia. Biographical edition. N.Y., Harper, 1899. 340p.

2456 A counterfeit presentiment. 5th ed. Boston, Ticknor, 1877. 199p.

2457 A hazard of new fortunes. With a new introduction by George W. Arms. N.Y., Dutton, 1952. 552p. (Everyman's library.)

2458 A hazard of new fortunes. With an introduction by Van Wyck Brooks. N.Y., Bantam Books, 1960.

2459 A hazard of new fortunes. With an introduction by Alexander Harvey. N.Y., Boni and Liveright, 1889.

2460 A hazard of new fortunes. With an introduction by Tony
      Tanner. London, Oxford, 1967.
2461 A hazard of new fortunes. N.Y., New American Li-
      brary of World Literature, 1965.
      Contains an afterword by Benjamin De Mott.
2462 Indian summer. With an introduction by William M.
      Gibson. N.Y., Dutton, 1951. (Everyman's library.)
2463 Italian journeys. With illustrations by Joseph Pennell.
      Cambridge, Mass., Riverside Press, 1901. 380p.
2464 The leatherwood god ... with illustrations by Henry
      Raleigh. N.Y., Century, 1916. 236p.
2465 Life of Abraham Lincoln; this campaign biography cor-
      rected by the hand of Abraham Lincoln in the summer
      of 1860 is reproduced here with careful attention to
      the appearance of the original volume. Springfield,
      Illinois, Abraham Lincoln Association, 1938. 17-94p.
      The facsimile is a part of the original edition which
      has title: Lives and speeches of Abraham Lincoln
      and Hannibal Hamlin. Columbus, Follett, Foster,
      1860. Twelve hundred fifty copies were published.
2466 Life of Abraham Lincoln. Bloomington, Indiana Univer-
      sity Press, 1960. 17-94p.
      "This campaign biography corrected by the hand of
      Abraham Lincoln in the summer of 1860 is repro-
      duced here with careful attention to the appearance
      of the original volume. The book is a reproduction
      of Samuel C. Parks' copy of a work with title page.
      Lives and speeches of Abraham Lincoln and Hannibal
      Hamlin. Columbus, Follett, Foster, 1860.
2466a Literary friends and acquaintance; a personal retro-
      spect of American authorship. Edited by David F.
      Hiatt and others. Bloomington, Indiana University
      Press, 1968. 397p. (A selected edition of W.D.
      Howells, v.32.)
2466b A modern instance. Edited with introduction and notes
      by William M. Gibson. Boston, Houghton Mifflin,
      1957. 362p.
2466c A modern instance. N.Y., New American Library of
      World Literature, 1964. (Signet classic.)
      Contains an afterword by Wallace Brockway.
2467 My literary passions [and] Criticism and fiction. N.Y.,
      Harper, 1911. 292p.
2468 "An edition of W.D. Howells' My Mark Twain." In-
      troduction and notes by Marilyn Austin Baldwin. Ph.D.
      dissertation, Rutgers University, 1963. 276p.
2469 My Mark Twain: reminiscences and criticisms.
      Edited with an introduction by Marilyn Austin Baldwin.

Baton Rouge, Louisiana State University, 1967.
189p.
2470 Poems. Boston, Ticknor, 1886. 223p.
2471 The rise of Silas Lapham. With an introduction by
George Arms. N.Y., Rinehart, 1949. 394p. (Rinehart editions, no.19.)
2472 The rise of Silas Lapham. Edited with an introduction
by Edwin H. Cady. Boston, Houghton Mifflin, 1957.
298p.
2473 The rise of Silas Lapham. With an introduction by
Everett Carter. N.Y., Harper, 1958. 380p. (Harper's
modern classics.)
2474 The rise of Silas Lapham. With an introduction by
Everett Carter, and a bibliography. N.Y., Harper and
Row, 1965. 333p. (A Perennial classic.)
2475 The rise of Silas Lapham. With an introduction by
Harry H. Clark. N.Y., Random House, 1951. 324p.
(Modern library of the world's best books.)
2476 The rise of Silas Lapham. With an introduction by
Henry Steele Commager, and illustrations by Mimi
Korach. N.Y., Printed for the members of the Limited Editions Club, 1961. 365p.
2477 The rise of Silas Lapham. With an introduction by
Rudolf and Clara Kirk. N.Y., Collier Books, 1962.
2478 The rise of Silas Lapham. With biographical illustrations and pictures of the selling of the book, together
with an introduction by C. David Mead. N.Y., Dodd,
Mead, 1964. 367p. (Great illustrated classics.)
2479 The rise of Silas Lapham. With an introduction by
Howard Mumford. N.Y., Oxford, 1948. 398p.
(World's classics.)
2480 The rise of Silas Lapham. Centenary edition. With
an introduction by Booth Tarkington. Boston, Houghton
Mifflin, 1937.
2481 The rise of Silas Lapham; new edition, with notes,
questions, topics for themes and suggestions for dramatization, by James M. Spinning. Boston, Houghton
Mifflin, 1928. 546p. (Riverside literature series.)
2481a The rise of Silas Lapham. Introductory biographical
sketch and selection of commentaries by Robert L.
Hough. N.Y., Bantam, 1971 [c1965]. 366p.
2481b The rise of Silas Lapham. Introduction and notes to
the text by Walter J. Meserve. Text established by
Walter J. Meserve and David J. Nordloh. Bloomington, Indiana University Press, 1971. 402p. (A selected edition of W.D. Howells, vol.12.)

2482   The rise of Silas Lapham.   N.Y., New American Li-
       brary of World Literature, 1963.   350p.   (Signet
       classic.)
       Contains an afterword by Harry T. Moore.
2483   The rise of Silas Lapham.   N.Y., Washington Square
       Press, 1966.   314, 47p.   (Collateral classic, CC705.)
       Contains a "Reader's supplement to The rise of
       Silas Lapham," 47 pages at end.
2484   The rise of Silas Lapham; simplified and adapted by
       Robert J. Dixson in collaboration with Lewis T. Davis.
       With exercises for study and vocabulary drill.   N.Y.,
       Regents Publishing Co., 1954.   123p.   (American
       classics, book 8.)
2485   A selected edition of W.D. Howells.   Bloomington, In-
       diana University Press, 1968.
       Edwin H. Cady, general editor; Ronald Gottesman,
       textual editor; Scott Bennett and David J. Nordloh,
       associate textual editors.   The edition is appearing
       volume by volume.   The titles are noted in this
       section.
2486   The shadow of a dream, and An imperative duty.
       Edited with notes and introduction by Edwin H. Cady.
       N.Y., Twayne, 1962.   235p.
2486a The shadow of a dream; and, An imperative duty.
       Introduction and notes to the text by Martha Banta.
       Text established by Martha Banta and others.   Bloom-
       ington, Indiana University Press, 1970.   2v. in 1.
2487   The son of Royal Langbrith.   Introduction and notes
       to the text by David Burrows.   Text established by
       David Burrows, Ronald Gottesman, and David J.
       Nordloh.   Bloomington, Indiana University Press,
       1969.   318p.   (A selected edition of W.D. Howells,
       v. 26.)
2488   Suburban sketches.   New and enl. ed.   Boston, Os-
       good, 1872.
2489   Their wedding journey ... with an additional chapter
       on Niagara revisited.   Illustrations by Augustus Hop-
       pin.   Boston, Houghton Mifflin, 1888.   319p.
2490   Their wedding journey.   Edited by John K. Reeves.
       Bloomington, Indiana University Press, 1968.   (A
       selected edition of W.D. Howells, v.5.)
2491   A traveler from Altruria.   With an introduction by
       Howard M. Jones.   N.Y., Sagamore Press, 1957.
       211p.
2492   Tuscan cities.   Illustrations from drawings and etch-
       ings of Joseph Pennell and others.   Boston, Ticknor,
       1886 [1885].   251p.

2493 Venetian life. 2d ed. N.Y., Hurd and Houghton,
     1867. 401p.
     Contains a new chapter on the history of Venetian
     commerce.

2494 Venetian life. New and enl. ed. Boston, Osgood,
     1872. 437p.
     Reprint except for "Our last year in Venice,"
     p. 399-434.

2495 Venetian life ... with illustrations from original water
     colors.... Cambridge, Mass., Riverside Press,
     1892 [1891]. 2v.
     Two hundred fifty copies were printed.

2496 Venetian life. Rev. and enl. ed. with twenty illustra-
     tions in color by Edmund H. Garrett. Boston,
     Houghton Mifflin, 1907. 423p.

2497 Selected writings. Edited with an introduction by
     Henry Steele Commager. N.Y., Random House,
     1950. 946p.
     Contains The rise of Silas Lapham, A modern in-
     stance, A boy's town, and My Mark Twain.

2498 William Dean Howells; representative selections. In-
     troduction, bibliography, and notes by Clara Marburg
     Kirk and Rudolf Kirk. N.Y., American Book Co.,
     1950. 394p. (American writers series.)

2499 "A critical edition of W.D. Howells' Years of my
     youth." By David J. Nordloh. Ph.D. dissertation,
     Indiana University, 1969. 450p.

2500 The Writings of William Dean Howells, Library edition.
     N.Y., Harper, 1906. 6v.
     Thirty-two volumes were projected but only six
     were published. Vol. I: My literary passions
     [and] Criticism of fiction. Vol. II: The landlord
     at Lion's Head. Vol. III: Literature and life.
     Vol. IV: London films and Certain delightful Eng-
     lish towns. Vol. V: Literary friends and ac-
     quaintance. Vol. VI: A hazard of new fortunes.
     Each volume contains a new introduction. Con-
     cerning this Library edition Robert W. Walts wrote
     "William Dean Howells and his 'Library edition'."
     Papers of the Bibliographical Society of America
     52:283-94, 4th quarter 1958.

TRANSLATIONS OF HOWELLS' WORKS

2501 Louis Fréchette ... une rencontre roman de deux touristes sur le Saint-Laurent et le Saguenay. Montréal, Société des Publications Françaises, 1897. 132p. [A chance acquaintance.]

2502 Pflichtgefühl. Tr. by A. Wiedemann. Stuttgart, Engelhorn, 1895. 159p. [A fearful responsibility and An imperative duty.]

2503 Voreilige Schlüsse. Tr. by Minna Wesselhoeft. Stuttgart, Auerbach, 1876. 327p. [A foregone conclusion.]

2504 La passagère de l'Aroostook, roman anglais. Paris, Hachette, 1884. 252p. [The lady of the Aroostook.]

2505 Bühnenspiel ohne Coulissen. Tr. by Heichen-Abenheim. Stuttgart, Abenheim, 1878. 443p. [Mrs. Farrell.]

2506 La fortune de Silas Lapham, roman américain. Traduit ... par Mariech. Paris, Hachette, 1890. 370p. [The rise of Silas Lapham.]

2507 Le fortune di Silas Lapham. Traduzione e introduzione di Cesare G. Cecioni. Opere Nuove, 1962. 484p. [The rise of Silas Lapham.]

2508 Di grosse Versuchung. Tr. by Eduard Klein. Berlin, Volk und Velt, 1958. 511p. [The rise of Silas Lapham.]

2509 Lune de Miel. Tr. by Gustave Van der Veken. Kapellen-Anvers, W. Beckers, 1968. 265p. [Their wedding journey.]

PORTRAITS

2510 Bookman 38:123, Oct. 1913.

2511 Bookman (London) 16:168, Sept. 1899.

2512 Collier's magazine 58:12, Nov. 18, 1916.

2513 Harper's weekly 40:655-56, July 4, 1896. (Contains an engraving by E. Schladitz.)

2514 Harper's weekly 47:579, Apr. 1911.

2515 Lamp 28:26-31, Feb. 1904. (Contains a full-page picture showing Howells sitting with book in hands, taken from a photo by Zaida Ben-Yusuf.)

2516 Metropolitan magazine 30:673, Sept. 1909.

2517 McClure 20:59, Nov. 1902.

2518 Printing art 31:118, Apr. 1918.

2519 Saturday review of literature 16:4, Aug. 7, 1937.

2520 Time 36:80, Aug. 19, 1940.

2521 Life in letters of William Dean Howells. Edited by Mildred Howells. Garden City, N.Y., Doubleday, Doran, 1928. vol. 1, p.10.

2522 Howells, William D. My literary passions. Criticism and fiction. N.Y., Harper, 1910. Opposite p.4. (Howells at 18 years of age.) Frontispiece has photograph of Howells at 70 years of age.

2523 Harper, Joseph H. The house of Harper. N.Y., Harper, 1912. Opposite p.328.

BIBLIOGRAPHIES

2524   Aaron, Daniel. "Howells' 'Maggie'." New England quarterly 38:85-90, Mar. 1965.

2525   Arms, George and Gibson, William M. "Selected bibliography." In William Dean Howells; representative selections. N.Y., American Book Co., 1950. p. clxviii-cxcix.

2526   Baatz, Wilmer H. "William Dean Howells' opera." University of Rochester bulletin 10:34-36, Winter 1955.

2527   Ballinger, Richard H. "A calendar of the William Dean Howells collection in the library of Harvard University." Ph. D. dissertation, Harvard University, 1953.

2528   Bennett, Scott. "Concealed printing in William Dean Howells." Papers of the Bibliographical Society of America 61:56-60, Jan. 1967.

2529   Blanck, Jacob N. "William Dean Howells." In his Bibliography of American literature. New Haven, Yale University, 1963. vol. 4, p. 384-448.
Contains a full description of the first editions and lists a great many of his short writings, including introductions to books, anecdotes, speeches, letters, poems, etc.; locates many of them in libraries; does not include periodical writings except when they later appeared in books. Contains a short list of biographical, bibliographical, and critical works.

2530   Blodgett, Harold. "A note on Mark Twain's Library of humor." American literature 10:78-80, Mar. 1938.

2531   Brenni, Vito J. "William Dean Howells: a checklist of his poetry, 1852-1920." Master's thesis, State University College, New Paltz, N.Y., 1970. 13p.

2532   Burrows, David J. "Manuscript and typescript material relating to Howells's The son of Royal Langbrith." Journal of the Rutgers University Library 29:56-58, 1966.

2533   Cady, Edwin H. "Howells bibliography: a "find" and a clarification." Studies in bibliography 12:230-33, 1959.

2534 _____ "William Dean Howells in Italy: some bibliographic notes." Symposium 7:147-53, May 1953.

2535 Cameron, Kenneth W. "Literary manuscripts in the
Trinity College Library." Emerson Society quarterly,
no. 14, p. 18, First quarter 1959.

2536 Carpenter, Kenneth E. "Copyright renewal deposit
copies." Papers of the Bibliographical Society of
America 60:473-74, Oct. 1966.

2537 Foster, J. Herbert. The library of the late J. Herbert Foster of Providence, R. I. The most extensive
collection in existence of first editions of writings of
William Dean Howells, nearly every volume auto-
graphed or inscribed by the author. N. Y., The
Anderson Galleries, 1922.

2538 Gibson, William M. and Arms, George. A bibliography of William Dean Howells. N. Y., New York
Public Library, 1948. 182p.
    The bibliography is a chronological list of his
    writings in both book and periodical form. Full
    description is given for first editions. For publi-
    cations previously published original source is
    given. Contains a selected list of criticism. The
    bibliography originally appeared in the New York
    Public Library bulletin, Sept. 1946-Feb. 1947.
    Some revisions and corrections were made.

2539 Graham, Philip. "American first editions at Texas
University xi William Dean Howells (1837-1920)" Li-
brary chronicle of the University of Texas 6:17-21,
Spring 1958.

2540 Howells, William D. "Howells's unpublished prefaces."
Edited by George Arms. New England quarterly 17:
580-91, Dec. 1944.
    Contains prefaces for The coast of Bohemia and
    The story of a play; Heroines of fiction; The shad-
    ow of a dream; The son of Royal Langbrith; A
    traveler from Altruria and Through the eye of the
    needle.

2541 The Howells sentinel. New Brunswick, N. J., Rutgers
University.
    Issued irregularly in mimeograph form beginning
    in 1951. Compiled by Rudolf and Clara Kirk for
    The Howells Group of the Modern Language Asso-
    ciation.

2542 Johnson, Merle. "William Dean Howells." In his
American first editions. 4th ed. Rev. and enl. by
Jacob Blanck. N. Y., Bowker, 1942. p. 268-73.

2543 Kirk, Rudolf and Kirk, Clara. "Poems of two
friends." Journal of the Rutgers University Library

4:33-44, June 1941.

2544 Lee, Albert. "A bibliography of first editions of
William Dean Howells." Book buyer 14:143-47, Mar.
1897.

2545 Monteiro, George. "Howells on Lowell: an unas-
cribed review." New England quarterly 38:508-09,
Dec. 1965.

2546 _____. "William Dean Howells and The breadwinners." Studies in bibliography 15:267-68, 1962.
The breadwinners was written by John Hay.

2547 _____. "William Dean Howells: two mistaken
attributions." Papers of the Bibliographical Society
of America 56:254-57, 1962.
The article is about two essays in the "contributor's column" of the Atlantic monthly, Feb. and
Mar. of 1879. Mr. Monteiro believes that John
Hay, a close friend of Howells, wrote them.

2548 _____. "William Dean Howells: a bibliographical
amendment." Papers of the Bibliographical Society
of America 58:468-69, 1964.

2549 Quinn, Arthur H. "Tracking down two lost manuscripts." New York Post Literary review, Oct. 10,
1925.

2550 Reeves, John K. "Howells divided." Autograph col-
lectors' journal 5:55-56, Winter 1953.

2551 _____, comp. "The literary manuscripts of William Dean Howells: a descriptive finding list." Bulletin of the New York Public Library 62:267-78, June
1958; 62:350-63, July 1958.

2552 _____. "The literary manuscripts of W. D. Howells:
a supplement to the descriptive finding list." Bulletin
of the New York Public Library 65:465-76, Sept. 1961.

2553 Stafford, William T. "The two Henry Jameses: a
bibliographical mix-up." Bulletin of bibliography 21:
135, Jan.--Apr. 1955.
The essay is about an article "James and his secret" in the Saturday review of literature 8:759,
May 28, 1932. The author claims the article
should be in the bibliography of Howells and the
elder Henry James (1811-82).

2554 Virginia. University Library. The Barrett Library:
W. D. Howells: a checklist of printed and manuscript
works of William Dean Howells in the Library. Compiled by Fannie Mae Elliott and Lucy Clark. Char-
lottesville, University of Virginia Press, 1959. 68p.

2555 Walbridge, Earle F. "The whole family and Henry

James." Papers of the Bibliographical Society of America 52:144-45, Second quarter 1958.
————The whole family (N.Y., Harper, 1908) is a composite novel written by a dozen authors of the day, including William D. Howells.

2556 Walts, Robert W. "Howells' plans for two travel books." Papers of the Bibliographical Society of America 57:453-59, 1963.

2557 ————. "William Dean Howells and his 'Library edition'." Papers of the Bibliographical Society of America 52:283-94, 4th quarter 1958.

2558 Wilcox, Marrion. "Works of William Dean Howells (1860-96)" Harper's weekly 40:655-56, July 4, 1896.
Contains an engraving by E. Schladitz

2559 "William Dean Howells." In Dizionario universale della letteratura contemporanea. Milan, Arnaldo Mandadori Editora, 1960. vol. E-K, p.766-68.

2560 Woodress, James. "The Dean's comeback: four decades of Howells scholarship." Texas studies in language and literature 2:115-23, Spring 1960.
————Also in Eble, Kenneth E., ed. Howells, a century of criticism. Dallas, Texas, Southern Methodist University Press, 1962. p.236-47.

2561 ————. "A note on Lowell bibliography: the review of Howells' Venetian life. Studies in bibliography 4:210-11, 1951-52.

2562 ————and Anderson, Stanley P. A bibliography of writings about William Dean Howells. American literary realism 1870-1910. Special no. 1969. 139p.

SUBJECT INDEX
to "Editor's Study," "Editor's Easy Chair,"
"Minor Topics," and "Life and Letters"

The following abbreviations are used:

ES "Editor's Study," Harper's monthly
EC "Editor's Easy Chair," Harper's monthly
LL "Life and Letters," Harper's weekly
MT "Minor Topics," Nation

Adams, Maude. LL, Nov. 9, 1895
Adultery. LL, June 29, 1895
Age. EC, June 1905, Nov. 1905
Alden, Henry M. EC, Dec. 1919
Allen, Grant. ES, July 1890
American English. ES, Jan. 1886
American literature. ES, Sept. 1887, Feb. 1887, Aug. 1891;
    EC, Oct. 1902
Anglophobia. EC, Feb. 1901
Animals. EC, Apr. 1906
Arnold, Matthew. ES, July 1888; LL, May 2, 1896
Art. LL, May 11, 1895
Artists. LL, Apr. 18, 1896
Austen, Jane. EC, Nov. 1913
Austin, Alfred. LL, Jan. 25, 1896
Authors. ES, Dec. 1890; EC, May 1903
Autobiography. EC, Apr. 1911
Automobiling. EC, Dec. 1916, Jan. 1917

Beer drinking. MT, Jan. 4, 1866
Bennett, Arnold. EC, Mar. 1911
Berea College. EC, June 1915
Bishop, W.H. ES, Sept. 1887
Books. EC, Apr. 1901, July 1902, May 1911; ES, Jan. 1890
Boy singer. MT, Jan. 25, 1866
Boyesen, H.H. ES, Aug. 1889
Brownell, W.C. EC, Nov. 1902

Cable, G.W. ES, Sept. 1887
Cahan, Abraham. EC, May 1915

192

Fenian Brotherhood. MT, Dec. 21, 1865
Fiction. EC, Oct. 1908; Mar. 1913; LL, Mar. 14, 1896
Firearms. EC, Oct. 1911
Fiske, Mrs. Maddern. LL, Mar. 20, 1897
Florida. EC, July 1916

Glass, Montague. EC, May 1915
Great Lakes. EC, Apr. 1908
Greeks. EC, Dec. 1906
Greeley, Horace. MT, Apr. 12, 1866

Hair. MT, Jan. 18, 1866
Haliburton, T.C. EC, Feb. 1917
Hall, Stanley. EC, Nov. 1901
Happiness. EC, Aug. 1907
Harland, Henry. EC, Feb. 1911
Harper's monthly. EC, June 1917
Harvey, George. EC, Sept. 1908
Hats. LL, Feb. 1, 1896
Heroes and heroines (fictional). EC, Aug. 1905
History. EC, Mar. 1906
Home economics. LL, June 20, 1896
Hoppin, Augustus. LL, May 2, 1896
Horticulture. EC, Mar. 1908
Hotels. EC, July 1919; LL, Aug. 17, 1895, Aug. 24, 1895
Howells, William D. ES, Mar. 1886; EC, Nov. 1919
Hughes, Thomas. LL, May 2, 1896
Hugo, Victor. ES, Dec. 1888
Humor. EC, July 1911, Feb. 1917
Hunting. EC, Nov. 1910
Hurst, Fannie. EC, May 1915

Ibanez, Blasco. EC, Nov. 1915
Immortality. ED, June 1903, Aug. 1919
Inns. EC, Jan. 1917
Insanity. MT, Apr. 5, 1866
Insects. EC, Sept. 1913
International government. EC, Nov. 1916
Internationalism. EC, Nov. 1907

James, Henry. ES, Sept. 1887, Oct. 1888
Japan. EC, Nov. 1907
Jefferson, Joseph. LL, May 11, 1895, Nov. 9, 1895
Jews. EC, May 1915
Johnson, Andrew. MT, Mar. 8, 1866
Journalism. MT, Apr. 19, 1866; EC, Sept. 1908
Justice. MT, Apr. 26, 1866

Painting. MT, Mar. 22, 1866
Parks. LL, Sept. 7, 1895
Peace. EC, Aug. 1911
Phelps, E.J. ES, Mar. 1890
Philanthropy. EC, May 1913
Piatt, J.J. EC, July 1917
Pioneers. EC, Mar. 1905
Poetry. EC, Sept. 1902, Nov. 1903, June 1907, July 1912;
    ES, Mar. 1887
Post-war conditons. EC, Apr. 1920
Poverty. MT, Mar. 29, 1866
Presidency. EC, Aug. 1909
Presidential campaign. EC, Dec. 1912
Prisons. EC, Nov. 1911, Sept. 1914
Prohibition. EC, Apr. 1919
Proudhon. MT, Mar. 8, 1866

Reading. ES, Aug. 1887
Religion. EC, Jan. 1915
Rich people. EC, Feb. 1902
Richardson, Samuel. EC, Aug. 1902
Riots. EC, June 1913
Roosevelt, Theodore R. EC, Nov. 1910
Ruskin, John. ES, Dec. 1888

Saturday Press. EC, Mar. 1906
Savage, M.J. ES, Oct. 1887
Science and religion. ES, Nov. 1890
Scott, Sir Walter. ES, May 1889
Scudder, H.E. EC, Apr. 1902
Shaking hands. MT, Mar. 1, 1866
Shakespeare. EC, Sept. 1905
Shaw, G.B.S. EC, Sept. 1905
Ships. EC, Oct. 1907, July 1909
Socialism. EC, Nov. 1918, May 1918
Society of Colonial Dames. LL, Feb. 15, 1896
Spanish literature. EC, Nov. 1911
Spelling. EC, Sept. 1906; LL, June 8, 1895, Nov. 2, 1895
Spiritualism. EC, Nov. 1912
Spitting. LL, Jan. 25, 1896
Stewart, A.T. MT, Feb. 15, 1866
Stoddard, C.W. EC, Dec. 1917
Subscription books. ES, Dec. 1886
Suffrage. EC, Oct. 1916

Teachers' employment agencies. MT, Feb. 15, 1866
Tennyson, Alfred Lord. ES, Sept. 1888

SUBJECT AND AUTHOR INDEX